Nadia Revisited

This book re-examines the case of Nadia, discovered as a child aged six, who had been drawing with phenomenal skill and visual realism from the age of three, despite having autism and severe learning difficulties. The original research was published in 1977 and caused great international interest. *Nadia Revisited* updates her story and reconsiders the theories that endeavour to explain her extraordinary talent.

As well as summarising the central issues from the original case study and presenting her remarkable drawings, the book explains Nadia's subsequent development and present situation in light of the recent research on autistic spectrum disorders and representational drawing in children. The book also considers the phenomenon of savant syndrome, the condition in which those with autism or other learning disabilities have areas of unusual talent that contrast dramatically with their general functioning.

Lorna Selfe uses this single case study to discuss theories of developmental psychology and considers the possible links between prodigious talent and underlying neurological dysfunction. The book is especially valuable for students and teachers of developmental psychology and neuropsychology, education and special education, as well as art and art education. Parents of autistic children or those with related disorders, learning difficulties or special needs will also be interested in the discussions presented in this book.

Lorna Selfe is a child psychologist with extensive experience of working with children and families in Local Authority and NHS settings. She has published several books on various aspects of special needs. She was Principal Educational Psychologist for Herefordshire.

Nadia Revisited

A Longitudinal Study of an Autistic Savant

Lorna Selfe

Psychology Press
Taylor & Francis Group

LONDON AND NEW YORK

First published 2011
by Psychology Press
27 Church Road, Hove, East Sussex BN3 2FA

Simultaneously published in the USA and Canada
by Psychology Press
711 Third Avenue, New York NY 10017

Psychology Press is an imprint of the Taylor & Francis Group, an Informa business

Typeset in Times by RefineCatch Limited, Bungay, Suffolk
Printed and bound in Great Britain by TJ International Limited, Padstow, Cornwall
Cover design by Lisa Dynan
Nadia's archive is held in Bethlem Royal Hospital Archives & Museum. The cover image (LD833–59) was drawn by Nadia at the age of 5 years and 6 months.

This publication has been produced with paper manufactured to strict environmental standards and with pulp derived from sustainable forests.

British Library Cataloguing in Publication Data
A catalogue record for this book is available from the British Library

Library of Congress Cataloging in Publication Data
Selfe, Lorna.
  Nadia revisited : a longitudinal study of an autistic savant / Lorna Selfe.
    p. cm.
  Includes bibliographical references and index.
  ISBN 978–1–84872–038–1 (hb)
  1. Autism–Longitudinal studies. 2. Savant syndrome–Longitudinal studies. I. Title.
  RC553.A88S45 2011
  616.85′882–dc22   2010039647

ISBN: 978–1–84872–038–1 (hbk)
ISBN: 978–0–203–82576–1 (ebk)

The book is dedicated to Paul, Jessie and Amy
Also to John and Elizabeth Newson

Contents

List of figures   *ix*
Acknowledgements   *xv*

Introduction   **1**

Nadia over 30 years   1
Structure of the book   3
*New developments in understanding graphic representation
    and ASD   4*
Problems with terminology and conceptualisation   6
Conventions in the book   7

1   Nadia then and now   **8**

Nadia's development in early childhood   8
Original study   14
Nadia's development in late childhood   16
Nadia's life from the age of 19 years   19
Nadia in 2010   22

2   Nadia's drawings   **28**

Drawings of animals   29
Drawings of humans   44
The decline in Nadia's talent   56

3   Nadia and representational drawing   **58**

Modern theories of graphic representation   58
Developmental progress in depiction   63
Drawing and ASD   82
Final words   85

4   Nadia and autistic spectrum disorder   87

  Introduction   87
  The prevalence of ASD   89
  The diagnosis and treatment of autism   90
  Theories of autism   95
  Conclusions   109

5   Savant syndrome   111

  Introduction   111
  Characteristics of savant syndrome   112
  Incidence of savant syndrome   113
  Some problems of definition and reporting   114
  *The areas in which savants most frequently display
     extraordinary ability   115*
  Who are some of the most extraordinary savants?   116
  Conclusion   138

6   Theories of savant syndrome   140

  How do they do it?   140
  Theories to account for savant syndrome   141
  Cognitive theories of savant syndrome   141
  Genetic and neurological theories   157
  Theories specific to savants who are autistic   165
  Conclusion   171

7   Gifted children: precocious artists   172

  Introduction   172
  Examples of non-savant artistic prodigies   174
  *What can the drawings of gifted children inform us about
     the skills of savants?   200*
  Conclusions   201

8   The challenge of Nadia   203

  Overview   203
  Theories: how they relate to Nadia   205
  Nadia and modern theories of graphic representation   215
  Towards a revised theory   216
  More questions than answers   221
  Final words: why did Nadia's skills wane?   222

  References   225
  Author index   241
  Subject index   247

Figures

1.1   Nadia aged 6   8
1.2   Two carousel horses drawn between 3 and 4 years   10
1.3   Guardsman on a horse from a Ladybird book that inspired
      Nadia   11
1.4   Nadia's galloping horse drawn at the age of 4. Contrast this
      with the statuesque horse and rider drawn by Leonardo da Vinci
      (Figure 1.5)   13
1.5   Horse and Rider by Leonardo da Vinci   13
1.6   The Jockey by Henri de Toulouse-Lautrec, which inspired
      Nadia's drawing (Figure 1.7)   17
1.7   Nadia's drawing of a horse and rider inspired by Toulouse-
      Lautrec's The Jockey; she was aged 11   17
1.8   A picture of a horse and a figure. This drawing illustrates how
      Nadia, by the age of 8–9 years still retained some of her earlier
      skill seen in the horse   18
1.9   Woman; drawn at the age of 10   19
1.10 Horse and rider leaping a barrier; drawn at the age of 10   19
1.11 A dog running; drawn at the age of 10   19
1.12 A horse drawn by Nadia in her early 20s that resembles the
      drawing of a child below the age of 5   21
1.13 A sheep drawn at about 24 years old. It shows something of her
      old ability   22
1.14 Nadia aged 38   22
1.15 Nadia aged 42 in 2009   27
2.1   Fairground horses; these were among Nadia's earliest drawings
      (from the age of 3 years 5 months)   29
2.2   Fairground horse; drawn at approximately 4 years of age   29
2.3   The heads of two horses; drawn at approximately 5 years of age   30
2.4   Three horses' heads; drawn at approximately 5 years of age   30
2.5   A line-by-line reconstruction of a horse's head drawn by Nadia,
      made with the aid of a videotaped observation   31
2.6   Enlarged version of the completed drawing of a horse's head
      shown in Figure 2.5   31

2.7   Horse and rider completed at approximately 5 years 6 months   32
2.8   Two horses and riders; drawn by Nadia when she was aged
        between 5 and 6   33
2.9   Rider with trumpet; drawn at the age of 5   34
2.10   Two riders drawn by non-autistic children aged 6 years   35
2.11   Front view of a horse and rider. This was drawn at the age of 5   36
2.12   Cockerel from one of Nadia's picture books   37
2.13   Cockerel drawn by Nadia at about 6 years of age   37
2.14   Horses, cockerel, and a cat; drawn by Nadia at about 6 years
        3 months   37
2.15   Two cockerels; one upside down. These were drawn at about
        the age of 6   38
2.16   Cockerel and chicken; drawn when Nadia was about 6   39
2.17   Cockerel and beaks; drawn at the age of 6 years 4 months   40
2.18   Three cockerels with beaks open; drawn at the age of 6 years
        4 months   40
2.19   Cockerel facing right, with beak open; drawn at the age of
        6 years 4 months   40
2.20   Illustration of pelicans from a Woolworths children's colouring-
        in book   41
2.21   Pelicans drawn by Nadia at 6 years 7 months   41
2.22   Cockerel and pelicans typical of drawings by an average
        6-year-old   41
2.23   Two dogs; drawn between the ages of 4 and 5   42
2.24   A dog with menacing face; drawn between the ages of 4 and 5   42
2.25   Cover picture of a lion from a Ladybird book that inspired
        Nadia   42
2.26   Nadia's drawing of a lion on the back of the book in Figure 2.25   42
2.27   A drawing possibly of an okapi; drawn between the ages of
        5 and 6   43
2.28   A reindeer; drawn when Nadia was about 6 years 3 months   43
2.29   A giraffe; drawn at about the age of 5   43
2.30   Possibly footballers and a rider; drawn at the age of about 5   44
2.31   Two dancing figures (or perhaps footballers); drawn at the
        age of 5   45
2.32   Two figures: one appears to be dancing (left) and the other one an
        unfinished rider. Nadia was about 5 years old when she drew these   46
2.33   A diver or a climber; drawn at approximately 4 years of age   47
2.34   A vivid impression of action: dancing, fighting, or playing
        football; drawn when Nadia was aged 5   48
2.35   A baby in a pram; drawn at approximately 4 years of age   49
2.36   A baby in a pram; drawn much later at about the age of 12   49
2.37   A face; Nadia was under the age of 6 when she made this
        drawing   50
2.38   Drawing of the author; drawn at the age of 6 years 8 months   50

2.39 A disturbing face; Nadia was about 6 years of age when she drew this 51

2.40 A left and a right facing shoe; Nadia drew this between the ages of 6 and 7 52

2.41 Shoes, including two sketches of crossed legs; drawn between the ages of 6 and 7. Note the foot balancing the slipper and the 'wedgie' shoe popular in the 1970s 52

2.42 Two sketches of legs, feet and shoes; drawn between the ages of 6 and 7 53

2.43 Further drawings of legs, feet and shoes, including a full figure and part of a horse; drawn between the ages of 6 and 7 54

2.44 A leg drawn on the football league table in a newspaper; drawn at 6 years 8 months 55

2.45 Carousel; drawn at the age of 10 56

2.46 A horse; drawn by Nadia in her early 20s 56

2.47 A garden; drawn by Nadia in her early 20s 57

3.1 Roof tops; drawn by a young child, aged 5, with autistic spectrum disorder who has mastered complex rules of perspective and view centred depiction without training 58

3.2 Train; drawn by a 6-year-old with learning difficulties and autistic spectrum disorder, showing extraordinary ability for linear perspective 58

3.3 Scribbles such as this are produced from about the age of 18 months 64

3.4 Circular scribbles develop shortly after those seen in Figure 3.3 64

3.5 The child described the drawing as 'a rabbit hopping'; he was aged 3 years 65

3.6 Tadpole figure with border 66

3.7 Tadpole figure 66

3.8 Tadpole figure with arms 67

3.9 Tadpole figure with large eyes 67

3.10 These drawings by a child aged 5 are of animals in a zoo 68

3.11 Clark's hat pin experiment 69

3.12 A self-portrait by a precociously gifted boy aged 11 (Brian Hatton) 72

3.13 A drawing of a man by a typically developing child of 11 years 72

3.14 A drawing by an autistic savant of 11 years of age 72

3.15 Drawing of a house: canonical flat view 74

3.16 Drawing of a house: right-angle side elevation with no attempt at an oblique angle 74

3.17 Drawing of a house: multiple squares used to depict several sides 74

3.18 Drawing of a house: oblique angle used to depict side elevation 74

3.19 A farm scene, by a child aged 6 years old, showing objects along a base line with little regard to the relative size between objects and no attempt at depicting relative size with distance 75

3.20   Diminishing size with distance; experimental stimulus   77
3.21   Seven possible graphic solutions used by children to draw one
       apple behind another   78
3.22   (a) Experiment 5: all children were asked to 'copy this picture
       as exactly as you can'. (b) Experiment 6: all children were
       asked to 'copy this pattern'   79
3.23   Child's solution to drawing a cube: flat square   80
3.24   Child's solution to drawing a cube: adjacent rectangle and
       square   80
3.25   Child's solution to drawing a cube: fold outs   80
3.26   Child's solution to drawing a cube: attempt at oblique projection 80
3.27   Child's solution to drawing a cube: attempt at linear perspective 80
3.28   Cubes and cube-like patterns with the same number of lines and
       angles   81
4.1   Titchener circles. This is a visual illusion whereby the centre circle
       on the left appears to be larger than the centre circle on the right   102
4.2   Navon figures. Navon (1977) suggested that there is a prefer-
       ence, in normal perception, for processing the whole field
       initially rather than detail   103
5.1   Derek Paravacini   119
5.2   Gottfried Mind's (1768–1814) watercolour of cats   126
5.3   A carved ship made by Pullen in Earlswood Asylum, known as
       the Mystic Representation of the World   129
5.4   Representation of Pullen's life, made up of individual drawings
       in which he recorded important incidents   129
5.5   A happy memory of Pullen's schooldays   130
5.6   Pullen recalls sailing a boat on a pond   130
5.7   Pullen observes a bridge across the Thames   130
5.8   Pullen draws a sad memory of his days in a classroom   130
5.9   The Capitol Building. Painted by Ping Lian Yeak at the
       age of 11   131
5.10   Cockerel. Painted by Ping Lian Yeak at the age of 11   132
5.11   A view of Moscow drawn by Stephen Wiltshire at the age of 15   133
5.12   St Pancras Station by Stephen Wiltshire, drawn before the
       age of 12   134
5.13   St Pancras Station by Stephen Wiltshire with photograph (inset
       top right), drawn before the age of 12 years   135
5.14   View of Amsterdam railway station by Stephen Wiltshire. This
       was drawn at the age of 15   135
5.15   Stephen Wiltshire in front of his huge canvas on which he is
       drawing his recollections of the scene of New York viewed
       from a helicopter   137
6.1   Model shown to an autistic savant. He was asked to draw
       what he thought the view would be like from another angle
       (Figure 6.2)   151

6.2   Drawing produced by an autistic savant who has looked at the
      model in Figure 6.1 and was asked to draw what he thought the
      view would be like from another angle   152
7.1   Jan Lieven's Allegory of the Five Senses (1622), painted when
      he was 15 years old   179
7.2   A fox in profile produced when Landseer was 5 years of age in
      1807   180
7.3   Head of a horse with nosebag (circa 1810–1812), drawn by
      Landseer at the age of 8–10   181
7.4   A cockerel, drawn by Landseer at about the age of 8–10
      (1810–1812)   181
7.5   Childhood painting by John Scarlett Davis, aged between 12
      and 14 years, of a street in Leominster painted on a wooden
      panel in his bedroom   183
7.6   The Head of Michelangelo by John Scarlett Davis, drawn when
      aged 12   184
7.7   A cavalryman on horseback (circa 1837) by John Everett
      Millais drawn at the age of 7   185
7.8   A man carrying a sack by John Everett Millais (1837), drawn at
      the age of 7   185
7.9   Carriage and Horses (Chateau de Bosc) drawn by Henri de
      Toulouse-Lautrec at about the age of 6–7   187
7.10 Pablo Picasso (aged 9) Bull Fight and Pigeons, 1890   188
7.11 Drawing of a horse and rider by Hatton, aged between 7 and
      8 years old   190
7.12 A collage indicating something of Hatton's sense of humour
      from a young age, drawn between the ages of 7 and 8   190
7.13 Drawing by Hatton of horses being led that was drawn between
      the ages of 7 and 8 and again shows his early talent for move-
      ment and the complexity of the subject matter   190
7.14 Drawing of sheep and a shepherd, drawn by Hatton between the
      ages of 10 and 11, showing his increasing maturity as an artist   190
7.15 Sketches by Hatton of views from his window in Swansea,
      probably of the Mumbles railway and related events. These
      were included in a letter he wrote to his parents at the age of 10   191
7.16 A galloping horse drawn by Hatton at the age of 7 or 8   192
7.17 Church drawn by David Downes at the age of 5   193
7.18 Scene drawn by David Downes at the age of 5 years 9
      months   193
7.19 A sketch of a local church by David Downes at the age of 5   194
7.20 The Albert Bridge by David Downes as a mature artist   195
7.21 Watercolour of houses by Kieron Williamson completed at the
      age of 6   196
7.22 Watercolour of a church by Kieron Williamson completed at
      the age of 6   197

8.1   Nadia's drawing of a horse when she was aged 22   216
8.2   Nadia's drawing of a galloping horse when she was aged
        about 5   216
8.3   Nadia, aged 42, with the author at their meeting in Nottingham
        in 2009   223

Acknowledgements

I wish to acknowledge the help and encouragement that I received in this project from my family. I am also grateful to Frances Kelly, my agent and to the editorial team at Routledge, in particular, Tara Stebnicky and her colleagues and Annalisa Welch. The thorough guidance that they provided has been invaluable in completing the project. I also received helpful and positive responses from many holders of copyright throughout the world, who provided the necessary images. The archivists and curators of galleries and museums, especially in Hereford and Surrey, were most generous with their time in discussing the artwork that was available in their collections. I also wish to acknowledge the help provided by Mr Michael Phillips of the Bethlem Royal Hospital Archives and Museum Service in which the archive of Nadia's work is held. I am grateful to many academics and professionals working in the field with whom I had valuable discussions. They include Dr Linda Pring, Margaret Oke, Peter Lane, and colleagues in the Powys Health Authority, together with some of the artists whose work appears in the book. Naturally, this project could not have proceeded without the full agreement of the team in NORSACA (Nottingham Regional Society for Autistic Children and Adults) who look after Nadia, with such care and dedication. The author royalties from the sale of this book will support this charity.

Introduction

Nadia over 30 years

This book is a longitudinal study of a remarkable individual. The story is in some ways a sad one but it is also a story of resilience and dedicated care. Nadia was a special, and possibly, uniquely gifted child. Commencing at the age of 3 years, she drew pictures of fairground horses with astonishing skill and realism. She bypassed all the usual rules for the development of drawing ability in children and by the age of 5 she had a repertoire of subjects, mainly animals, that she drew rapidly and fluently, preferably in biro. But at the same age Nadia had no communicative speech. She was excessively slow in her movements and fine and gross motor development was delayed. She could not dress herself and she could not manage a knife and fork. She was mainly a passive child but she could also have destructive tantrums. In short she had severe learning difficulties. I met Nadia when she was 6 years old and had come to the Child Development Research Unit for an assessment with John and Elizabeth Newson. After the assessment session, when it had been evident that Nadia had severe learning difficulties, I was shown a sheaf of beautiful, accomplished drawings that Nadia's mother claimed had been drawn by Nadia. I declared that this was impossible and was gently challenged to find out. The events of the following day gave me a new subject for my thesis and a life-long interest in graphic representation in children, savant syndrome and autistic spectrum disorders. I studied Nadia in detail over the next 5 months and marvelled at the skill she displayed. This study was published as a book in 1977.

In the years following my first study, and throughout her school days, Nadia was given intensive help especially with language development and her ability to communicate improved with the production of two/three word sentences. She also started to draw like an infant so that, for a period, two styles coexisted and sometimes on the same piece of paper. Gradually and inexorably she lost the ability to draw realistically. Unlike some savant artists such as Stephen Wiltshire, who has gone from strength to strength with his drawing, Nadia's ability appeared to peter out. She is now middle aged and lives in a specialist care home but for many years she has simply refused to draw. Her wonderful pictures adorn the walls of the hallway where she lives, but she shows no interest in them. She spends her days quietly but is totally dependent on others and has to be supervised for most activities. However, this is also an optimistic story of the love and care of the family who raised her and of the people who now care for Nadia. She is in the safe and competent hands of dedicated staff who devote themselves to the care of people who are unable to look after themselves.

In the 1960s and 1970s when I was a student, psychology was still an emerging science. It was still regarded as a branch of philosophy in some British universities and as many arts degrees (BA) as science degrees (BSc) were awarded in the discipline. Experimental psychologists were also trying to readjust the reputation created by psychodynamic and psychoanalytic interpretations of human behaviour. I was fortunate in having excellent teachers; especially Professors Alan Clarke and later, John and Elizabeth Newson. All three were thoroughgoing scientists and I was schooled in scientific method and empiricism. Experience, evidence, observations of the natural world and hypothesis testing were central to any endeavour in psychology. The training I received emphasised both caution and scepticism. Metaphysical concepts were regarded with suspicion. At the same time, this was also the era of Chomsky, with his groundbreaking theory of linguistics, the 'return to mind' movement (Joynson, 1972) and the cognitive revolution. A single case study of a child with extraordinary drawing ability and severe disabilities caught the public imagination as well as that of the community of psychologists, especially in the USA. Looking back, I can now see that the publication was timely. After years of the domination of behaviourism in psychology, Nadia chimed in with the zeitgeist. There was a tradition of single case studies, notably the study of S by Luria (*The Mind of a Mnemonist*, 1968), but idiographic approaches were generally unfashionable. A case of exceptional drawing ability in infancy, like Nadia, had not been reported before although a few retrospective studies of adults with artistic savant skills existed. The academic fraternity remained intrigued and interest in the case has reverberated for many years, up to the present.

In the early 1980s, I was at a conference on autistic spectrum disorder (ASD) presenting a paper on Nadia. At the end of my presentation a somewhat distressed father of an autistic child approached me. He said that it was all well and good presenting the case of one, atypical autistic child who had an outstanding skill but this did not help with his understanding of his own child nor did I give any pointers for intervention strategies or ways of coping with the day-to-day problems of raising an autistic child. His gentle admonishment stayed with me. I have spent my professional life as an educational psychologist working in a Local Authority with children with special educational needs. Most of them are disadvantaged in one way or another in terms of the ordinary success criteria of the society in which they live. It is also privileged work because of the faith, hope and endeavour I encounter in these children, their parents and teachers on a daily basis. The challenge I received from that parent that day helped me confirm my future direction and work. The central challenge for psychologists working directly with children with ASD is to find the best intervention strategies for them, develop their capabilities as far as possible and help to ameliorate their difficulties. As well as helping the child, the practitioner also tries to relieve the intense stress that parents experience in coping with autism. This is essentially the practitioner's code of practice and this remains the day-to-day concern of Nadia's carers. She may have been a *wunderkind* but this is incidental to her needs both as a child and as an adult.

So, in this Introduction I would like to record that I agree with Happé and Frith (2009) who warn that, 'The public fascination with savant skills may have dangerous consequences that striking skills are expected of everyone on the autistic spectrum' (p. 1346). Although many autistic children have been shown to have islets of ability (Howlin, Goode, Hutton, & Rutter, 2009), 'prodigious talent' remains a very rare phenomenon (Treffert, 2009). Unfortunately, however, it does receive undue attention especially in the media. Draaisma (2009) explored the presentation of autism in fictional narrative in such films as 'Rain Man' and concluded that savant skills are vastly overemphasised in this genre. Again, he points out that this can be distressing for parents of a low-functioning child with autism who does not show any special talent. Hacking (2009) too, argues that lay conceptions of autism are dominated by autobiographical accounts of the syndrome but that such accounts may inadvertently give a misleading picture of autism, which is depressing for the parents struggling with a classically autistic child. People who have both the insight and the ability to write about their autism are very exceptional. In some cases their communication skills are so good that any diagnosis of autism seems to be contradictory.

Having acknowledged that the case of Nadia should not detract from the seriousness of the problems encountered in ASD, I would point out that Nadia is, in any case, an example of the low-functioning end of the spectrum. Nadia, however, exists and it falls to me to write about her because I was the main witness to an extraordinary event, her drawing ability at the height of her powers. This book is not written to amaze the reader and I hope that it will not add to the false impression about ASD described above. I have attempted to investigate a highly unusual phenomenon and to relate the facts of the case to theories about representation and cognition.

Structure of the book

In writing the book there was an obvious logical structure. The first chapter deals with Nadia's history and present status. The second chapter presents her remarkable drawings mainly from her early years but with later drawings in addition. The drawings are the evidence for all I have to say about Nadia and readers will undoubtedly begin by surveying them. In the third chapter I review research since 1980 on representational drawing development in normally functioning children and discuss some recent research that is particularly relevant to explanations for Nadia's ability. The fourth chapter considers developments in research into autism and ASD, since this is Nadia's principal diagnosis. The fifth and sixth chapters are about savant syndrome. The sixth chapter describes twelve theories that have been advanced to explain savant syndrome. The seventh chapter looks at the early work of child prodigy artists many of whom went on to become renowned artists. The last chapter attempts to relate the new theories and findings to all the facts we have about Nadia; her extraordinary ability and its gradual decline.

New developments in understanding graphic representation and ASD

Research on representational drawing has been moving forward at a sedate pace so that we now have new, robust theories of representational drawing allied to theories of perception and cognition. Research on autism or ASD, on the other hand, has exploded. Where, in the 1970s, it was very much a minority interest, it has now become a veritable industry with articles in the press on a weekly basis, a dedicated glossy magazine available in the high street stores (The Autism File) and frequent television programmes. There is so much research that one eminent authority recently lamented that it was now impossible to read all that is written. Theories and studies have proliferated. Belmonte, Allen, Beckel-Mitchener, Boulanger, Carper, and Webb (2004, p. 9228) summed up my own concerns:

> It has been said that people with autism suffer from a lack of 'central coherence,' the cognitive ability to bind together a jumble of separate features into a single, coherent object or concept (Frith, 1989). Ironically, the same can be said of the field of autism research, which all too often seems a fragmented tapestry stitched from differing analytical threads and theoretical patterns. Defined and diagnosed by purely behavioural criteria, autism was first described and investigated using the tools of behavioural psychology. More recent years have added brain anatomy and physiology, genetics, and biochemistry, but results from these new domains have not been fully integrated with what is known about autistic behaviour.

When I started out in the field in the 1970s there were no specific assessments for the diagnosis of autism apart from checklists of autistic features such as Creak's nine-point scale (1961). Diagnosis was often solely the province of the local child psychiatrist. This has changed. Multiprofessional assessment is now advocated by the Department for Children, Schools and Families. As a clinician specialising in ASD, I have been involved in the diagnosis of hundreds of children. I have witnessed the development of numerous excellent diagnostic tools; particularly those devised by Wing and Gould (Diagnostic Interview for Social and Communication Disorders [DISCO], 1991); Bishop and her associates (Developmental, dimensional and diagnostic interview [3di]; Skuse, Warrington, Bishop, Chowdhury, Mandy, & Place, 2004) and the Autism Diagnostic Interview (ADI–(R)), developed by Rutter, Le Couteur, and Lord (2003). The latter has been reported as the 'gold standard' for the assessment of ASD. But all rely on behavioural criteria reported by parents. There is no definitive, objective, independent test for the spectrum of conditions.

Some confusion over diagnosis will be discussed in this book. It has arisen from my practical experiences. Since I wrote my first book on Nadia, there has been a widening of diagnostic categorisation to include children who are relatively high functioning but have problems with social interaction and communication. Asperger's syndrome was added to the *Diagnostic and Statistical Manual of Mental Disorders* (DSM) fourth edition in 1994 (American Psychiatric Association (APA)). We now have a spectrum of disorders; a proliferation of children diagnosed with ASD and an increasing number of professionals who are trained to make the diagnosis. The spectrum of children receiving the diagnosis is now so wide as to be meaningless in informing specific treatment or intervention (Selfe, 2002). Most children with ASD have some learning difficulties but the range of intelligence quotient (IQ) of children with ASD spans from the exceptionally able to the profoundly and multiply disabled. Sheppard, Ropar, and Mitchell (2009) have pointed out the relative independence of the three major diagnostic categories so that children with a diagnosis may have few features in common. Happé, Ronald, and Plomin (2006) have suggested that the search for a single model for causation for autism may be doomed to failure because the subjects are not homogeneous. Children with ASD are heterogeneous in many respects so that research may find general rules that do not apply to any given individual.

It has been exciting to follow the growing interest and research into savant syndrome. Many books have appeared since my work on Nadia, the most notable being Howe's work entitled *Fragments of Genius* (1989) and Hermelin's *Bright Splinters of the Mind* (2001). Hermelin and O'Connor (1970) laid the ground for research with their studies on cognition in children with severe learning difficulties (together with Alan and Anne Clarke and Jack and Barbara Tizard). They were the first psychologists to use experimental methods with groups of children with learning difficulties to understand how they learned and how their learning could be optimised. Hermelin and O'Connor extended their studies to look at savants (1986, 1990, 1991; O'Connor & Hermelin, 1987a, 1987b, 1989b; Hermelin, O'Connor, & Lee, 1987; Hermelin, Pring, Buhler, Wolff, & Heaton, 1999). Among other achievements, they elucidated the mechanisms involved in calendar calculation. Treffert (1989) provides an overview of the subject with his accounts of musical, mathematical and calendar calculation as well as savant artists. Mottron has worked on savant syndrome, especially on savant artists, and his work, as Pring (2008) suggests, provides a convincing account of the acquisition of savant abilities. It seemed to me to be both opportune and symbolic that the first full-scale review devoted to autism and talent was held in London at The Royal Society as part of their Philosophical Transactions in May 2009. The papers from these discussions have informed this work and have now been published as a book (Happé & Frith, 2010).

Finally, advances in the understanding of the underlying neurology of the brain and its structural and functional correlates, have been dramatic, especially since magnetic resonance imaging scanning was developed in the late 1970s. Every year mind and brain inch closer together so that psychology is more allied to neurology rather than philosophy. Connectionism, mathematical and computational models of human behaviour hardly existed in the 1970s but such models show us how complex human behaviour can be correlated to the functions of neural networks in the brain. It has been a brilliant and privileged journey and I feel that Nadia has been on the path with me metaphorically nudging me occasionally and asking, 'Well, and where do I fit in?' Some savants have the most exceptional abilities with amazing powers of memory. Any new theory in developmental psychology or neuropsychology has to allow for the possibility of savants such as Nadia. Savants offer an alternative glimpse into human cognition and they present a major challenge to psychological theory.

Problems with terminology and conceptualisation

Conducting the research for this book has been mainly fascinating and illuminating but it has not been without some frustrations. I have already described aspects of my fascination. Frustration arose from the problems of terminology and conceptualisation. Psychology is a rewarding and powerful discipline with roots that reach in all directions. Eminent researchers come from different backgrounds and traditions. John Willats had a background in engineering; Maureen Cox was a teacher with a background in art and education, and Norman Freeman took a natural science tripos at Cambridge. All three have subsequently written and researched children's drawing development in university departments. All three use different terminology in describing their findings that relate to their original training and to their preferred school of psychology. This may be confusing for the lay reader and for other psychologists who have to hold the various schools in mind and translate between theoretical models that do not always quite coincide. Is 'object centred description' (Willats, 2005) the same as the search for 'equivalent graphic forms' (Arnheim, 1974) or 'invariant structures' (Cox, 2005, after Gibson)? Willats' formulation relates to computer models of graphic depiction while Arnheim's derives from Gestalt psychology.

As already discussed, the matter of defining ASD is a complex one. Autism is a spectrum of disorders. At one end we have a person like Nadia. At the other end of the continuum there are people who function very effectively independently. In between these poles are all those who have been diagnosed as ASD; 10% will have a special talent but most do not. Treffert (2009) suggests that about 50% of savants have ASD (p. 1352).

Attempts to define savant syndrome are more accessible and clear but not without some problems. Howe (1989) made a useful distinction between types of children with extraordinary talent. He distinguishes between savants, who are individuals with generalised intellectual deficits, and normally functioning prodigies, in terms of their relative mental capacities. He names Mozart and Macaulay, as examples of the latter. Savants are generally defined in terms of a discrepancy between an outstanding skill in certain specific areas, together with severe intellectual deficits. Treffert distinguishes between prodigious savants, such as Nadia, and talented savants. Prodigious savants are defined as savants whose level of skill is well beyond what could be accomplished by the most gifted normally functioning child. The talented savant's skill is out of step with their general intelligence level but not necessarily remarkable compared with the ability of normally functioning children. The distinctions work well but problems of definition arise when the IQ profile of the savant is very uneven as in the case of some individuals with Asperger's syndrome who can have very specific deficits and be very bright individuals with a range of obsessional interests that have become talents. One such person known to me would be insulted to be labelled as a savant. I suspect it is for a similar reason that Baron-Cohen, Ashwin, Ashwin, Tavassoli, and Chakrabarti (2009) use the term savant sparingly and why at the beginning of their paper they state that they define savantism as prodigious talent, thus blurring Treffert's and Howe's fundamental distinction.

Metaphysics, defined as the study of being and existence without reference to fact and evidence, was regarded with caution when I was a psychology student. Notions about privileged access, unconscious motivation, lower order processing and even, hyper-systemising seem to me to be metaphysical theories rather than scientific facts. It may of course, just be a question of time before these theories become testable but currently definitions, predictions and experiments that could establish the scientific validity of the concepts appear tenuous. Over the next 30 years we may well be able to use scanning techniques to look inside the 'black box' of the brain and delineate exactly what privileged access amounts to and sketch the neural pathways involved in systemising, but until then one should proceed with caution. Of course, understanding Nadia was never going to be an easy matter. Her case remains an enigmatic one that may be resolved by future generations of psychologists.

Conventions in the book

The current definition of savant identifies the syndrome as talent in association with learning disability. With the possible exception of Baron-Cohen, all researchers currently in the field use this definition, which rests on a discrepancy. Treffert's definitions are adopted in this book. Recent research has offered the term autistic spectrum condition (ASC) in preference to the older term ASD. However, it has been decided to use the older terminology in this book because it is used more commonly and because savants, by definition, have learning difficulties and are usually at the more disabled end of the continuum. It is very likely that the revision of the principal diagnostic manual (DSM–5) will retain the term 'disorder', too.

1 Nadia then and now

Nadia's development in early childhood

1967–1970: her family background and early development

Nadia (Figure 1.1) was born in Nottingham in 1967. She was the second child in a family of three children, having an older brother and a younger sister. Both her parents were science graduates from the Ukraine, then part of the USSR, who had emigrated to Britain. Her father had a degree in engineering and her mother graduated in chemistry. Mr Chomyn came to Britain after the war. His wife completed her studies at the University of Lvov arriving in Britain sometime later. At home in Nottingham the family spoke Ukrainian so the other two children grew up to be bilingual. Nadia was born full term after a normal pregnancy but her mother reported that she was an unduly passive baby with poor muscle tone. Her developmental milestones were substantially delayed and she did not walk independently until she was 2 years old. However, she developed single words at

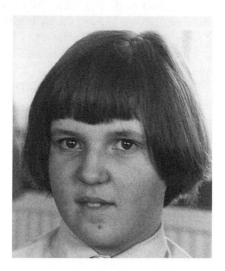

Figure 1.1 Nadia aged 6. Photograph by Sam Grainger.

around 9 months. When Nadia was 1 year old her mother commenced a full-time job and Nadia was looked after by her paternal grandmother. In Nadia's second year of life Mr and Mrs Chomyn began to have increasing concerns about her development as her motor milestones were delayed. The single words she had spoken gradually petered out and two-word, generative language did not emerge so that by the age of 2½ Nadia was virtually mute. Her ritualistic and restricted behaviours were also giving increasing cause for concern.

Nadia's younger sister was born when Nadia was 20 months old. When she was 2 years old Nadia had a particularly bad attack of measles and during this period her family noticed that she was becoming increasingly isolated and unresponsive. Just before Nadia was 3 years old her mother was diagnosed with breast cancer and had to begin a long period of hospitalisation and chemotherapy. Mrs Chomyn was in and out of hospital and away from home for 3 months. Her grandmother cared for the three children during this difficult period. During the time when Mrs Chomyn finally returned from hospital and was recuperating at home, Nadia began to draw. She was, therefore, 3 years old when she commenced her drawings and from the outset these were marked by their extraordinary visual realism. Nadia did not go through the usual stages of scribbling with the usual emergence of circles and prototype human tadpole figures typical of normal children, as described in Chapter 3 (see Figures 3.6–3.9.).

Nadia's first subjects were horses and frequently fairground carousel horses (Figure 1.2). She had very limited actual experience of these, visiting the Goose Fair in Nottingham once or twice and a local large park that had a carousel. Her inspiration seems to have come mainly from picture books, especially the Ladybird series, whose pictures were frequently based on photographic images (Figure 1.3).

Her mother reported to me that she had been amazed at Nadia's dexterity in drawing. Her manual skill was in stark contrast to the otherwise clumsy and poorly coordinated child who still had difficulties in feeding herself.

1971–1973: her early diagnosis and schooling

When Nadia was 4½ years old the local general practitioner referred her to a paediatrician who diagnosed severe learning difficulties and a place was found for Nadia in Clifton Day Special School in Nottingham. The headteacher of the school remembered that Nadia was toilet trained when she commenced school but could only feed herself with a spoon. She was physically large for her age and slow and ponderous in all her movements. She had occasional screaming tantrums and could be destructive. She had very little language with fewer than ten spoken single words, which would be heard occasionally. However, she showed persistence and interest in a range of perceptual motor activities including jigsaw and inset boards. It was quickly discovered that she had phenomenal drawing skills.

Nadia settled into school where her typical behaviour in the classroom was one of withdrawal into her own private world and passive cooperation with her teachers and occasional tantrums. Nadia would sit for a long time staring into

Figure 1.2 Two carousel horses drawn between 3 and 4 years.

Figure 1.3 Guardsman on a horse from a Ladybird book that inspired Nadia. Reprinted with kind permission of Ladybird Books Ltd, Loughborough, UK.

space. She was excessively slow in all her movements and rarely initiated any contact with adults or children, although she developed a liking for one other child who she would follow about. Her behaviour at home at this stage was very similar.

When she was 5 in 1972 she was seen by a senior clinical psychologist in Nottingham who remarked on her exceptionally skilful drawings. Nadia was then referred to the Hospital for Sick Children in Great Ormond Street for further assessments. It was during this assessment that the suggestion of autism was first raised.

1974: the Child Development Research Unit

When Nadia was 6 years old she was referred to the Child Development Research Unit (CDRU) in the University of Nottingham and it was here that I first met her. The unit had been set up by Professor John and Dr Elizabeth Newson to assess individual children, conduct research on child development and to train postgraduate students. The diagnostic clinic at the CDRU was groundbreaking at that time and utilised state of the art equipment such as video cameras and a one-way vision screen. The set-up comprised an observation playroom, which had one wall as a one-way vision screen so that student psychologists, parents and academic staff could sit behind it and observe. I was one of these students who was expected to volunteer to observe or work directly with a child for an afternoon clinic session.

Nadia attended the unit with her mother. I remember meeting a stolid, silent little girl with short brown hair. I had volunteered to work directly with her and we went into the playroom while several students, the unit founders and directors, John and Elizabeth Newson and Nadia's mother observed. Her behaviour was very much as described by her school. She was very slow and seemed to be in a world of her own, avoiding eye contact and staring into the middle distance for periods of time up to 1 minute. It was extremely difficult to get her attention although she would passively cooperate in being led around the playroom. She turned her head and looked fleetingly after coaxing and calling her name repeatedly, but she rarely maintained attention.

I attempted to engage her in a wide range of activities as the playroom had every conceivable toy and activity provided. Construction toys, inset puzzles, posting toys, bubble mixture, and the Wendy House were all utilised. I introduced dolls and cars for symbolic play and large apparatus, scooters, and tricycles to assess gross motor control. Nadia showed a fleeting interest in some of these but spent most of the time staring into space. Although she was passive and unresponsive she did not appear to be unduly upset or anxious. She did not attempt to look for her mother. One or two spoken utterances were heard all afternoon and these were unintelligible words. At one stage during the long play session Nadia was given a thick style wax crayon and paper for her to draw on. She scrubbed up and down on the paper using a fist grip and with no evident ability to draw. I formed the strong impression of a child with severe global developmental delay.

I was astonished and frankly sceptical after the session when Elizabeth Newson showed me a sheath of beautiful drawings of cockerels, horses and horse and riders. Nadia's mother had told Elizabeth that Nadia had drawn these. Among the group of psychologists who stayed behind to discuss Nadia I was the 'doubting Thomas'. I rashly stated, 'If that little girl is capable of this work, I will study her for my Master's project'. Elizabeth Newson challenged me to follow this up. The next day I drove out to Nadia's school and the head, with a polite smile, took me to Nadia's classroom. She explained that Nadia would only draw with a fine biro pen. I sat down beside Nadia and watched in wonder and astonishment while she drew a most beautiful cockerel followed by a horse and rider. There have been few such moments in my life of pure astonishment and this was one. I had been a primary school teacher for several years and I had considerable knowledge and experience of children's drawings as well as of severe learning difficulties. Here was a clumsy, non-verbal child with severe learning difficulties drawing like Leonardo da Vinci (Figures 1.4 and 1.5).

I returned to the CDRU with the news and with a new topic for my dissertation. Elizabeth Newson wrote in her report at the time,

> Nadia's drawing is inspired by pictures and apparently sometimes solid objects, which she has seen. But she does not have a model in front of her while drawing, nor does she have had to have seen it recently. Different versions of the same model seem very similar in details. But it may be that she changes the orientation in some of the details. She sometimes scribbles finely on part of the model. Even if one posits the tracing of an eidetic image (which presents theoretical difficulties of time span and image dimension), her motor coordination is quite incredibly fine for a normal child of this age. She draws very fast, can return to the exact point necessary on an interrupted line, may 'finish' a picture and then return and add detail of decoration.

Figure 1.4
Nadia's galloping horse drawn at the age of 4. Contrast this with the statuesque horse
and rider drawn by Leonardo da Vinci (Figure 1.5).

Figure 1.5
Horse and Rider by Leonardo da Vinci. Reprinted with kind permission from The
Royal Collection © 2010 Her Majesty Queen Elizabeth.

Elizabeth Newson concluded,

> This extremely unusual child needs much more investigation. Her autistic features, as they stand, would probably not be sufficient to warrant a definite diagnosis of autism; yet her quite extraordinary drawing ability, however it is eventually explained, shows the label of non-specific, severe subnormality to be totally inadequate.

'Subnormality' was the official term used for severe learning difficulty at this time (1974) prior to the 1981 Education Act.

Original study

I studied Nadia intensively for the next 5 months. My findings became the subject of a book published in 1977. Throughout the period in which I was working with her, she was drawing prolifically and with a wide variety of subject matter. Some of these drawings are presented in the next chapter together with drawings her mother had collected from earlier years. When I began working with Nadia she regularly drew cockerels and horses, especially horses and riders, but in addition I saw the evolution of several new subjects such as her drawings of a pelican (see Figure 2.21). These evolved from her examination of a cheap picture book illustration. A few weeks later she suddenly produced the image of a pelican which I recognised at once. Over the following few weeks the image appeared several times in different sizes and occasionally as a complete mirror image. She then stopped drawing pelicans and as far as I am aware, she never drew another one.

I also witnessed the evolution of a series of drawings of legs and shoes that may have been inspired from life. She became very interested in shoes (this was the era of high wedged heels and raised soles; see Figures 2.40, 2.41 and 2.42. But she did not look at these subjects when she was drawing and appeared to draw entirely from memory. She always drew with remarkable speed, rarely taking more than a few minutes to complete the drawing, which she would then cast aside. She could cover many sheets of paper in one session and would draw for up to an hour at a time but she always signalled the end of a session by getting up and pushing the paper aside. During the drawing session Nadia would become very animated and was evidently happy and excited to be drawing. At the height of her drawing phase she would draw on the walls and on cereal packets or any paper that was available so that her parents found it quite difficult to manage. On one occasion, when I was with her, she drew on a tablecloth. She chose the subjects but she would occasionally draw subjects to request usually prompted by a picture of a previous drawing and even drew my profile on one occasion (Figure 2.38).

Cognitive assessment

Over the months I worked with Nadia I assessed her on a wide range of standardised tests. This was a very difficult task because her cooperation was extremely variable. Anyone who has worked with autistic children will recognise the problem of knowing whether the child 'will not' or 'cannot' do the task. Occasionally, there are moments of cooperation when an autistic child will suddenly do a task they have refused to do previously. Testing Nadia was protracted and the usual rules and time constraints were abandoned. At this age (6 years 9 months) Nadia would not cooperate with testing on any of the subtests on the Wechsler Intelligence Scale for Children (revised version, 1974) or the preschool version including the block design test, regularly reported to be a test in which autistic children do relatively well (Howlin et al., 2009). Nadia failed to understand and/or cooperate with the Frostig Developmental Test of Visual Perception (Frostig, 1964) and the Columbia Mental Maturity Scale (Burgemeister, Blum, & Lorge, 1959). Her language ability was assessed using a number of tests including the Reynell Developmental Language Scale (1969). It was possible to record all the single words and holophrases she had used. She had a very limited vocabulary of about ten words in English and fewer in Ukrainian. She had a few repetitive two/three word phrases often produced as echolalia and out of context such as 'bedtime'; 'good girl'; 'shut door'. Verbal expression was assessed as being between 1 year and 18 months. At this stage, too, Nadia produced some babbling and scribble talk usually heard when she was happy or excited, particularly when she was drawing. Nadia's comprehension of language was similarly severely restricted. Repeated testing on the Reynell using English and Ukrainian instructions failed to bring Nadia's score higher than a 6-month level of verbal comprehension. However, I found that Nadia's comprehension was greatly enhanced when there was a context for the instruction and when there were visual prompts including gesture and pictures, to aid comprehension.

Nadia's cognitive abilities were also assessed using the Merrill Palmer Mental Measurement of Preschool Children (Stutsman, 1931). Verbal abilities were commensurate with findings on the Reynell but the Merrill Palmer was particularly appropriate because it has many tests of motor coordination and visual perception that appeared to be her strengths. Nadia proved to be much better at such tasks, particularly at jigsaws and inset form boards and at copying tasks. She was able to pass some items at just below her chronological age.

Theories and explanations available in 1974

Nadia's exceptional ability was explored in relation to theories current at that time (1974). It was evident that she did not follow the normal developmental path of graphic representation fully examined and described by Goodenough (1926) and Harris (1963). Theories about the developmental trajectories of cognitive skills had often made the distinction between verbal and linguistic processes and thinking that employed images and visual perception (Bruner, Olver, & Greenfield, 1966; Piaget & Inhelder, 1956). Indeed the Wechsler Intelligence Scales (1974) had divided the test into verbal processes and performance skills. It was noticed that verbal skills involved sequential processing over time while imagery and perception involved spatial processing. Over the next 35 years this dichotomy was developed in great depth (O'Connor & Hermelin, 1978; Paivio, 1971) and is now largely taken for granted today. The large discrepancy in Nadia's verbal skills and her perceptual abilities, as evidenced by her drawings, was explored and the possibility of an underlying neurological and physiological explanation was considered. The notion that all behaviours had their neurological correlates was still a contentious philosophical issue in the 1970s. Studies of the neurological networks in the brain relied on electroencephalographs (EEGs) since magnetic resonance imaging (MRI) scanning was in its infancy. But the notion that functions were lateralised and verbal abilities were largely controlled by the left hemisphere and perceptual functions by the right in most people, including left-handed people, was gaining popularity at the time. Since this time of course, research and techniques of examining the brain have proliferated and been refined so that specific functions have been mapped to electrical activity in specific areas of the brain. Neurological findings have been developed into a dominant theory used to explain savant syndrome (Treffert, 2009) and are considered in Chapter 5. In the 1970s the simplistic but logical notion was that damage to the left hemisphere and the verbal centres in the brain may lead to compensatory effects in perceptual development presumed to be a right hemisphere activity. Evidence, however, was contradictory since Nadia's EEG hospital records had shown that there was abnormal activity in her right cerebral hemisphere.

From all of these speculations I developed a theory that linked the lack of language skills and the ability to classify and conceptualise with Nadia's precocious ability to draw objects from one fixed viewpoint in perspective and with a high degree of photographic realism. The inability to form internal representations of objects as categories and thereby order her experiences, allowed Nadia to draw the visual world untrammelled by cognitive processes, which systematised and imposed structure.

I conducted my own investigations into the theory that Nadia's severe limitations in categorisation may have been linked to her drawing ability. Nadia was trained to match pictures of individual objects presented on cards to a static array of all possible cards. Nadia quickly learned to match the cards to identical pictures. I then presented the same task but used just the silhouettes of the objects. Nadia had no difficulties with this task. Nadia was next presented with the same pictorial array but with miniature objects taken from the Reynell test (these included a toy table and chair, knife, spoon and plate). Nadia was able to match the miniature object to its picture. Cards of different types of objects, for example, chairs (armchairs, deckchair, kitchen chairs) were then presented to Nadia. She was unable to match objects according to a functional dimension 'all objects for sitting on' and simply failed to understand what was required. I concluded that Nadia encountered increasing problems when the possibility of perceptual matching diminished and when the need for conceptual matching increased.

Nadia's development in late childhood

When I left Nottingham other trainee clinical psychologists took over my role in working with Nadia and her drawing skill continued to be promoted but it was

Figure 1.6
The Jockey by Henri de Toulouse-Lautrec, which inspired Nadia's drawing (Figure 1.7). Reprinted with kind permission © The Trustees of the British Museum and also Worcester Art Museum, Massachusetts, USA.

Figure 1.7
Nadia's drawing of a horse and rider inspired by Toulouse-Lautrec's The Jockey; she was aged 11. Note the attention to detail in her drawing, which was not copied. She has recalled the ribbons on the rider's hat and the hoof that is scarcely visible. But she has ignored the second horse and rider and the context in which the action occurs.

decided that Nadia's priority need was to develop some communicative language skills and suitable programmes were instituted. Nadia changed schools and, following a positive diagnosis of autism by Elizabeth Newson, was placed in a specialist school for autistic children (Sutherland House in Nottingham).

Nadia's language abilities started to improve marginally and she developed short telegraphic sentences and began to communicate her basic needs through language. She was encouraged to draw and her therapist used art books to stimulate her interest. For example, one of her favourite art works, The Jockey, was by Toulouse-Lautrec (Figures 1.6 and 1.7).

At this time Nadia appeared to notice and copy other children's drawings so that there was a prolonged period when she was producing her fine, visually realistic drawings and also childlike drawings (Figure 1.8).

When Nadia was 9 years old her mother succumbed to the cancer that she had been bravely fighting over the intervening years. It is difficult to assess the

Figure 1.8 A picture of a horse and a figure. This drawing illustrates how Nadia, by the age of 8–9 years still retained some of her earlier skill seen in the horse; but she was also reverting to a more typical childlike drawing as in the figure above the horse.

impact this had on Nadia and on her drawing. This was a close and loving family and Nadia clearly grieved for her mother. Her mother had also been the spur and inspiration for the early flowering of her prodigious talent. Some commentators have linked Nadia's decline in drawing ability to her mother's death. However, I am of the opinion that a change in her style and ability was already discernible before her mother's death as is evident in Figure 1.8. Thereafter, Nadia appears to have wrestled increasingly in finding the image and she frequently drew over and over a line as if searching for the exact line. Alternatively she increasingly drew childlike canonical drawings and sometime on the same page as in Figure 1.8.

A year later, my book about Nadia was published and Nadia's life was disrupted by a period of media interest. She was the subject of several films and television broadcasts and was recorded making some of her drawings on film by CBS. An attempt was made by Walter Cronkite to interview her for television in the USA.

Nadia was still drawing with some flair and considerable skill at this time but as she entered adolescence her drawings became increasingly childlike, using symbolic representation. Occasionally, her old flair for visually realistic, single viewpoint depictions appeared. Figures 1.9–1.11 were drawn at the age of 10. Some elements of her early skill are discernible in the horse and rider leaping the barrier, also in the light and very deft capture of a running dog; whereas Figure 1.9 is not untypical of a gifted 9-year-old's work.

I went on to conduct further research into savant syndrome finding a very small group of autistic children with outstanding drawing ability, although none had shown Nadia's level of skill at a very young age. Nadia's progress was reviewed

Figure 1.9
Woman; drawn at
the age of 10.

Figure 1.10
Horse and rider leaping a
barrier; drawn at the age of 10.

Figure 1.11
A dog running; drawn
at the age of 10.

as part of this and the study was published in 1983. As part of this research Nadia was reassessed when she was 12 years old using a wide range of tests of cognitive functioning. Nadia had maintained some spoken language and her vocabulary of single words had increased to 200 to 300 words. She could put simple sentences together but often her language was echolalic and conversation was extremely limited. In retrospect, this was the era when Nadia was most cooperative and her general development had dramatically improved. However, the testing showed severe deficits in all aspects of cognitive skills especially those related to language and verbal processes. She showed relative strengths with block design tasks and with the ability to recall and reproduce a geometric design. Even these abilities were below average compared with the performance of average normal subjects.

The theories that I had formed in my original study had evolved and modified but the central idea of the domination of conceptual processes in normal children's drawings and the possibility of access to more visually realistic perspective depictions in children with savant syndrome prevailed. At this time the dichotomy between linguistic, discursive thinking and perceptual/imaginal thinking was being actively proposed and investigated by several psychologists (Paivio, 1971; Pylyshyn, 1973) and this concept fitted nicely with my research. Research on autism was still awaiting major unifying and explanatory theories such as 'Theory of Mind' (Baron-Cohen, Leslie, & Frith, 1985).

Nadia's life from the age of 19 years

When Nadia was a young adult she moved from Sutherland House, where she had remained until she was 19, to a residential adult care unit under the auspices of the East Midlands Regional Autistic Society. She has remained within this community to this day although her address has changed. I reviewed Nadia's development again when she was 25. At this time I interviewed care staff within the home and visited Nadia and asked her father to complete a question-naire on her progress. It was evident that Nadia would require supervision and support throughout her life and she would not achieve the degree of self-sufficiency that would allow her to be independent. Nadia could feed herself competently, wash, dress, and undress unaided. She could prepare a simple meal for herself and carry out basic household activities if given a modicum of super-vision. However, she could not plan to carry out simple activities without careful supervision. She was unable to tell the time or understand money, use public transport, or go about the neighbourhood unsupervised. Nadia was totally dependent on others. She was able to respond to one-commission requests ('Go and get your coat') and occasionally offered answers to questions in two or three word utterances or more commonly, in single words. Her language abilities were extremely restricted and had not developed from the initial flowering around 9 and 10 years of age.

During this period Nadia had regular art therapy but if she was left to her own devices she would spend time scribbling concentric circles. Representa-tional drawings were only done occasionally and had to be coaxed out of her. She otherwise passively refused to cooperate. When she could be induced to cooperate most of her productions were crude, childlike canonical representations corre-sponding to those of a child of around 5 to 6 years. Very occasionally, however, a drawing would appear that echoed her old skills. I concluded at that time that her wonderful burgeoning talent had not been fulfilled and not from lack of oppor-tunity or nurturing. 'Nadia has had a series of excellent dedicated teachers who have taken pains to encourage her. One cannot but feel dismay, comparing her drawing then and now . . . But the story must be told and now with such an ending, we have a new enigma. Why such a disastrous withering?' (Selfe, 1995, p. 221).

I published a chapter in a book edited by Claire Golomb (1995), where I reviewed Nadia's development to that date and attempted to offer some tentative comments about the case. Nadia's language and intelligence had not improved. Her cognitive and conceptual development was extremely impoverished. I suggested that Nadia's 'view specific' drawings may have been a symptom of pathological development rather than the drawings of 'frozen intelligence'. I was able to contrast her development with that of Stephen Wiltshire, another talented savant with extraordinary drawing ability who, unlike Nadia, has gone on to improve his graphic skills (see Chapter 5). He had not shown such prodigious talent in his very early years, however. I also reviewed the research on ordinary children's drawing in the intervening years, which had established that young children could be encouraged to draw in perspective when they had been given lines to copy that were parts of objects (such as a table) but where an object for depiction had not been named (Light & MacIntosh, 1980; Phillips, Hobbs, & Pratt, 1978). This research had shown that the act of labelling or attaching meaning to the production influenced the output and whether the representation would be canonical rather than visually realistic.

Research into autism had also proliferated. The diagnostic criteria had changed substantially, as defined by the *Diagnostic and Statistical Manual*, 3rd edition of the American Psychiatric Association (DSM–III; 1980) and was characterised by impairment of social interaction; impairment of communication and restricted, repetitive and stereotyped patterns of behaviour. Classical autism, which was Nadia's original diagnosis, was included in a group of pervasive developmental disorders. It was also widely accepted that autism had a neurological basis although exact mechanisms remained elusive. Theories about the underlying cognitive deficits in ASD were just emerging beginning with Baron-Cohen, Leslie, and Frith's work on 'Theory of Mind' (1985). Other theories proposed that children with ASD have weak central coherence and utilise a localised, specific processing strategy rather than seeing the whole picture (Frith, 1989). Whereas in the USA Ozonoff and her colleagues (Ozonoff & Miller, 1996; Ozonoff, Strayer, McMahon, & Filloux, 1994), working in the early 1990s, had suggested that autistic subjects had executive functioning difficulties. That is they had difficulties with higher order top–down functions such as planning, sequencing and organising. This was a very exciting and productive period in research on ASD but much of it did not appear to relate to Nadia because she had severe and global learning difficulties.

By this age (around the age of 20) Nadia's drawings were consistently in line with her severe intellectual impairments, with very rare exceptions. Figure 1.12 is of a horse drawn by Nadia at about the age of 22. She had lost her former skill by this time. This horse resembles the drawing of a child below the age of 5 years. Note how the horse has only two legs, in contrast with her dramatic representations under the age of 6 years. Figure 1.13 is a drawing of a sheep made when she was about 24 and shows something of her old ability. The photograph (Figure 1.14) shows Nadia as an adult.

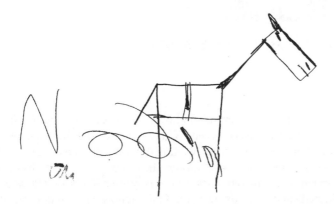

Figure 1.12 A horse drawn by Nadia in her early 20s that resembles the drawing of a child below the age of 5.

Figure 1.13 A sheep drawn at about 24 years old. It shows something of her old ability.

Figure 1.14 Nadia aged 38. Photograph by Andy Beech.

Nadia in 2010

Nadia was then 42 years old and entering middle age. I visited her in her residential home in order to conduct a reassessment. When I entered the main reception area at her placement house, Nadia was waiting for me. She has changed in appearance from our last meeting. I did not recognise her at first. She has lost weight becoming much more angular. Rather little is written about middle adulthood and ageing in ASD and I was interested to find out how she had developed.

Members of staff told me that Nadia had been excited by my proposed visit. Consequently, she had not been sleeping well; she had been up in the night for several lengthy periods. I was also told that her medication had been changed that day.

I spent about 15 minutes attempting to talk to Nadia as a prelude to an assessment. She looked at me once or twice, fleetingly and sat down opposite me but I cannot say she showed any sign of recognition. I had bought her a box of biscuits and she was very keen that the staff should open the tin. Once this had been done she immediately took a handful and quickly ate them while I tried to talk to her. She appeared to listen to me; she vocalised occasionally but the only coherent words I heard during the assessment session, which last more than 3 hours was, 'Cup tea'.

I had arrived close to lunchtime and it was evident that Nadia was preoccupied with being hungry. I was informed that she would be much more responsive once she had eaten lunch. We went to the kitchen area and Nadia took a number of sandwiches on a plate returning to the lounge to eat them. She went back to the kitchen twice to locate more sandwiches and a dessert. I noticed she enjoyed cracking empty plastic containers and she did this with empty plastic cups. This appeared to be one of her repetitive, ritualistic activities. I recalled that when she was 6 years old she enjoyed the sound of breaking glass. This has persisted to the present day so that staff at the care home have to keep glass, pottery and porcelain away from Nadia's reach. If she has the opportunity she will drop jars of jam or bottles. She is, therefore, provided with unbreakable containers. Nevertheless, she has found a way of crushing plastic to achieve a similar sharp cracking sound.

After her lunch I went with her to the lounge and attempted to explain using words and gesture as I had years before that I hoped she might help me with some simple tasks. I had brought with me a number of test items for her to try. It was soon evident that she was unable to cooperate in any way. She listened to me passively but gave me no eye contact or sign that she understood what I was saying. Shortly afterwards the unit manager pointed out to me that Nadia was 'nodding off'. Within a minute, in an upright position, Nadia had fallen asleep. We moved her to a comfortable armchair where she spent the next hour and a half sleeping, while I interviewed the staff. Nadia's current status and functioning can be considered under the following headings:

General health

Staff at the home reported that Nadia is generally healthy and very rarely has a cold. Over the last 15 years she has had no hospitalisations and no seizures. Recently she has lost some weight. She was overweight but staff had instituted a regime of healthy eating and regular exercise in the form of walks, which have improved Nadia's general health. She takes several medications to help to control difficult behaviours and anxiety.

Cognitive functioning

Staff confirmed that it was their opinion that Nadia has severe learning difficulties. They confirmed that she is unable to cooperate with any formal assessment but her measured intelligence would be estimated to be below IQ 40 and in the DSM–IV classification corresponding to F72.9 Severe Retardation. DSM–IV describes this group as follows (APA, 1994, p. 41).

> The group with Severe Mental Retardation constitutes 3%–4% of individuals with Mental Retardation. During the early childhood years, they acquire little or no communicative speech. During the school-age period they may learn to talk and can be trained in elementary self-care skills. They profit to only a limited extent from instruction in pre-academic subjects, such as familiarity with the alphabet and simple counting, but can master skills such as learning sight reading of some "survival" words. In their adult years, they may be able to perform simple tasks in closely supervized settings. Most adapt well to life in the community, in group homes or with their families, unless they have an associated handicap that requires specialized nursing or other care.

The revised version of DSM–IV, DSM–5 (2013), will replace the term 'mental retardation' with 'intellectual disability'. This is an accurate description of Nadia's level of functioning.

Expressive language

Nadia was virtually mute during my visit. Staff at the home confirmed that there is no meaningful conversation. Nadia will respond with single words sometimes. She can babble and string words and phrases together unrelated to the context. Nadia vocalises less when she is under stress. Staff reported that when Nadia is not agitated she can become more vocal, streaming words together that very rarely relate to the events that are current. The stream of words often relate to activities she enjoys such as 'Go to Goose Fair. Go now. Go out in the bus'. The statements are not echolalic but are often repetitive, well-rehearsed statements about her desires and things she would like to be doing or eating.

When she needs to communicate her needs Nadia uses single words. She also gestures and points to things she wants. Staff stated that beyond meeting immediate basic needs, there is no real social interaction using language. They believed that there has been a slight regression in her ability to use language effectively and I was able to confirm this for myself.

Verbal comprehension

Nadia's comprehension of language appears to be better developed. Staff said that Nadia will respond to requests requiring two or three commissions, for example: 'Go upstairs and fetch your coat'. She understands the routines of the day and can understand a request within this context. She is easily confused by non-routine requests. She becomes agitated very easily and during this she will flap and whine, grumbling and mumbling to herself.

Nadia has never been interested in the television or radio and this remains the case. However, she has an abiding passion for books and particularly pictures and illustrations. In her early twenties Nadia enjoyed looking at fashion magazines and listening to pop music. She is now less involved with fashion but will study adverts. Unfortunately, her enjoyment of music appears to have waned and she will no longer seek this out as an occupation.

Motor control (fine and gross)

Fine motor skills

Nadia prefers to use a spoon for eating. She is a messy eater and can use a knife but uses it in a tearing motion rather than a cutting one. She will finger feed for preference. Nadia can unwrap a chocolate bar without problems. She used to stitch tapestry if the needle was threaded for her and the tapestry had large holes (as constructed for children) but staff reported that she is no longer interested in doing this. Nadia learnt to tie shoelaces and enjoys this activity in the home, offering to tie other people's shoelaces. Her obsession with shoes and feet was established in childhood and has persisted. Nadia wrote her name for me in the fashion she used many years ago and which she acquired in her teenage years. She uses a fine tripod grip with her left hand. However, most other fine motor skills show no special dexterity.

Gross motor skills

Nadia's gross motor skills remain poorly developed. She remains very clumsy in her gait. She is unable to stand on one leg and her balance is very poor. She can, however, walk downstairs one foot per tread. She makes a good attempt to throw and catch a large ball. She has never learned to ride a two-wheeler bike and was described by the staff as physically 'cumbersome'. However, I was informed that she swims well.

Social and behavioural factors

Nadia knows and distinguishes certain people who are very familiar to her. She also recognises old friends who have been her carers or fellow residents from the past. She shows her pleasure by increased motor activity, flapping, stamping and smiling. Staff reported that she used to say their names and approach such people, but she does not do this any more. She shows initial pleasure by smiling and shaking her hands then lapses into a reverie or resumes the occupation in which she was previously involved.

As the years have progressed Nadia seems less interested in communicating with other people. She has bouts of anxiety marked by flapping and barging and occasionally pushing people with her shoulders. Hand flapping can take on an aggressive aspect at such times. She can also wail and shout. These activities are especially difficult at night-times when she will disturb the whole house and neighbours.

Nadia will break any breakable objects as described above. She can be generally destructive with any object in her room so that it has had to be kept bare. There are times when she cannot be left on her own. She has smashed televisions and stamped on objects including cutlery, which she can bend. She will shred paper particularly. Fortunately, Nadia has never indulged in self-harm, although she has a patch on her right cheek that she repeatedly scratches.

The staff remarked that Nadia shows very little interest now in other people or attachment behaviour to others. When her father died, the staff reported that Nadia appeared to be relatively unconcerned although she had been visiting him on a weekly basis.

Daily routine

Nadia is reported to be a very poor sleeper. She rarely sleeps through the night and can be very disruptive in the household. She gets up regularly in the night and shouts and chunters until someone takes her back to bed and settles her down. Her morning routine is to get up and have a bath, supervised by a carer. She has breakfast and various activities are arranged for her in the morning including, swimming, horse riding, walking and attending group-based activities such as colouring and making collages. Nadia is very fond of food and drinks. These activities dominate her day as she gets hungry before meal times and she cannot tell the time. She usually has a sandwich lunch. After this, there are again community-based activities including walking and road awareness. She has tea and may socialise in the lounge with other residents. She shows no interest in watching television but looks at favourite magazines. She has dinner at about 6.00 pm and in the summer evenings will go for a walk with a member of staff occasionally stopping in a pub before returning to the home to go to bed. The routine at the weekends is very similar except that Nadia is allowed to get up when she wants. She goes swimming on a Sunday and has occasional trips out to bowling or to take country walks. Holidays are also arranged through the local autistic society.

Self-help skills

Nadia can undress and dress herself and has been able to do this for many years. She can manage buttons and zips and will help other residents with their zips. She can wash herself and bathe with support only. Members of staff wash her hair. She has to be supervised to clean her teeth although she is left to use the bathroom facilities unaided.

Nadia has been encouraged to help with simple household tasks. She understands how to sweep and to mop and hang out washing. She can prepare very simple meals. She can butter sandwiches, make a cup of tea and make beans on toast but is generally supervised in these tasks. Nadia is totally dependent on others. She could be a danger to herself and others if left unattended. She is unable to use local transport, use money, or go shopping unsupervised.

Leisure and hobbies

Nadia's principal hobbies and pastimes are colouring, looking at magazines and pictures, going for walks, swimming, and horse riding. She has an obsession with spinning, with moving chairs and whenever she has the opportunity with breaking glass and plastic objects to hear the smashing sound. Finally, I asked about any drawing activities that she undertakes. I was told that she does very little now. She will not draw to request and has been known to break pencils and ballpoint pens to demonstrate her annoyance at being asked. When she does draw, her drawings are at a mental age of 2–3 years, as illustrated in Chapters 1 and 2. Members of staff have framed several of her best drawings from her early childhood and these are placed in the hallway of the Home. The staff told me sadly that Nadia shows no recognition or interest in her early remarkable ability. The drawings are ignored by her. I walked past them with her to the kitchen and pointed them out and Nadia made no gesture of interest or recognition. However, Nadia still enjoys looking at pictures; she looks at them avidly. She loves photographs in particular and clearly recognises objects and people in photographs of familiar surroundings.

In conclusion

All in all Nadia is now an unremarkable person with severe learning difficulties who needs constant support and supervision for all her basic needs (Figure 1.15). Nadia has certainly regressed since she was last assessed at the age of 26. I had taken assessment materials with me in order to attempt a formal reassessment of Nadia's cognitive abilities. It was evident, however, that any formal testing was impossible because she would not give me basic cooperation or eye contact and certainly would not focus on anything I had to show her. I would judge her current abilities to be at the low end of the severe learning difficulties range in educational terms and in the Severe Retardation category using DSM–IV (APA, 1994).

Figure 1.15 Nadia aged 42 in 2009. Photograph by Andy Beech.

2 Nadia's drawings

Nadia always preferred to draw in fine point biro pen on white paper; she showed no interest in the use of colour (or in colouring in); she did not enjoy using paint, which only frustrated her as did the flow of ink, which she smudged causing her to discard a drawing. The pictures have not been reproduced at their original size and those of her drawings made in pencil on poor quality paper have been difficult to reproduce with great clarity. Some photocopied illustrations are included because they have relevance for the development of her work.

Drawings of animals

Horses

Figure 2.1 Fairground horses; these were among Nadia's earliest drawings (from the age of 3 years 5 months).

Figure 2.2 Fairground horse; drawn at approximately 4 years of age.

Figure 2.3 The heads of two horses; drawn at approximately 5 years of age.

Figure 2.4 Three horses' heads; drawn at approximately 5 years of age.

Figure 2.5
A line-by-line reconstruction of a horse's head drawn by Nadia, made with the aid of
a videotaped observation.

Figure 2.6
Enlarged version of the completed drawing of a horse's head shown in Figure 2.5.

Figure 2.7 Horse and rider completed at approximately 5 years 6 months.

ure 2.8 Two horses and riders; drawn by Nadia when she was aged between 5 and 6.

Figure 2.9 Rider with trumpet; drawn at the age of 5.

Figure 2.10 Two riders drawn by non-autistic children aged 6 years. From the author's own collection.

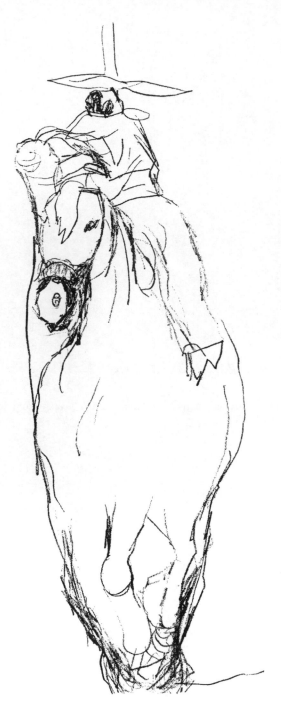

Figure 2.11 Front view of a horse and rider. This was drawn at the age of 5.

Birds

Figure 2.12
Cockerel from one of Nadia's picture books. By kind
permission of Ladybird Books Ltd, Loughborough, UK.

Figure 2.13
Cockerel; drawn by Nadia at
about 6 years of age.

Figure 2.14 Horses, cockerel, and a cat; drawn by Nadia at about 6 years 3 months.

Figure 2.15 Two cockerels; one upside down. These were drawn at about the age of 6.

Figure 2.16 Cockerel and chicken; drawn when Nadia was about 6.

Figure 2.17 Cockerel and beaks; drawn at the age of 6
years 4 months.

Figure 2.18 Three cockerels with beaks open;
drawn at the age of 6 years 4 months.

Figure 2.19 Cockerel facing right, with beak open;
drawn at the age of 6 years 4 months.

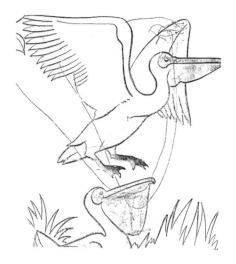

Figure 2.20 Illustration of pelicans from a Woolworths children's colouring-in book (circa 1970) which served as the inspiration for Nadia's drawing (see Figure 2.21).

Figure 2.21 Pelicans drawn by Nadia at 6 years 7 months.

Figure 2.22 Cockerel and pelicans typical of drawings by an average 6-year-old. From the author's own collection.

Other animal drawings

Figure 2.23
Two dogs; drawn between the ages of 4 and 5.

Figure 2.24
A dog with menacing face; drawn between the ages of 4 and 5.

A LADYBIRD
Fifth Picture Book
by ETHEL and
HARRY WINGFIELD

The Ladybird Picture Books are ideally suited for use with the Ladybird 'Under Five' series—'Learning with Mother' and its associated Playbooks.

Figure 2.25
Cover picture of a lion from a Ladybird book that inspired Nadia. By kind permission of Ladybird Books Ltd, Loughborough, UK.

Figure 2.26
Nadia's drawing of a lion on the back of the book in Figure 2.25.

Figure 2.27
A drawing possibly of an okapi; drawn between the ages of 5 and 6.

Figure 2.28
A reindeer; drawn when Nadia was about 6 years 3 months.

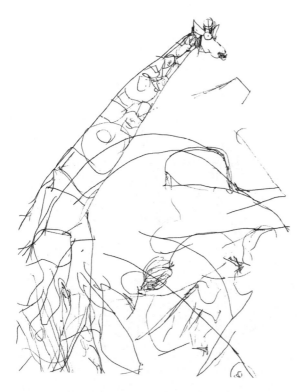

Figure 2.29 A giraffe; drawn at about the age of 5.

Drawings of humans

Figures

Figure 2.30 Possibly footballers and a rider; drawn at the age of about 5.

Figure 2.31 Two dancing figures (or perhaps footballers); drawn at the age of 5.

Figure 2.32 Two figures: one appears to be dancing (left) and the other one an unfinished rider. Nadia was about 5 years old when she drew these.

Figure 2.33 A diver or a climber; drawn at approximately 4 years of age.

Figure 2.34 A vivid impression of action: dancing, fighting, or playing football; drawn when Nadia was aged 5.

Figure 2.35 A baby in a pram; drawn at approximately 4 years of age.

Figure 2.36 A baby in a pram; drawn much later at about the age of 12.

Faces

Figure 2.37 A face; Nadia was under the age of 6 when she made this drawing.

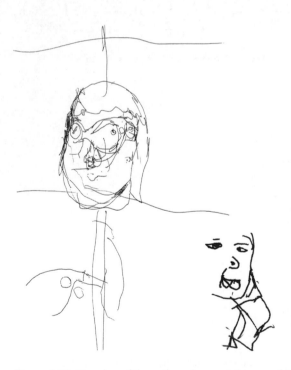

Figure 2.38 Drawing of the author; drawn at the age of 6 years 8 months.

Figure 2.39 A disturbing face; Nadia was about 6 years of age when she drew this.

Feet and shoes

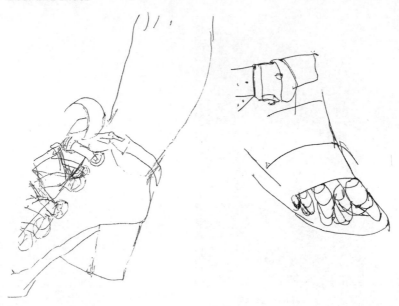

Figure 2.40 A left and a right facing shoe; Nadia drew this between the ages of 6 and 7.

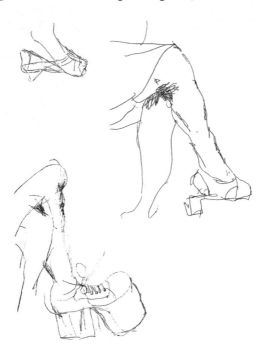

Figure 2.41 Shoes, including two sketches of crossed legs; drawn between the ages of 6 and 7. Note the foot balancing the slipper and the 'wedgie' shoe popular in the 1970s.

Figure 2.42 Two sketches of legs, feet and shoes; drawn between the ages of 6 and 7. Note the detailed drawing of the laces and the way in which the ankle of the crossed leg is angled to the floor.

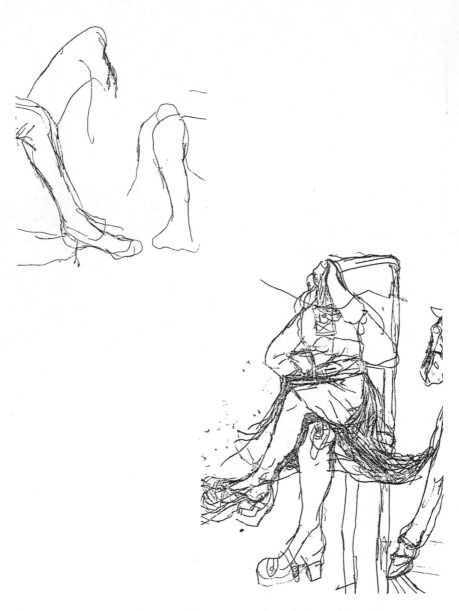

Figure 2.43 Further drawings of legs, feet and shoes, including a full figure and part of a horse; drawn between the ages of 6 and 7.

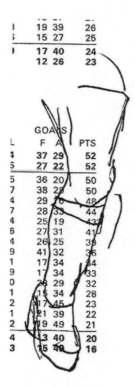

	19	39		26
	15	27		25
	17	40		24
	12	26		23

		GOALS		
L	F	A		PTS
4	37	29		52
5	27	22		52
5	36	20		50
7	38	28		50
4	29	26		48
7	28	33		44
4	25	19		43
6	27	31		41
4	26	25		39
9	41	32		36
1	17	34		34
9	17	34		33
0	26	29		32
1	15	34		28
2	17	45		23
1	21	39		22
2	19	49		21
4	13	40		20
3	15	39		16

Figure 2.44 A leg drawn on the football league table in a newspaper; drawn at 6 years 8 months.

The decline in Nadia's talent

Figure 2.45 Carousel; drawn at the age of 10.

Figure 2.46 A horse; drawn by Nadia in her early 20s.

Figure 2.47 A garden; drawn by Nadia in her early 20s.

3   Nadia and representational drawing

Modern theories of graphic representation

Nadia's drawings are instantly arresting and everyone viewing them is astonished to learn her age when the drawings were executed. They show foreshortening, linear perspective, overlapping and the correct use of proportion within and between objects. The drawings are much closer to the one single viewpoint, photographically realistic drawings, of art students in a life drawing class than to the drawings typical of young children of the same age. Figures 3.1 and 3.2 illustrate the ways in which young children with autistic spectrum disorder (ASD) can master complex rules of perspective and view centred depiction without training under the age of 7 years (Selfe, 1983).

Figure 3.1
Roof tops; drawn by a young child, aged 5, with autistic spectrum disorder, who has mastered complex rules of perspective and view centred depiction without training. Reprinted from Selfe (1983) from the author's own collection.

Figure 3.2
Train; drawn by a 6-year-old with learning difficulties and autistic spectrum disorder, showing extraordinary ability for linear perspective. Reprinted from Selfe (1983) from the author's own collection.

In the late 1970s, as a result of my original study of Nadia and to try to objectify and elucidate the phenomenon, I undertook research and reviewed the literature on the development of representational drawing in normal children (*Normal and Anomalous Representational Drawing Ability in Children*, 1983). What has happened in the intervening years? Compared with other areas of investigation in cognitive psychology, there are comparatively few psychologists conducting research into how normal children set about solving the problems of representing their three-dimensional visual world onto a two-dimensional paper surface. The psychologists who have made the most important contribution to the field are considered in this chapter.

Claire Golomb is a leading authority; she was a pupil of Rudolph Arnheim and comes from the Gestalt tradition of psychology. She has developed Arnheim's theory of 'graphic equivalents' to understand the development of drawing skills in children. Arnheim (1956, 1970, 1974) asserted that the process of drawing in children required a search for structural equivalents. The process is a symbolic one in which the child discovers graphic symbols that stand for an object or part of an object. Perception is viewed as being dependent on the relationship between elements in a scene that we perceive as whole forms or Gestalten. The process follows certain laws that reflect the way the brain functions. Gestalt theory delineates a number of laws of organisation. For example, we tend to complete figures or objects that have gaps in them. This is the law of closure. Arnheim suggests that pictorial forms in drawings grow organically from the simplest, undifferentiated form to the inclusion of increasingly complex elements as the child grows older.

Norman Freeman has been influential in bringing empiricism to the study of children's drawings. He looked at the depiction of objects in terms of the planning problems the child has to overcome with a limited repertoire of skills. Freeman introduced the term 'canonical representation' to describe young children's drawings of objects. He proposed that the child depicts an object as containing all the salient structural features in the right spatial relationship to one another, necessary for recognition (Freeman, 1980). He elucidated the rules that children appear to employ in the placement and alignment of objects and their parts on a two-dimensional surface such as paper, addressing questions such as 'why do young children draw tadpole forms?' (A human figure with head and trunk fused. See Figures 3.6–3.9.)

John Willats (1997, 2005) was a leading authority on the development of drawing systems in children. He collaborated with Dubery initially and they produced a new theory of pictures and pictorial representation and developed a precise vocabulary for describing representational systems in drawing and painting (Dubery & Willats, 1972, 1983). Later in his book, *Art and Representation: New Principles in the Analysis of Pictures* (1997), Willats put together his studies of drawing in terms of the planning problems encountered in representing visual perception on a two-dimensional surface. In order to describe drawing systems he made extensive use of a developmental sequence. Originally an engineer and also an accomplished sculptor, Willats was a polymath. He used theories from the psychology of visual perception and artificial intelligence as well as from art, especially those of Gombrich (1960), and from engineering to develop a language and theory of the development of graphic representation in children and adults. In particular Willats drew upon the work of David Marr (1982) in visual perception and linked this to the work of Noam Chomsky (1972) in psycholinguistics. Chomsky proposed an account of how children develop speech and language based on a hard-wired system of rules (deep structure) so that as words are learnt they operate within a grammatical structure or syntax, which is generative, flexible, and creative. According to Willats, Marr suggested a parallel account for visual perception.

Willats pointed out that before David Marr produced his book *Vision* (1982), most theories of visual perception had at their heart an optical theory of vision that assumed that the brain received, stored, and retrieved images rather like a photograph album. Paul Light (Light & Humphreys, 1981; Light & MacIntosh, 1980) produced research on children's drawing in which he characterised the difference between canonical representation and visual realism as 'object specific' and 'view specific'. This was the first time that a distinction between the knowledge of an object derived from a single viewpoint and the knowledge derived from multiple viewpoints and derived over time had been made. David Marr's theory of visual perception was therefore, anticipated by other researchers. Clearly the 1970s and early 1980s was a time when theories of perception were changing radically and research into children's drawings was proliferating.

Marr's theory of vision

Typically developing young children attempt to draw the most salient or characteristic features of an object. Hence a car, for example, would be represented as a box in profile with four wheels along the bottom side, which is a view that is impossible from any fixed viewpoint. David Marr (1982), produced a theory of vision in which internal representations of objects and scenes can take two possible forms. Marr termed these 'viewer centred' and 'object centred' internal descriptions. Viewer centred descriptions provide us with an account of objects as they appear from one fixed viewpoint, so that a car viewed from one specific viewpoint may have two wheels or even one wheel; or the top of a table could be described as being like a trapezium. Willats (2005) claimed that Marr's 'viewer centred descriptions' are not unlike the photographic image and the retinal image notions proposed by former theorists but Marr also suggested that we need to be able to store internal representations of 'object centred' descriptions. These would be based on the invariant structures of objects; Marr argued that the primary function of the eyes and the visual cortex of the brain is to translate the ever changing, 'viewer centred' field available at the retina into permanent 'object centred' descriptions that can be stored in memory and retrieved instantly so that objects are recognised in multiple orientations or lighting conditions. Willats argues that Marr's account has parallels with the acquisition of words and the development of an underlying syntax. Willats suggested that children's drawings are derived from 'object centred' internal descriptions rather than from fixed viewpoints. In learning to draw, he says, children have to find ways of mapping three-dimensional internal descriptions of objects onto a two-dimensional surface, and they do this by acquiring increasingly complex and effective drawing rules.

Piaget and Inhelder (1956), suggested that developmental stages in the child's conception of space could be described in terms of a hierarchy of geometries in the following order; topological geometry, projective geometry, affine geometry, and Euclidean geometry. As children develop they gradually acquire more sophisticated ways of representing space from a superficial regard for surface appearance to understanding and representing underlying geometry and linear perspective. Willats acknowledged his debt to Piaget but developed his theory making use of Marr's descriptions and using Minsky and Papert's (1972) ideas from artificial intelligence. They had suggested that children derive their 'object centred' depiction in a similar manner to computer graphics. Pictures drawn by computers are derived from three-dimensional 'object centred' descriptions in which spatial relationships are described mathematically in terms of length, orientation, and coordinates. Willats points out that objects usually have volumetric properties unless and unusually, they are flat. It is this property that children depict in their object centred drawings.

Willats' theory of drawing systems

Willats (1997, 2005) has assessed how different drawing systems are used at different ages from orthographic projections through to linear perspective. He produced the following developmental description:

1   *No projection system:* a base line may be used (e.g., for a table). Mean age 7 years 5 months.

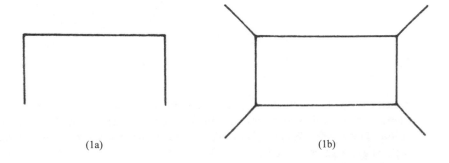

(1a)   (1b)

2   *Orthographic projection:* in which objects are depicted as flat projections in which all lines, contours, or edges of the object are given their proportions as in life. Objects, therefore, are drawn without reference to a spectator or a fixed viewpoint as if every part of the object was seen head-on. Mean age 9 years 8 months.

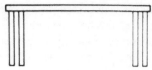

3   *Oblique projection:* here objects are viewed from the front and the side and a compromise is achieved between elements of linear perspective and the geometrical properties of the objects depicted. For example, a table in oblique projection would be depicted with the front and rear edges in the top/bottom plane being of equal length. This, of course, transgresses the linear perspective view, but retains a known, geometrical relationship. Linear perspective may be used in the right–left or left–right plane, however. No one fixed viewpoint is possible with this projection. Mean age 11 years 11 months.

4   *Naive perspective:* where perspective is used but foreshortening is often incorrectly applied and obliques do not all converge to a central vanishing point. Mean age 14 years 4 months.

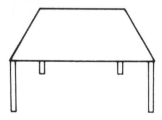

5   *Linear perspective:* this is a systematic method of pictorial illusion relating directly to discernible regularities in our common visual experience (Gombrich, 1960). Dubery and Willats claim that it is the most abstract drawing system. Mean age 13 years 7 months.

Gibson's contribution

Another influential figure in our understanding of visual perception, and graphic representation is J. J. Gibson. In his last book, published in 1979, he also rejected what he termed 'the retinal image' notion of visual perception in favour of an ecological approach. Gibson describes drawings in terms of the child representing 'invariant features of an optic array'. He says: 'By gradual stages human children begin to draw in the full meaning of the term . . . The child delineates for himself and others something he has apprehended or experienced. The traces that the child leaves on the paper are not just lines or forms, they are the distinguishing features of the environment' (Gibson, 1979, p. 278).

One of Gibson's key concepts is that of 'invariants of structure'. These are those elements in the optic array that come to have significance for the viewer, such as edges, contours, light, shade, and form. Most of the time the optic array is constantly changing as the person moves around but the child comes to attend to invariants that are relevant to him. In his early drawing the child is attempting to record these invariants. Gibson says about picture production, for example, that 'invariants display a world with nobody in it' (1979, p. 284). This is a multifaceted world derived from many visual experiences, whereas the perspective drawing displays where the observer is in the world. He, too, recognised a distinction between the dynamic experience of objects and the one fixed static view. Gibson pointed out the strangeness of pictures because they are flat two-dimensional depictions of our dynamic, constantly changing optical experience.

Gibson's notion of 'invariants of structure' has echoes of Freeman's concept of 'canonical forms', Arnheim's of 'equivalents' and Willats' ideas derived from Marr of 'object centred depictions'. The difference is that Gibson's description is integral to his ecological theory of perception. Most theories proposed are constructivist in so far as perception is conceived as the child seeing an object and instantly matching it to an internal catalogue of representations. These internal representations are constructed from all of our visual experiences of that object hitherto. Gibson proposed that the optic array 'afforded' recognition and that meaning lay outside our heads and in the physical world.

These researchers are using different terminology depending on their preferred tradition in psychology (Gestalt, empiricist, Piagetian, artificial intelligence, Gibsonian, etc.) to describe the same phenomenon expressed crudely by the old maxim 'the child draws what he knows not what he sees'. The savants I encountered were the exception to this general rule. They were able to depict objects from the viewer centred, single, fixed viewpoint as illustrated in Figures 3.1 and 3.2 on page 58. The drawings are in perspective; they show foreshortening, houses are overlapped and proportions between and within objects are observed.

Developmental progress in depiction

Maureen Cox has researched and written extensively on children's drawings and the development of graphic representation over the past three decades. She takes an eclectic approach critically examining the evidence from all sources. However, she prefers the term 'invariants' and is influenced by J. J. Gibson's ecological theory of perception. Cox (2005), comprehensively reviewed the research on all aspects of children's representational drawing in her book, *The Pictorial World of the Child*. She describes the development of drawing in normal children. She draws on evidence from much earlier studies, particularly those of Luquet (1927/2001), Burt (1921), Buhler (1930/1949), Goodenough (1926), and Harris (1963). Cox suggests that many children begin to draw from about 12 months onwards. She states that they may notice their parents or siblings making marks on paper or writing. Their first marks are often made with fingers on a table with spilled liquid; on a steamed up window or with a stick in the garden. They are soon offered paper and mark making develops into scribbling (Figures 3.3 and 3.4).

Scribbling stage

Early commentators pointed out that scribbling in infancy is often an enjoyable activity involving motor movements. Children will also show interest and delight in watching others drawing, especially when this involves interacting with them. Willats reported on a study by Matthews (1984, 2003) who made careful observations of the development of drawing in his own son Ben. He noted that Ben produced a series of mark-making movements characterised by vertical downward sweeps; horizontal sideward sweeps and push–pull scrubbing movements. Later, and at the age of 18 months, Ben gained more control over these mark-making, intentional, directional movements. The push–pull movements became rotational, producing spirals and eventually a closed shape. Random scribbles thereby become steadily more controlled so that intentional closed shapes, which are usually circular, emerge. This was termed 'the mandala' by Kellogg (1969) and is universally seen as the beginning of object depiction. Matthews (1999) claimed that these forms of motor activity are observable in different cultures and using different tools. Harris (1963) for example, collected children's drawings and artwork from around the world, including scribbles in

Figure 3.3
Scribbles such as this are produced from about the age of 18 months. From the author's own collection.

Figure 3.4
Circular scribbles develop shortly after those seen in Figure 3.3. From the author's own collection.

charcoal on rock faces and demonstrated the universality in early development. Matthews (1999) suggested that early representations were not necessarily of objects. He found that children demonstrated 'action representation', for example, a rabbit hopping, where the child mimics the jumping action of the animal. The child clearly did not intend to capture a visual likeness of the object but was representing its hopping action; an example of such a drawing is seen in Figure 3.5.

Representation of objects

Children quickly learn from observation of pictures; also by watching other children draw and by comments from their parents as to what kind of drawings they are expected to produce. Representation of objects is one of the key aims of the process. Luquet (1927/2001) observed that children's scribbles may accidentally appear to represent something in the visual world and the child will label it. Luquet termed this 'fortuitous realism'. He suggested that children discover the possibility of depicting objects through this process. It is doubtful that all children discover representational drawing in this manner or that the impetus to draw objects derives entirely from this experience as Luquet suggested. It is equally likely that children begin to draw in a representational way because they intend to depict objects of their experience (Thomas & Silk, 1990). They have observed older children drawing objects; moreover, their parents suggest representational forms when mother asks, 'Have you drawn Daddy?' In my own experience too, in observing hundreds of children drawing, if the child at the scribble stage (under 2–3 years) is asked to describe what they have drawn, they will usually oblige

Figure 3.5 The child described the drawing as 'a rabbit hopping'; he was aged 3 years. The wavy lines he made illustrate how a child can represent movement as well as static visual appearance. From the author's own collection.

by seeing something vaguely representational in their scribbles and labelling it, but this is a *post hoc* experience.

The real impetus to draw representationally appears to proceed from the magic moment when the child masters the closed form. This occurs around the age of 2–3 years (Cox, 2005; Harris, 1963). Golomb (1992) pointed out that the closed form is a contour against a background that thereby suggests an object. The child has discovered a prototype for many different objects. Matthews (1984) has stated that with the development of the closed form the child has constructed an enclosed pictorial space and thereafter can add lines inside or outside the figure.

Alignment and attachment

Children typically draw human figures first. The circular shape is given facial features (eyes, nose, mouth) or attachments (usually legs) producing the famous tadpole figure. Figures 3.6–3.9 show tadpole figures; this stage of drawing development normally takes place between the ages of 2 and 3 years. Luquet (1927/2001) discerned a stage of synthetic incapacity when children attempt to elaborate the closed form but cannot manage to place the attachments correctly. With practice, however, the child learns a more precise alignment and attachment. Young children are creating 'equivalents' that stand for objects or parts of objects in their experience (Arnheim, 1974). Freeman (1972) used the term 'canonical representation' and Luquet used the term 'intellectual realism' for this stage (3 to 7 years). All three commentators were making the same point that representational drawing at this age is a symbolic activity where the child discovers or

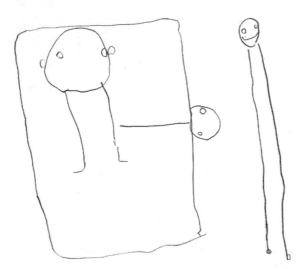

Figure 3.6
Tadpole figure with border. From the author's own collection.

Figure 3.7
Tadpole figure. From the author's own collection.

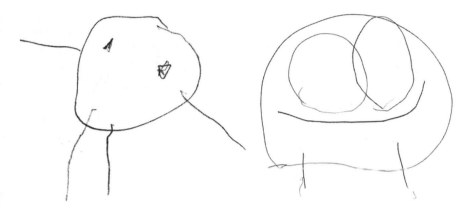

Figure 3.8
Tadpole figure with arms. From the author's own collection.

Figure 3.9
Tadpole figure with large eyes. From the author's own collection.

invents forms that stand for objects. This has echoes of the discovery of a 'vocabulary' of representation and this metaphor of language acquisition influenced Willats. The child quickly learns to use basic shapes and attachments to draw a range of objects such as people, houses, animals, trees, and cars. The range of shapes and attachments grows with increasing mastery as can be seen in Figure 3.10.

The notion of stages of development with the implication of a fixed progression may be misplaced (Cox, 2005). She also states that few researchers would dispute that there are developmental changes over this early period of drawing. Cox (2005, p. 87) notes the 'gradually emerging repertoire of drawing devices that the child can call upon when drawing'. There is a shift from early uncontrolled markings and scribbling towards more controlled distinct lines and forms that appear regularly, to the closed form and the beginnings of representational drawing. When older children living in cultures where they do not have access to drawing materials are given these tools there is a short period of experimentation before recognisable representations are produced (Cox, 2005).

Development of representational drawing

From the beginning of interest in children's drawings, writers and researchers such as Ricci (1887), Sully (1895) and Kerschensteiner (1905) noted that when infants begin to draw representationally they draw 'what they know rather than what they can see'. Luquet (1927/2001) distinguished, therefore, between intellectual realism and contrasted this with visual realism in children's depictions. Intellectual realism gives us information about the invariant structure of objects. For example, human figures have a head, two arms; a trunk or torso and two legs. Luquet also pointed out that young children will rarely look at a model in the drawing process preferring to use their internal model. 'Visual realism' describes objects

Figure 3.10 These drawings by a child aged 5 are of animals in a zoo. From the author's own collection.

from a single fixed viewpoint and records how that object appears but, as with the photograph of a car, information about the invariant structure of the object will be lost. Some of the original experimentation about the preference for drawing what is known rather than what is actually seen, was conducted by Clark (1897). He asked young children to draw an apple with a hatpin inserted through the core. Children under the age of 8 typically draw the apple with the hatpin visible through the whole apple as illustrated in Figure 3.11.

Freeman (1972), investigated this phenomenon of failing to eliminate the hidden line. He used a cup presented with the handle invisible to the viewer. Again children under the age of 8 generally drew a canonical representation of the cup with the handle drawn in. In reviewing this work, Cox (2005) pointed out that children as young as 5 can be persuaded to abandon a canonical representation for a more visually realistic one. Davies (1983) asked children to draw two cups from real-life models; one had its handle to the side and visible and the other cup had its handle turned away from the viewer. When the children were presented with this contrast they were prompted to represent this distinction in their drawings and some children as young as 4 to 6 years did so. When left to their own devices, of course, young children prefer canonical forms in their graphic depiction but when constrained, they can produce view specific forms.

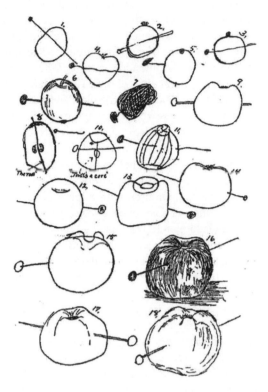

Figure 3.11 Clark's hat pin experiment. The illustration shows that younger children draw the occluded part of the hatpin. Older children were more likely to draw the hat pin as occluded.

In my own studies of typically developing children of average intelligence I found that the overriding need to present canonical views of objects dominated their productions even when children are encouraged to produce view specific representations and given the instructions to draw 'exactly what you can see'.

The shift to realism

Children younger than 6 or 7, at the intellectual stage of realism, use their prior knowledge or 'internal model' of an item when they represent an object (Ford & Rees, 2008; Luquet, 1927/2001). In this way, the child's perception of the important features of the object will be produced on the page (Boyatzis, Michaelson, & Lyle, 1995; Picard & Durand, 2005). The young child's tadpole drawing consists only of a head with arms and legs. These parts represent what the child thinks are the most vital features (Boyatzis et al., 1995). Other theorists (Karmiloff-Smith, 1990) have suggested that tadpole drawers cannot adapt their figures to integrate additional features during the drawing process. She argues that this is because children develop routines and methods that enable them to depict objects. Representation is believed to be based on 'figurative graphic schemes' (Morra, 2005). Consequently, children are constrained to use inflexible procedures that generate stereotyped drawings, with body parts omitted (Karmiloff-Smith, 1990). As a child matures, however, the intention is to provide the most realistic representation of an object or a person (Cox, 2005; Gombrich, 1960). Other writers such as Goodnow (1977) and Thomas and Silk (1990) state that children will eventually endeavour to find more realistic ways of representing objects and that a shift towards greater visual realism occurs around the age of 7 to 8 years.

This shift coincides with the notion of Piaget and Inhelder that children become aware of another person's perspective at around this age as demonstrated by the famous three mountains task. They presented children with a three-dimensional model of a landscape with three mountains and positioned a doll at various points around the model. The child had to select a picture that matched the doll's viewpoint. Young children make an egocentric choice but older children understand and choose pictures that show the doll's view (Piaget & Inhelder, 1956). This also coincides with the fact that children start to spend more time observing a model before them in the drawing process (Willats, 2005).

Karmiloff-Smith (1990, 2008) discusses the change to more visually realistic schemas in terms of the child's increasing cognitive abilities. She suggested that the limitation in young children's working memory capacity could be a reason why they rely on well-practised schemas stored in long-term memory. Short-term memory capacity increases with age (Miller, 1963) and appears to be related to other cognitive abilities such as language and verbal skills (Baddeley, 2004). The assumption is that depiction involves a series of motor movements that set down the elements of the object and which have to be remembered in sequence. As the child becomes more competent with information processing and planning, working memory capacity increases, so they are able to expand their repertoire of equivalents or invariant structures. The number of steps in the depiction increases until eventually the competent drawer can also take into account view specific information and include it in their drawing. Cox (2005) also suggested that another impetus for children to become more critical of their own productions and strive towards visual realism is their increasing exposure to photographs and linear perspective in mature drawings. By the age of 7 to 8 years children show more interest in and admiration for visually realistic pictures. Their aim in drawing appears to shift towards learning to represent objects from a fixed viewpoint.

From 'canon' to linear perspective

In my own series of studies (Selfe, 1983), I attempted to investigate some of the features of visual realism depicted in the drawings of my sample of children with savant syndrome. All the children in my small sample had learning difficulties and most were diagnosed with autism. However, they were all able to draw photographically realistic objects and scenes as if from a single fixed viewpoint using approximations to linear perspective, from a very early age and well before standard norms for normal average children. I attempted to define the differences between their depictions and those produced by normally developing children. In the savants, these features were as follows:

- The use of the paper surface as a plane where the bottom edge represented near distance and the top, far distance, so that objects could be arranged to represent near and far.
- The development of the representation of photographically realistic proportions within an object in children's human figure drawing.
- The depiction of the dimensions of an object (such as a cube) as a means of representing depth in a single object.
- The depiction of relative size between objects along the same base line or viewed at equal distance from the viewer.
- The development of overlapping as a device in the representation of photographic realism. This is the ability to place one object behind another in depiction thereby creating partial occlusion.
- The representation of diminishing size with distance between objects as a means of depicting depth in drawing and the beginnings of linear perspective.
- The use of a projection system as defined by Willats.
- Photographically accurate proportions between and within elements of drawing following the principles of linear perspective.

It is important to note that by no means all adults use linear perspective in their depictions where lines converge to a vanishing point. Studies concerned with the use of perspective in adolescent drawers generally confirm that children have continuing problems with the graphic depiction of space. Leroy (1951) found that only 65% of her sample of 14 year olds were able to use perspective precisely (according to her 'table of exactitude'). Willats (2005) found that even by the age of 17 years, a proportion of students did not use linear perspective in their drawings and Cox (1986) found that one-third of adult subjects continued to depict a cube as two squares.

Proportion within objects

In order to draw more realistically a child would need to have understood the notion that parts of an object have a size that is relative to other parts of the same object (proportion) and mastered this in their depictions. Freeman (1975) commented on the young child's 'immense tendency' to draw a head larger than the trunk in human figure drawings well into middle childhood. Harris (1963) had reported on some very early Dutch research and noted that with increasing age the proportions of the parts of the human body, as drawn by children, approached more visually realistic standards. In a series of studies, I investigated the depictions of proportions between head and trunk in drawings of a man in typically developing children of average range intelligence. I found that children between the ages of 5 to 10 years produce more photographically realistic proportions with age. On average children aged between 5 and 6 draw the head larger than the trunk whereas, by the age of 8 the trunk is larger than the head. However, even by the age of 10, the average child produces a trunk that is three times larger than the head. The actual head:trunk ratio in most photographs of adult people is approximately 1:6. The relative size of the head in children's free human figure drawing is exaggerated well into adolescence and possibly into adulthood. See Figure 3.12 for a drawing by a gifted 11-year-old and compare this with a drawing by a typical 11-year-old (Figure 3.13) and that of an autistic savant of the same age (Figure 3.14).

Problems of representing depth within and between objects

Other psychologists have attempted to elucidate both the planning problems (production order, attachment and alignment, paper size constraints, for example)

Figure 3.12
A self-portrait by a precociously gifted boy aged 11 (Brian Hatton). Reprinted with the kind permission of Hereford Museum, Herefordshire Heritage Services, UK.

Figure 3.13
A drawing of a man by a typically developing child of 11 years. From the author's own collection.

Figure 3.14
A drawing by an autistic savant of 11 years of age. From the author's own collection.

and the rules that children adopt in size scaling in human figure drawing (Allik & Laak, 1985; Thomas & Silk, 1990). One obvious difficulty with depicting accurate proportions in human figures is that children's heads are larger in proportion to their bodies and their drawing schemas could be derived from their perception of other children as much as from observing adults. However, unless the child attempts to portray approximately accurate proportions (often by using comparative measurements), there is obviously a substantial bar to more realistic depiction. The use of proportions and the depiction of depth is best investigated using objects, such as the cube, with the most simple volumetric rules. Cox (2005) claims that children spontaneously attempt to create the illusion of depth in the depiction of three-dimensional objects from the age of 7. She uses the example of a drawing of a house where a side elevation may be added to the canonical flat frontal elevation typical of younger children.

I found that in the free drawing of houses, normal children of 5 to 6 years of age did not attempt to represent any side other than the usual flat rectangle plus roof but by the age of 9 to 10 the majority of children attempted an elaboration of the canonical view by incorporating sides. I used three-dimensional models of houses presented to the children at an oblique angle so that two sides were visible. Significantly more children at 7 to 8 and 9 to 10 years produced further dimensions in their drawings when a model was presented thereby showing that it was possible to promote the depiction of further dimensions in children from 7 years on. I concluded that after the age of 7 years some children have a more elaborate representation of an object well within their competence but do not always choose to use it.

Some further experiments were conducted designed to optimise the opportunity to represent depth in a single object (Selfe, 1983). Children were presented with a box and a flat rectangle and requested to draw them and 'to show how they are different'. It was found that there was a significant trend towards representing further dimensions with age. If the children did not have a schema for representing another elevation within their repertoire they failed to produce a further dimension although many of these children of 7 to 8 and 9 to 10 showed by their comments that they had understood the difficulty and realised the problem of depiction being presented.

There is a developmental trend in the way children depict depth in three-dimensional objects (Thomas & Silk, 1990) (see Figures 3.15–3.18). One problem to be overcome in the depiction of cubes and houses is representing a right angle as an oblique (Cox, 2005). Younger children draw depth lines that are perpendicular to a base line (Freeman, 1980) (Figure 3.15). At the next stage, children attach a second elevation that is still parallel to the base line as in Figure 3.16. The next step is to draw depth lines that are still parallel to each other but oblique to the base line as in Figure 3.18. There are of course many variations to this development as in Figure 3.17. Cox (2005) comments that only a few older children and not all adults converge depth lines to produce converging obliques and still fewer use linear convergence perspective. She concludes that young

Figure 3.15
Drawing of a house: canonical flat view. Age 5 years. From the author's own collection.

Figure 3.16
Drawing of a house: right-angle side elevation with no attempt at an oblique angle. Age 7 years. From the author's own collection.

Figure 3.17
Drawing of a house: multiple squares used to depict several sides. Age 7 years. From the author's own collection.

Figure 3.18
Drawing of a house: oblique angle used to depict side elevation. Age 10 years. From the author's own collection.

children (5 to 6-year-olds) can draw converging obliques and can be shown to be sensitive to changes in the orientation and projection of an object but in drawing they appear to be intent on preserving the invariant structure of an object; particularly the right angle. Drawing the edges of a cube as acute angles infringe what they know about the structure of cube-like objects. It is not until the age of 9 years plus that typically developing children begin to be able to represent objects in perspective projection. This was also the conclusion of Willats in his studies.

Proportions between objects

Research has also been undertaken on understanding the child's growing aware-ness in depiction of the relative size of objects and how this also relates to their distance from the viewer (Cox, 2005; Freeman & Cox, 1985; Goodnow, 1977; Thomas & Silk, 1990). This involves the development of using the paper as a near/far plane where the lower portion of the paper is closer to the viewer and the top is farther away or represents the horizon. Depth can thereby be indicated. The relative size between objects within a supposed near/far picture plane has been investigated.

Before the age of 7 years children usually make few attempts to represent relative size *between* objects. They operate with other imperatives such as the rule 'to each its own space' first discussed by Goodnow (1977) where objects are separated. Young children frequently place single objects along a base line when they start to attempt to depict scenes; the lower half of the page is frequently used as a base line to represent near objects and the upper section is used to place objects that are farther away, thereby creating the illusion of depth. But typically little account of the relative size of the separate objects is apparent as seen in Figure 3.19.

Figure 3.19 A farm scene, by a child aged 6 years old, showing objects along a base line with little regard to the relative size between objects and no attempt at depicting relative size with distance. From the author's own collection.

Understanding that objects have a relative size when they are the same distance from the viewer develops slowly in children but there is a discernible trend for more realistic proportions to be depicted with increasing age along the base line (Selfe, 1983). However, understanding that the size of an object is also related to the distance from the viewer is altogether more difficult. From the age of 10 typically developing children of average-range intelligence start to experiment with roads and railways receding into the distance or in drawing people, cars, or animals as smaller and smaller with distance. Arguably, operating these two rules simultaneously, requires considerable cognitive maturity (relative size between objects at the same distance from the viewer and relative size between objects at different distances). This problem has similarities with the balance problem presented to children where they had to judge which way a balance would tip when the distance from the pivot was varied along with the size of the weights (Siegler, 1981). Siegler found that children are unable to integrate two rules until the age of 12 (Piaget's stage of formal operations).

In my original studies I set out to investigate the child's notions of representing relative size with increasing distance (Selfe, 1983). I tried to make the task as basic as possible to optimise the opportunity for visually accurate representation. I used a drawing in linear perspective of a road with lamp posts at regular intervals but diminishing in size with the illusion of distance in accordance with linear perspective. The middle lamp post was omitted from the drawing but its correct position was strongly indicated (Figure 3.20). The subjects were asked to draw in the missing lamp post and the opportunity to demonstrate an understanding of diminishing size with distance was thus optimised. The subjects were in three groups: 5–6 years; 7–8 years and 9–10 years. All the subjects, without exception, drew a lamp post that was smaller than the adjacent larger (and closer) lamp post and larger than the adjacent smaller lamp post, (further from the supposed viewer). This demonstrated that all the children had an understanding of the principle and were capable of relational responding to more than one feature in the array. That is to say, they were able to scale to both the larger and the smaller lamp post but accuracy varied with age.

There was a statistically significant difference between the younger group and the two older groups. The younger children consistently underestimated the correct length of the lamp post. The possible reasons for these findings were discussed in terms of a notable caution in adding detail to complete a drawing. Young children appear to be tentative about adding a detail and draw smaller than actual size and smaller than their own unconstrained productions. This is also seen in their attempts to complete a human figure drawing. The older children were much more accurate but even at 9–10 years not all the subjects could scale with precision even in this simple task.

Hidden line elimination

Freeman and Janikoun (1972) reawakened interest in occlusion or hidden line elimination kindled by Clark's classic study (1897). Young children have a major

Figure 3.20 Diminishing size with distance; experimental stimulus.

problem in depicting one object in front of another. Most commonly they will separate overlapping objects or draw X-ray or transparency drawings, as first noted by Clark (1897). In Willats' terms this is unsurprising if they are representing 'object centred' descriptions. The need to depict the invariant structure will take precedence over depicting the fixed viewpoint where invariance may be disregarded and vital elements of the structure occluded. Freeman, Eiser, and Sayers (1977) reported that the methods of representing occlusion showed incremental changes with age and they concluded that hidden line elimination, as demonstrated in a variety of conditions (hatpin task, cups task, apples task), was usually only mastered by age 9 with precursors of interposition and enclosure occurring (as illustrated in Figure 3.21) from the age of 7 years onwards. Freeman conducted a series of experiments on hidden line elimination described in his book *Strategies of Representation in Young Children* (1980).

Promoting the use of hidden line elimination in children

I conducted my own experiments on hidden line elimination (1983) using Freeman et al.'s (1977), experimental situation of drawing apples 'one behind the other'. The children were between 5 and 10 years old. I varied the conditions and

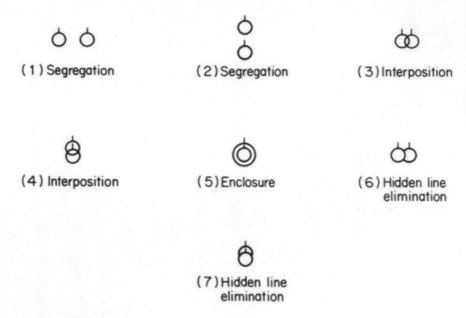

Figure 3.21 Seven possible graphic solutions used by children to draw one apple behind
another. Reprinted from Selfe (1983) after Freeman et al. (1977).

presentations in order to optimise the opportunity to depict overlapping since
this was a key feature of the drawings of my savant subjects as seen in Figures 3.1
and 3.2. I found that the younger children were stubbornly persistent in representing two separated apples and appeared to avoid drawing one apple overlapping and occluding the other. In my final experiment I decided to present the
children with a drawing of two apples one behind the other, where all possible
ambiguities in the task were reduced, including verbal instructions, since the
children were presented with a drawing of two apples one overlapping the other
to copy and were merely asked 'Please copy this picture exactly as you can'
(Figure 3.22). It was remarkable to watch a substantial proportion of children at
7–8 years and 9–10 years drawing the apples as two separated objects. I concluded
that Freeman's findings about the difficulties of hidden line elimination in
children up to 10 years were extremely robust. Even with the solution to copy
many older children ignored the overlapping and produced separated apples. The
tendency to produce occlusion, however, did increase with age. (See also Thomas
& Silk, 1990, for a useful discussion about hidden line elimination.)

Further studies were conducted on occlusion to probe whether very young
children segregate apples in Freeman's task because they are dominated by the
need to represent the invariant structure of apples (i.e., that they are round, solid
objects), or whether the problem of drawing occlusion is one of motor control and
alignment. The complexity of the task was reduced once again. I gave 5- to 6-year

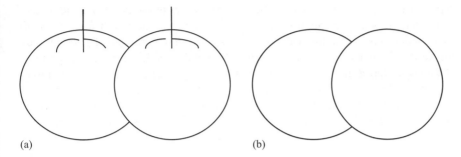

Figure 3.22 (a) Experiment 5: all children were asked to 'copy this picture as exactly as you can'. (b) Experiment 6: all children were asked to 'copy this pattern'. From the author's own collection.

olds the picture of circles as in Figure 3.22b, but I omitted the apple stalk included in Experiment 5, which might well have acted as a signifier, and I asked the children to 'Copy this pattern'. Under this condition most of these younger children produced a circle with a half moon shape attached. In addition, after they had completed their drawings, I asked all the children what they had drawn. The majority of the children who had achieved the half moon attached to a circle said they had drawn 'a pattern'. Those who had segregated the two circles labelled the drawing and said they had drawn 'apples' or 'cherries'. It would appear that redefining the lines to be drawn as objects rather than as a pattern has a profound effect on representation. I concluded then, that young children did not lack the necessary motor or alignment skills to draw hidden line elimination but that they were dominated by the need to represent the invariant structure of the object of depiction. These studies and my findings would be of no surprise to John Willats in view of his theory of object centred depiction.

Objects versus patterns

In the late 1970s other studies showed that young children could be promoted to produce and copy complex patterns but that when the pattern resembled an object and was labelled as an object, children would be constrained to produce a canonical or object centred representation. Phillips et al. (1978), for example, compared children's drawings of cubes copied from pictures and the child's copies of similar but non-object designs. They were concerned to see whether the structural accuracy of simple line drawings copied by children depended on whether the pictures are seen as objects or as designs.

Phillips et al. (1978) found that children copied drawings of objects less accurately than when they copied similar designs. They offered two possible explanations for their findings and for the dominance of intellectual realism in young children's drawings. They suggested that it would seem plausible that the computations necessary to translate an internal visual description into a drawing would be more complex when the internal description is of a solid object than when it is a description of a flat two-dimensional design. There are depth descriptors to be taken into account and resolved in the drawing. The child, they suggested, is reluctant to distort or omit the solid three-dimensional property of the object. They argued that the drawings of young children tend to display three-dimensional properties of the object when simple and obvious computations can be made on what they termed the 'object data structures'. Some of this anticipates Marr's book (1982) on visual perception. Their solutions to drawing a cube can involve fold outs, etc., as illustrated in Figures 3.23–3.27.

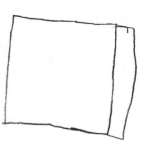

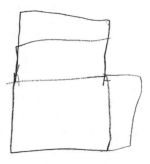

Figure 3.23
Child's solution to drawing a cube: flat square. Drawing by a child aged 5 years. From the author's own collection.

Figure 3.24
Child's solution to drawing a cube: adjacent rectangle and square. Drawing by a child aged 6 years. From the author's own collection.

Figure 3.25
Child's solution to drawing a cube: fold outs. Drawing by a child aged 7 years. From the author's own collection.

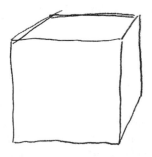

Figure 3.26
Child's solution to drawing a cube: attempt at oblique projection. Drawing by a child aged 9 years. From the author's own collection.

Figure 3.27
Child's solution to drawing a cube: attempt at linear perspective. Drawing by a child aged 10 years. From the author's own collection.

A second explanation for the findings is offered in terms of the motor programmes for the drawings that the child gradually acquires (Phillips et al., 1978). They refer to these as 'graphic motor schema'. This explanation proposes that when copying the drawing of an object the child uses the graphic motor schemas they have already learned for that object and similar objects. 'The drawing being copied serves only to select the graphic motor schema to be used and does not guide it thereafter' (p. 28).

This view is very close to Freeman's notion of canonical representation. In my original studies (1983) I argued that it seemed reasonable to conclude that the cause of the persistence of segregation in the depiction of overlapping objects was due to the dominance of the young child's need to represent simple complete canonical forms or, in Gibson's terms, their invariant structure. The representation of occlusion threatens the clear and unambiguous representation of the invariant features of the object.

At the time of my earlier research I was particularly interested in Phillips et al.'s study (1978) because there was a parallel between his findings and the drawings of the savant group. When objects were not longer perceived as such but were seen as patterns of lines children were able to draw complex patterns with a greater degree of accuracy (Figure 3.28). It is argued that notions about the lines representing a three-dimensional object with invariant structure, as opposed to a pattern, were not in the child's mind. It was only after the drawing was completed that the child may have seen a resemblance between the pattern and an object. The autistic savants I was studying were able to represent cubes (as houses, roofs, sheds, etc. illustrated in Figures 3.1 and 3.2) in linear perspective and from a young age. I proposed at the time that the drawings represented not so much

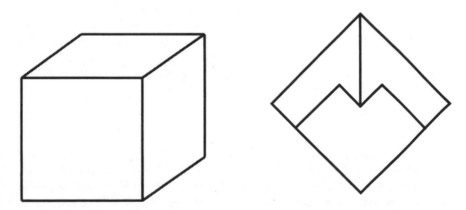

Figure 3.28 Cubes and cube-like patterns with the same number of lines and angles. From Phillips, Hobbs, and Pratt (1978). Intellectual realism in children's drawings of cubes. *Cognition, 6,* 15–33. © Elsevier (1978), reproduced with kind permission.

accelerated development, but a failure to produce canonical forms and to record invariant structure. I argued that the savant drawings had many similarities to the drawings of normally developing children when they believed they were drawing patterns as opposed to objects. The normal children's drawings of patterns were uncontaminated by the need to represent objects with their three-dimensional structure. In the case of the autistic savants more realistic depiction resulted from their lack of ability to form symbolic or canonical representations (Selfe, 1983).

These findings have largely been confirmed by subsequent studies (Lee, 1989; Moore, 1986; Sheppard, Mitchell, & Ropar, 2008). Research by Moore (1986) carried out some experiments with children of 7 to 9 years building on the work of Phillips et al. (1978). She asked them to copy line drawings that had three-dimensional interpretations. Some of the children were then given real three-dimensional objects that accorded with the line drawings (made out of polystyrene). All the children were asked to copy the line drawings again and those children who had been exposed to the three-dimensional objects drew less accurate copies. Children who had not been exposed to the models drew copies of the same standard as their first attempt. In accord with previous studies, Moore argued that exposure to the three-dimensional models made their depth properties more salient and they were thereby primed to attempt to represent this depth in their copies.

Cox (2005), however, cautions that depiction results from planning problems and the application of learned graphic devices rather than from perception. Apart from studies of the drawings of cubes, Cox and her associates undertook a series of studies on the depiction of converging lines using models and photographs of roads receding into the distance. Cox concludes (2005) that it seems that the use of oblique lines in depiction and particularly converging obliques is resisted by young children when drawing an object in depth. 'It is not because they cannot draw converging obliques nor because they are insensitive to the changes in projection of an object seen in depth. Rather they seem to be intent in preserving some of the invariant structure of the object and it is not until about the age of 9 years that they begin to be able to represent objects according to their correct perspective projection' (p. 126).

Drawing and ASD

It was only a matter of time before findings in the 1980s about the impact of the conceptual knowledge of an object on depiction were being examined in relation to all children with ASD as well as rare cases of savant syndrome such as Nadia. It was argued that the performance of savants may be due to differences in cognitive processing that relate to autism (Mottron & Belleville, 1993; Shah & Frith, 1993). Frith (2003) suggested that individuals with autism have impairments in concept formation that allows lower-level perceptual processing to prevail. Mottron and Belleville (1993, 1995) and Mottron, Burack, Stauder, and Robaey (1999) suggested that children with ASD had enhanced perceptual abilities and linked this with deficits in conceptual development to explain the ability of autistic savants to draw realistically.

Researchers investigated whether drawings by autistic children showed a greater degree of visual realism than drawings of normally functioning children matched for intellectual ability. Charman and Baron-Cohen (1993) administered three drawing tasks involving occlusion to children with and without autism. Surprisingly there was no difference between the groups in the number of visually realistic drawings produced as measured by indices of realism including hidden line elimination. All the participants produced drawings in line with their mental age. In another study a range of tasks was carried out with carefully matched controls but the children with autism were not more likely to produce visually realistic drawings (Eames & Cox, 1994). They concluded that there was no autism-specific propensity for visually realistic drawings. Similar results are reported by Ford and Rees (2008). However, Sheppard et al. (2008) state that this leads one to conclude that there are no differences between the drawings of non-savant individuals with autism and other individuals of the same mental age. In their studies they found differences between the performance of children with ASD and matched controls in certain conditions.

The problems of heterogeneity in ASD are discussed in Chapter 4 but in my view it is not surprising that these researchers found no significant result. The problem is that any group of children diagnosed with ASD will contain children with disparate cognitive profiles. They are not homogeneous in terms of their cognitive strengths and weaknesses. One-fifth of children with an ASD diagnosis have significant impairments with perceptual skills. Savant artists, who almost universally also have a diagnosis of autism, are thought to comprise a subgroup within the autistic spectrum and research established that they all had similar cognitive profiles with low scores on verbal tests and much higher scores on perceptual processing and memory items such as block design, object assembly and recall of designs (Selfe, 1983).

Sheppard and colleagues (Sheppard, Ropar, & Mitchell, 2007; Sheppard et al., 2008) suggest that there is a demonstrable difference between non-savant children with ASD and matched controls in graphic representational skills. They argue that this depends on the drawing task. In the tasks described by Charman and Baron-Cohen (1993) and by Eames and Cox (1994) the children were required to draw from a three-dimensional model or from imagination. Sheppard et al. found a difference when the task was copying an ambiguous line drawing of a pattern that had three-dimensional properties. They indicate that in such tasks children with ASD appear to be less susceptible to the influence of the knowledge the individual holds about the structure of the three-dimensional object that the line drawing could represent.

Recent studies on how autistic children depict depth

In recent years further work has been undertaken by Sheppard et al. (2008, 2009), on how autistic children depict depth (their subjects did not have any special drawing ability or savant syndrome). Sheppard and her colleagues originally wanted to test the notion that processing in perception is more localised in individuals with autism than in those without the condition. They set out to test two influential theories of perceptual processing in autism; these being the weak central coherence theory of Happé and Frith (2006) and the enhanced perceptual functioning theory of Mottron, Dawson, Soulieres, Hubert, and Burack (2006). This is discussed in detail in Chapter 4. In weak central coherence theory the suggestion is that autistic children process perceptual information at a specific and local level rather than at a global or generalised level. Mottron et al. (1999) had reported, in accordance with weak central coherence theory, that children with autism may begin their drawings with incidental details whereas normal children usually begin by sketching the outline of an object and adding detail thereafter. However, Mottron, Burack, Iarocci, Belleville, and Enns (2003) had gone on to develop a theory that autistic children show overall enhanced perception with more acute visual imagery and visual memory. Sheppard et al. (2007) decided to use drawings of a cube to investigate how autistic children would approach the task of depiction. If weak central coherence theory was an adequate explanation then one would expect the subjects to start depiction by adopting a localised depiction of part of the object. They would not draw an outline. If the theory of Mottron and colleagues (2003) was correct then they predicted that autistic children would adopt a strategy that would take into account the three-dimensional outline of the object and additionally, they would be able to represent 90 degree angles as acute (rather than the strategy adopted by normal children of drawing each face as a separate unit where the invariant right angle is preserved).

Sheppard et al. (2007) found that, contrary to predictions of weak central coherence, and in support of Mottron, the autistic children did not consistently use localised drawing strategies more than typically developing children matched for age and intelligence. A substantial number of the autistic subjects started by drawing the outline of the cube and did not focus on local detail.

Line drawings of three-dimensional objects such as cubes, are noted by Sheppard et al. (2007) to represent an interesting case. This is because the global properties of the drawing, when considered as a two-dimensional array (where right angles are represented as acute), differ from the global properties of the object (where all corners are right angles). Sheppard et al. claimed that when two aspects of perception are in conflict (as in drawing a cube where object centred versus view specific representations are possible), autistic subjects are less affected by concepts or by knowledge of the invariant structure of objects. Visual aspects rather than conceptual aspects of the cube take precedence. So that even when they are drawing an outline of a cube they are more likely to incorporate acute angles than matched controls without ASD. The odds of using the outline strategy where cubes are depicted as having acute angles, increased by a factor of nearly seven if the participant had autism. Sheppard et al. (2007) argue that their findings are concordant with research that implies that the perception of children with autism is less concept driven and their perceptions are enhanced. Those with autism have a tendency to disregard the conceptual properties of the three-dimensional objects they are depicting and their perception is less affected by higher order or top-down influences. This is in accordance with the enhanced perceptual functioning model suggested by Mottron et al. (2003).

In another experiment that borrowed from the earlier work of Moore (1987), Sheppard et al. (2008) reported differences between autistic and non-autistic children's depictions when they were asked to copy two-dimensional patterns with three-dimensional properties where three-dimensional properties had been pointed out. Children with ASD appeared to be more resistant to reinterpreting the lines as a three-dimensional object and their subsequent drawings were more accurate than those of children who had been primed to see the line drawings of geometric shapes as three-dimensional. Sheppard et al. linked these findings to Leslie's proposals (1987) that autistic children have great difficulties in forming secondary representations – that is, the ability to make one object stand for another object, as is seen in pretend play, e.g. using a banana as a telephone; using the fingers as 'piggies' or 'birds' in nursery rhymes. Another example is the use of metaphors in language that is a well-documented difficulty for children with ASD. Children with ASD have grave difficulties with pretend play and are very literal in their understanding of language. According to this research when presented with a geometrical line drawing children with ASD are less likely to see it as something other than a set of lines (Leslie, 1987).

Final words

In drawing a simple scene in linear perspective the normally developing adolescents are assumed to have been on a long journey learning and remembering skills, complex rules, and strategies of depiction. They have learned that realistic depiction is valued by their culture and they strive to draw what they see. It is not until they are much older and wiser that they will value symbolic depiction again. They have learned that a two-dimensional surface can be used to represent depth. They have noticed that objects have a relative size in relation to one another at the same distance from the observer, and a relative size in relation to the distance from the viewer. They can attempt to integrate this information in their drawing. They have also noticed that objects usually occur in front of or behind other objects in their visual field. They have been taught or more rarely have discovered that there are rules about diminishing size with distance and these are the rules of linear perspective. Closer objects are usually drawn first and drawing has become an activity requiring careful planning and sequencing where old solutions to problems of representation have to be remembered and applied. Even so, the gifted adolescent artist rarely works without an eraser. It is little wonder that many bright adolescents give up on drawing in frustration when confronted by this challenge to their powers of intelligence, planning, memory, motor control, and patience.

Autistic savants with exceptional drawing ability probably did not embark on this journey and simply travel through at an accelerated rate. They arrived by a different route (enhanced perception: view centred depiction or lack of susceptibility to interpreting lines as objects) but perhaps, the next step for such a savant is to learn how to draw symbolically, like a child. Picasso said that it took him a whole lifetime of making art to get back to drawing like a child.

4 Nadia and autistic spectrum disorder

Introduction

There is increasing agreement among knowledgeable academics and clinicians that there is no single condition that can designate someone as 'autistic'. At best there is a spectrum of autistic disorders (see also Happé et al.'s, 2006, account of heterogeneity in the genetic aetiology). This continuum can run from one extreme, a person with severe disabilities, unable to look after themselves (such as Nadia), to a person at the other extreme, who has some unusual behaviour but who can exist perfectly well in the general community. Such people may currently be described as having mild, atypical Asperger's syndrome.

Classical autism was first described by Kanner, a psychiatrist working in the USA, in 1943. He identified a group of 11 children who were characterised by abnormal behaviours that he later described as follows:

1   A profound lack of affective contact with other people.
2   An anxiously obsessive desire for the preservation of sameness.
3   A fascination with objects which are handled with skill.
4   Mutism or a kind of language that does not seem to intend to serve interpersonal communication.
5   Good cognitive potential manifested in those who can speak, by feats of memory.

Subsequently, classical autism has come to be marked by significant cognitive and communicative problems such as delays in or lack of language, which inhibits the individual from normal functioning. Someone with a diagnosis of Asperger's syndrome, on the other hand, may not show delays in language. In this sense it is a more subtle disorder and affected individuals will often only appear to be eccentric or unusual.

As autism came to be universally recognised and research proceeded, a pattern of three areas of impairments emerged. This became the triad of impairments enshrined in the diagnostic manuals (*Diagnostic and Statistical Manual* of the American Psychiatric Association [DSM–IV], 1994 and *The International Classification of Diseases–10* [ICD–10], World Health Organization, 1992). This triad of impairments is described in DSM–IV as being:

- • qualitative impairment in social interaction;
- • qualitative impairment in communication;
- • restricted, repetitive and stereotyped patterns of behaviour, interests and activities.

Currently features related to all three areas have to be present for a positive diagnosis.

Asperger's pioneering paper was published in German in 1944. He was a child psychiatrist working in Vienna. He identified and described a very similar group of children to Kanner (1943); however, his paper was largely overlooked in the post-war period. In his descriptions, Asperger's children were generally older and brighter than those described by Kanner, with normal language development but with pedantic speech, behaviour problems and difficulties with non-verbal communication. Asperger also suggested that his identified subjects were excessively clumsy. Otherwise there was a good deal of overlap between the two descriptions and Frith (1991) comments that, 'on all the major features of autism Kanner and Asperger are in agreement' (p. 10).

Asperger's syndrome tends to be subtler in its presentation. Whereas most people can interpret the behaviour and motives of others from body language, facial expression, previous actions, and so on, people diagnosed as having Asperger's syndrome have difficulty in making such interpretations and in reading cues. Some individuals with the syndrome cannot make eye contact; others have a more staring eye contact, both can affect normal social interactions. They lack the ability to see the subtleties involved in social discourse whereby people normally react to their interpretations of the behaviour of others as a guide to their own (Wing, 1996). Consequently, their own patterns of behaviour may be regarded by others as eccentric or odd, which in a school situation can lead to disharmony and antagonism from other pupils. While those with Asperger's may face obstacles in social relationships, many adjust to them and live effective, independent lives.

It was not until 1981 that Wing resurrected Asperger's original work and brought it to the attention of the medical and academic fraternity. Some clinicians believe Asperger's is a separate condition from autism. Others argue that there should be no dividing line between 'high-functioning' autism and Asperger's syndrome. They need similar treatment. In 1994 the revised DSM–IV described five discrete disorders under the category heading 'pervasive developmental disorders'. These included autism, Asperger's syndrome and Rett's syndrome. There is the possibility of a further diagnostic category of Pervasive Development Disorder: Not Specified that was used for conditions that resemble ASD but do not meet the full criteria necessary for a positive diagnosis. These disorders were then grouped by the National Autistic Society among others, collectively, under the heading autistic spectrum disorder (ASD). Currently Asperger's syndrome, classical autism and some other pathological conditions are described separately under the category of pervasive developmental disorder in DSM–IV (APA, 1994). The revision of DSM–IV, expected to be published in 2013 as DSM–5, is likely to merge all these conditions under one group, autistic spectrum disorder, and to institute a delineation based on the severity of symptoms.

In the 1990s discussions about some other conditions, particularly Rett's syndrome, tuberous sclerosis and homocystinurea, had focused on the similarities in presenting symptoms with autism. Children who could be described as autistic, therefore, varied widely in cognitive ability, in presenting symptomatology and underlying genetic or neurological status so that the notion of a spectrum or continuum of disorders linked by essential diagnostic criteria emerged and applies today. Every child diagnosed with ASD, therefore, is at a different point along this spectrum and Nadia is at the extreme in terms of severity. As the other children with artistic savant syndrome I have studied could be classified as either autistic or as having Asperger's syndrome I will use the term ASD in this chapter to encompass all the children in my original study.

Since my original study of Nadia we now have some robust theories about the underlying cognitive deficits in autism, which will be discussed in this chapter. We now have a great deal of agreement about the core impairments and we equally have general agreement about a neurological basis that postulates a final common pathway that must be damaged or dysfunctional within the brain. Autism is a neurodevelopmental disorder and the causes are likely to be congenital. There is now established evidence of a genetic susceptibility (Rutter, 2000) and also suggestions that some forms of autism may be linked to viral infections in the mother during the second trimester (Patterson, 2002).

The prevalence of ASD

The diagnosis of ASD has been rising steadily over the past 20 years. The prevalence figure used to be quoted as 7 children in 10,000 (Lotter, 1966). Wing and Gould (1979) reported on an epidemiological study in Camberwell and confirmed an incidence of 5 in 10,000 for children with classical autism (the study was conducted before Asperger's syndrome had been recognised), but suggested that there was a further, larger group of children with delayed and disordered language and social development. In the 1980s, Asperger's work was resurrected and a new category added to the definitions of autism. By the 1990s a figure as high as 58 in 10,000, or almost 6 in every 1000 children, was regularly quoted (Wing, 1996). Currently, the National Autistic Society suggest that the incidence is about 1 child in 100 derived from several sources including the latest research conducted by Baird, Simonoff, Pickles, Loucas, Meldrum, and Charman (2006), who found an incidence of 110 in 10,000. The incidence in the USA, as reported by Kogan, Blumberg, Schieve, Boyle, Perrin, Ghandour, et al. (2009), is a little lower, while official statistics from Italy report an incidence of 8 in 10,000, which is considerably lower. In all developed countries the incidence has been rising but few commentators have suggested that we are in the grip of an epidemic. The notion of what constitutes autism has widened to include people who are otherwise high functioning. Also our understanding of a spectrum of disorders that includes Asperger's syndrome, with common core features, has improved, together with diagnostic acumen. However, concerns are now being expressed about the possible over diagnosis of ASD (Goldstein, Naglieri, & Ozonoff, 2009) and the over-reliance on parental reporting as the main means of assessment.

The diagnosis and treatment of autism

The diagnosis of autism is based entirely on behavioural criteria set out in the international manuals of psychiatric disorders (ICD–10 [WHO], 1992 and DSM–IV [APA], 1994). There are no medical tests for the disorder although, increasingly, computerised tomography, (CT), magnetic resonance image (MRI) scanning, positron emission tomography (PET) scanning, diffusion tensor tracking and chromosome analysis is helping to elucidate underlying abnormalities and subtypes of the spectrum of disorders. Rett's syndrome, for example, has been found to be caused by abnormalities on the X chromosome (Amir, Stafford, Freshman, & Foa, 1998). Clinicians who have worked for many years diagnosing and assessing diverse children with autism understand that autism is not one homogeneous disorder. It is a collection of disorders. As the principal diagnostic instrument, the DSM–IV has dominated diagnosis and conceptualisation over the last 20 years. However, changes to this categorisation are envisaged by DSM–5 which will inevitably change the way that ASD is diagnosed and conceptualised.

Problems of diagnosis

Children with a diagnosis of ASD resemble one another only in so far as they could be expected to have some difficulties with communication, social interaction, and some restricted and repetitive behaviours. McGregor, Nunez, Williams, and Comez (2007) have pointed out that these behavioural symptoms are relatively independent of one another. As time and research has progressed it has become evident that there are distinct differences between children with an ASD diagnosis. Currently there is concern that this heterogeneity dooms research into cause and treatment to failure (Happé et al., 2006; Klin, 2009). Happé et al. (2006, p. 1218) state, 'There will be no single (genetic or cognitive) cause for the diverse symptoms defining autism . . . At the cognitive level, too, attempts at a single explanation for the symptoms of autism have failed'.

If 'between subject variance' is too great then resulting data is misleading; (a mean intelligence quotient [IQ] of 100 could be derived from children with vast differences in IQ and underlying brain dysfunction). Equally if variation is too wide the relevance of any suggested treatment will be doubtful in many cases. There is a wide difference in intelligence between those with a diagnosis of ASD. There are those with a diagnosis who are exceptionally bright individuals with university degrees and high level jobs and, more commonly, there are those who have severe learning difficulties, very low IQs and who require constant care, such as Nadia. There are those children with ASD whose expressive language develops relatively normally; there are those children whose language development is severely delayed and remains so. There are children who have delayed language development but who show catch-up effects and there are those children whose language develops normally but their language production fades away. There are children with ASD with evident motor impairments and those children who have no such impairments (McAlonan, Suckling, Wong, Cheung, Lienenkaemper, Cheung, et al., 2008).

The cognitive abilities profiles of children with ASD are varied. Most children with ASD have a discrepancy between their verbal abilities and their performance abilities (but not all). Most have significantly poorer verbal scores and higher scores on visual perceptual tasks and notably on block design. (This is a task where the child is presented with a picture of a pattern in red and white and is given red and white blocks to construct the two-dimensional pattern. The task is timed and additional points earned for speed in completion.) Problems with communication usually stem from delayed and abnormal language development but observation and visual processing is often a relative strength. However, there is a distinct group of children (between 15 and 20%) with an ASD diagnosis who have a cognitive abilities profile where verbal abilities are a relative strength and performance skills, including block design, are particularly weak. This derives from my own data collected over 25 years (Selfe, 2002), and corresponds with data reported by Howlin et al. (2009). Their cognitive profiles are radically different from the majority of autistic subjects.

These disparities are rarely addressed because it is recognised that ASD is an umbrella term. Differences in presentation are not usually acknowledged as indicative of the fact that there may be distinctly different groups of children who currently have the same diagnosis. It could be objected that it really does not matter whether cognitive levels and profiles are different in autistic children, if they respond to the same kind of treatment. But, although we have behavioural symptoms that resemble one another, we would not want to 'treat' the child with non-verbal difficulties in the same way as we 'treat' the child with a verbal impairment. Consider, for example, the child who is clumsy. We could construct a checklist of 'clumsy' behaviours but the underlying cause could be due to a number of very different factors such as, an impairment of motor control, a visual difficulty, or the child could simply be very young. Similar behaviours can result from different causes.

For all of these reasons there has been a call for distinguishing subtypes and subgroups that currently exist under the one ASD umbrella (Klin, 2009). This will lead to more careful assessments and, more importantly, more specific treatments and educational interventions. It is also proposed in the draft to the DSM–5 that the subgroups currently subsumed under pervasive developmental disorders, including Asperger's syndrome, be described under one heading, namely autistic spectrum disorder. However, a differentiation on the grounds of severity of symptoms will operate.

Problems of treatment

Children currently diagnosed with ASD do not all need the same treatment programme. The standard programmes for the child with ASD now accepted as being the most appropriate, emphasise visual structure and visual learning, particularly the picture exchange communication system (PECS) and treatment and education of autistic and related communication handicapped children (TEACCH). (Other approaches such as applied behavioural analysis (ABA) are not ASD specific.) Interventions specific to ASD make use of pictures or icons to teach words or actions. For the child with very poor visual perceptual skills diagnosed as having ASD, these programmes can be seriously inappropriate. The use of pictures and visually presented materials are precisely what they cannot understand. Diagnosis of ASD without a careful evaluation of the child's cognitive abilities and their strengths and weaknesses can lead to inappropriate treatment and ineffective educational intervention that could add further stress to an already confused and desperate youngster and their family.

Children with autism resemble one another in terms of essential criteria that are very broad in terms of problems with communication, social interaction, and stereotyped and ritualised behaviours. Autistic spectrum disorder is assessed using behavioural checklists based entirely on parents' reports. Naglieri and Chambers (2009) make the point that many of these instruments are poorly developed. There is a recognisable behavioural pattern of symptoms that relate to one another. For example, if a child has very delayed language production, it will follow that he or she will have confusions of pronouns, telegraphic sentences, echolalia, and so on. What is apparent in conducting assessments is that children with the same ASD diagnosis can have substantially different cognitive profiles and very rarely does any child meet all the criteria for ASD. Careful and thorough-going formulation of every child's functioning is needed to inform effective interventions.

Brain abnormalities and ASD

Autistic spectrum disorder is regularly reported to coexist with a wide range of other conditions where there are known brain abnormalities. Comorbid conditions include epilepsy, attention-deficit hyperactivity disorder, learning difficulties, and specific learning difficulties. Autistic spectrum disorder has also been diagnosed in children who have suffered with tuberosclerosis, homocystinuria, Jeune's syndrome, meningitis in the early months, Prader-Willi syndrome, Fragile X syndrome, and in children with non-verbal syndrome. In addition, children who have been known to have suffered very severe neglect, such as the Romanian orphans, and children who are the victims of severe emotional, physical, and sexual abuse have also been found to present with autistic-like behaviours (quasi-autism; Rutter, Anderson-Wood, Beckett, Bredenkamp, Pastel, Groothes, et al., 1999).

There is general agreement that ASD results from neurological dysfunction present from birth; although the causes of the dysfunction may be various the result is abnormal neurological functioning. Exact mechanisms and supposed differences in brain structure remain elusive but recent promising research has identified that a significant proportion of children with ASD have larger brains with thicker cortex (Courchesne & Pierce, 2005). This finding has led to hypotheses about connectivity differences in neural processing. Post-mortem studies, for example, have shown characteristic differences in the morphometry of radial cells minicolumns in autistic subjects. Minicolumns are multiples of neurons working together in a concerted fashion (Casanova, van Kooten, Switala, van Engeland, Heinsen, Steinbusch, et al., 2006; Casanova & Trippe, 2009). Autistic individuals may possess a defect in mirroring or copying actions performed by others (Tantam, 2009). In the 1990s, Rizzolatti and his colleagues examined the response of single cells in the prefrontal cortex when a monkey moved its hand to grasp a grape. Rizzolatti (1996) discovered that when the monkey observed a human experimenter reaching out to grasp the grape, the neurons also fired. These mirror neurons respond to the monkey's actions *and* the actions of others. The neurons of the monkey function in a system lacking language. However, the mirror neurons are in an area that is thought to be similar to Broca's speech area in humans. This might indicate that these neurons have evolved in humans to allow us to make a prediction about another's intentions (Gazzaniga, Ivry, & Mangun, 2002). Subsequent studies (Kilner & Frith, 2007) have found areas in the human brain that are similarly activated when observing and implementing movements. The mirror neuron system is considered to consist of three connected areas, the ventral premotor area, the inferior parietal lobule, and the superior temporal sulcus. There is also a presence of mirror neurons in the primary motor cortex. These neural architectures shed light upon the processing of information relating to observation and interaction (Kilner & Frith, 2007). This system may be disrupted or damaged in the autistic individual (Tantam, 2009).

It is assumed that there is a common site of damage in the brain in autism but there are many ways in which the damage can occur (Happé & Frith, 1996). These can include genetic factors, maternal disease, and toxic environmental factors. An alternative explanation is that there is no common site but a similar, observable behavioural result. There may be many different neurological pathways leading to the same behavioural consequences. A range of different underlying neurological changes or deficits could give rise to typical ASD behaviours, confusion and high anxiety, resulting in a retreat from social interaction and into obsessional and ritualistic behaviours.

The symptoms commonly associated with autism may result from a variety of different causes. This is very obviously the case with children with severe learning difficulty. Such children frequently also meet all the DSM–IV criteria for autism. It is unsurprising, therefore, that in all the neurological studies only a portion of subjects with ASD show the results under investigation.

Further issues relating to diagnosis

There are a number of other important issues to consider, especially from the perspective of a clinician. Although much progress has been made in our understanding of ASD, some aspects of diagnosis and assessment leave one with some disquiet. Eccentric children with a quirky view of the world and obsessional interests are now labelled as having Asperger's syndrome or, as the author recently read, 'atypical, mild Asperger's syndrome'. Fitzpatrick said in an article in

The Times (2009; p. 24): 'The tendency to label as autistic every computer geek or eccentric scientist, and every train spotter and stamp collector (compounded by the vogue for identifying historical figures and even contemporary celebrities as autistic) carries the danger that the spectrum becomes stretched so wide that autism loses its distinctiveness.'

Children as young as 18 months are being diagnosed in the interests of early intervention. Proponents of the Lovaas method are claiming recovery from autism (Lovaas, 1987). Extraordinarily articulate people are writing books or heading conferences explaining what it is like to be autistic. The very fact that these autistic individuals can describe and reflect on their autism is a contra-indication of the condition (Draaisma, 2009). It is perhaps unwise to make generalisations from the experiences described by high-functioning people diagnosed with ASD to the experiences of others who may often be unable to speak for themselves (Hacking, 2009). He warns that in reality, we cannot know what it is like to be 'inside the autistic mind'. Baron-Cohen has voiced his doubts that diagnosis of a 'disorder' in high-functioning people with Asperger's syndrome is either helpful or ethical (Orr, 2009).

It is all a different world from the 1970s when I was writing my first book and clinicians just had Kanner's (1943) original conception of autism to consider. Nowadays, psychiatrists seem to be under increasing pressure to diagnose ASD from worried parents since they believe that a diagnosis will bring rights to better resources or provisions. The pressure to diagnose is creating its own momentum. In the meanwhile parents of children with severe ASD and severe learning difficulties are becoming increasingly concerned that the public perception of the condition is dominated by that created by articulate and high-functioning individuals. The fear is that the needs of those children with severe autism are being neglected or marginalised.

Another concern is that assessment tools are almost always behavioural checklists used with parents (with the notable exception of the Autism Diagnostic Observation Schedule (ADOS; Lord, Rutter, Goode, Heemsbergen, Jordon, Mawhood, et al., 1989). The responses are, unfortunately, subjective and open to interpretation and bias. Parents of adolescent children are asked questions about their child in infancy relying on their memories when there may be three or four other children in the family. There is no medical test for autism – no objective, definitive test. Diagnosis relies solely upon behavioural criteria. Even in the best available diagnostic questionnaires there is no normative comparison, and little attempt to relate questions to the child's age or cognitive level. Frequently, the IQ level of the subject is ignored. Usually some sort of score is computed and cut-off points or bands of probability of a diagnosis of autism constructed. The questions are often applied to all children regardless of age or developmental level, and what is abnormal at one age is perfectly normal at another. For example, the obsessive need to line objects up at the age of 8 is unusual but it is a regular feature of pre-symbolic play in very young children.

Similarly, in the best assessments there is some attempt to weight assessment criteria beyond essential and non-essential but in many there is not. Failing to use pointing and gesture is far more significant in terms of diagnosis than tip-toe walking, but both are given the same weighting in many diagnostic checklists. Equally, the best checklists only give cut-off criteria for diagnosis with a simple choice of 'yes' or 'no' as to whether the child shows the specified behaviour. Diagnosis, then, depends largely on an assessment of observed behaviour as judged by the parent.

Labelling: benefits or costs?

As has been stated, the incidence of ASD has been rising. Recent suggestions have claimed 1 in 100 children with ASD (Baird et al., 2006). But is a diagnosis necessarily beneficial to all the children whom we are currently identifying? There is much psychological and sociological research that points out the dangers of labelling children. Expectations and perceptions can actually shape behaviour in children so the label becomes a self-fulfilling prophesy (Rubie-Davies, 2010). Therefore, applying any label to a child should never be undertaken lightly. Kogan et al. (2009) quote studies that show that 40% of children in the USA suspected by a health professional of having an ASD are not confirmed as having this disorder subsequently, and the rate of disconfirmed cases is highest among black children. This suggests that premature labelling of ASD is prevalent. Children's sociability improves with maturity and the label of ASD may be used inappropriately about children from other cultural backgrounds whose mores may be more difficult to comprehend.

Pilgrim (2000) reviews the problems of medical labelling and self-fulfilling prophesy effects, and argues for a context specific formulation of mental disorders. He argues that categorical descriptions are 'reductionist, impersonal and stigmatising', and he is critical of what could be regarded as the 'medicalisation' of personality. His arguments can be extended to the diagnosis of ASD. We have always had children who were 'loners', 'oddballs', 'different' and, in other contexts, people applaud the lone heroes who blazed trails or held some obsessive conviction against the odds. One problem with the widening definition of ASD is that it takes children who hitherto would have been regarded as eccentric, boys who train spot or keep collections of bugs, or like dinosaurs excessively, and turns their behaviour and their interests into 'symptoms'.

Nadia was diagnosed with autism when she was aged 7. She continues to meet the diagnostic criteria for ASD in her middle age. She has little interest or ability in communication beyond indicating her basic needs. She remains asocial, rarely initiating any social contact and she has a series of ritualistic obsessions and stereotyped behaviours. She has severe learning difficulties as is common with classical autism.

Theories of autism

Since my original studies, research into ASD has proliferated. I was able to read most of the literature written in English about autism in 1977 and did so. Today the task would be impossible. Several journals have emerged dedicated solely to the welter of research on ASD. Hardly a week goes by without an article in one of the quality newspapers on ASD and there are frequent television programmes.

Theories about the causes of ASD have been numerous: some have been promising and some frankly implausible. The range of theoretical explanations can be seen in these examples from press reports.

'Vinyl Flooring "doubles the chances of children being autistic", study shows'. *The Independent* April, 2009 (by Geoffrey Lean and Nina Lakhani). The authors discuss research that purports to find that children who live in homes with vinyl flooring have double the chance of being autistic. The study by scientists in Sweden, Denmark and the USA stumbled across the connection almost by accident. The new research, which traced nearly 5000 Swedish children from infancy to at least 6 years old, set out to investigate links between air pollution and asthma and other allergies. Their paper published in the journal, *Neurotoxicity*, describes the findings as 'puzzling'. A possible explanation they suggest, is that vinyl or PVC flooring produces dust full of phthalates that are then breathed in.

'Scientists throw fresh light on autism' – *Aberdeen University Magazine*, September, 2009 (Anon, p. 63). This report describes how researchers at Aberdeen have discovered abnormalities in a gene important for learning and memory and suggest this is a possible cause of autism. In a study published in the *Journal of Medical Genetics* the researchers, led by Dr Miedzybrodzka, reader in medical genetics at the university, explained how the investigations into the gene *EIF4E* began with the study of one child with severe autism (Neves-Pereira et al., 2009). The boy was found to have a rare rearrangement of chromosomes. Using state of the art genetic mapping techniques, they found the rearrangement had disrupted the *EIF4E* gene. They then looked in more detail at the make up of *EIF4E* in 120 other families with autism.

'MMR scare research withdrawn by "Lancet"'. *The Independent* February, 2010 (by Jeremy Laurance). He reported that the controversial research paper that sparked an international scare over the measles, mumps, rubella (MMR) vaccine was now withdrawn by *The Lancet* medical journal, 12 years after it was published. The decision followed a preliminary verdict by a disciplinary panel of the General Medical Council that found serious errors in the research, which linked the vaccine to the onset of autism. Laurance notes that the decision 'brings to a close one of the unhappiest chapters in medical research'. The 1998 paper, based on 12 children, some of whom had bowel disorders and autism that had developed following vaccine with MMR, was criticised from the start. But it triggered a sharp fall in vaccination rates and years of speculation about the safety of MMR vaccine, despite absence of evidence.

There are now several Masters level degrees on the subject. It remains an interesting question as to why there is such intense interest in ASD. Why do we not have the same number of journals dedicated to, say, Down's syndrome, where the diagnosis is much more clear-cut and where there is a known genetic abnormality? I think the answer to this is that ASD remains so puzzling. There is no certain cause and speculation fuels interest. Also fragments of normal functioning, which usually occur in the individual with ASD, often create the impression of a human jigsaw that could somehow be repaired. Most importantly, enquiries into ASD help us understand normal cognition. One powerful and well-tried method of learning about normal functioning in medicine, for example, is to study abnormal functioning. Some theories have emerged that now have a very solid evidence base and move our understanding of ASD and normal development forward and these are considered next.

Theory of mind

In non-autistic, typically developing individuals the capacity to attribute mental states to self and others, termed a theory of mind, arises at a very early age. Children as young as 4 can attain advanced concepts such as false belief, deception, white-lie, and double bluff (White, Hill, Happé, & Frith, 2009). Recent research on motivational states has revealed that even babies in their first year of life can attribute dispositions and goals to agents (Biro & Leslie, 2007; Song, Onishi, Baillargeon, & Fisher, 2008). Infants with autism show delayed or absent preconditions for the development of mentalising, such as attentional preferences for human faces, voices, and movements (Frith, 2001). Wimmer and Perner (1983) created a false belief task about the location of a bar of chocolate for a boy called Maxi, in order to test an individual's theory of mind. Baron-Cohen and his associates (1985) developed a simplified version termed the 'Sally Anne task'. A toy scene is set up involving small dolls (Sally and Anne). Sally has a basket and Ann has a box. Sally puts a marble into her basket and leaves the room. Anne moves the marble from the basket to her box. Sally comes back into the room. The child watching this scene is then asked, 'Where will Sally look for her marble?' This task requires a prediction to be made on the basis of attribution of false belief to another person. The prediction is incorrect if it is made on the basis of the child's own belief or knowledge. Essentially, in order to succeed at the task, the child has to be aware that different people can have different beliefs about a situation.

Baron-Cohen and colleagues (1985) found that 80% of their autistic subjects failed the test as compared with non-autistic children and Down's syndrome children, where over 80% passed the test. The results suggested that autistic children as a group fail to employ a theory of mind. There appears to be an inability to understand the mental states of others. This puts autistic individuals at a grave disadvantage when having to predict the behaviour of other people. Children with autism fail to understand mental states at an appropriate mental age. A 6-year delay was found between an ASD sample's theory of mind and a non-autistic group (Happé & Frith, 1996); 80% passed first order false belief tasks, whereby a prediction is made about what another believes, by 11 years instead of 5 years (Happé & Frith, 1996).

It has been argued that false belief tests, such as the 'Sally Anne task', require working memory and the ability to inhibit reality-oriented responses (Frith, 2001). To distinguish whether or not failure at this task is essentially a theory of mind deficit, an ASD sample must successfully complete similar tasks without the mentalising component. A picture task was used (Leslie & Thaiss, 1992), whereby, autistic children were shown a teddy bear sitting on a chair. A Polaroid photograph was taken of the scene. The photo was put aside. The teddy bear was then moved to a bed. The children were asked whether in the photograph the teddy was sitting on a chair or a bed. The contents of the photo no longer accords with current reality, just as with Sally in the 'Sally Anne task', who has a false belief about the position of the marble. The concept of mental states has been removed from the task, since participants are not asked to consider another's perspective. Autistic children could correctly state that the teddy was on the chair in the photograph. This suggests that autistic children do have the ability to inhibit a realism-oriented response and have the working memory capabilities to correctly respond in this picture task (Frith, 2001). Consequently, poor performance in the 'Sally Anne task' is likely to be due to specific difficulties in mentalising and appreciating another's mental states.

The neural basis for theory of mind has been investigated (Castelli, Frith, Happé, & Frith, 2002). In previous research (Abell, Happé, & Frith, 2000), silent animations on a computer had been created to assess the mentalising ability of an autistic sample. There were three sets of animations: a mentalising condition, whereby two triangles appear to play together on the computer screen; a goal-directed condition, whereby the triangles appear to chase one another; and a random animation condition, whereby the triangles move aimlessly about the screen. The ASD sample were very poor at attributing mental states to the triangles in the mentalising condition. In other research, ten autistic adults of average intelligence and ten non-autistic adults were scanned using functional MRI (fMRI), while they watched the three, silent animations (Castelli et al., 2002). The control sample evidenced peaks of activation in the medial prefrontal cortex, an area at the top of the superior, temporal gyrus and at the temporal poles adjacent to the amygdala. Importantly, the activity in these areas changed across conditions. Autistic individuals, during the mentalising condition, showed identical activation in the occipital gyrus as the controls. The autistic individuals appeared to dedicate more intense visual analysis to the animations. However, the connectivity between the occipital and temporo-parietal regions was weaker in the autistic group than in the controls. The apparent mind blindness in autism could be due to under-activation, occurring as a result of restricted access for interaction between lower and higher order perceptual processing areas (Frith, 2001).

It is important to note that Castelli et al.'s (2002) research was conducted with ASD adults of average intelligence, who are on this basis, atypical (Klinger, Klinger, & Pohlig, 2006). It has also been objected that the functioning of the mind is still so far removed from our understanding of the underlying physiology of the brain that it is premature to be concerned with which brain region is activated (Coltheart, 2006). Neuroimaging has been viewed as reductionist, concerned only with *where* and not *how* our cognitive processes arise. Coltheart (2006) suggests that functional imaging data are only applicable if there is organised mapping between which psychological process is occurring and where neural activity is changing.

Recently working with a little boy with a diagnosis of Asperger's syndrome he attempted to teach me a complicated card game involving a series of characters with magical powers. I wasn't getting on too well so that at one point he said to me, 'I'd play Excalibar Sonic if I was you.' I answered quizzically, 'Well, how do I know you're not tricking me into a bad move?' To which he replied, 'Well, you will have to trust me.' I replied, 'How do I know I can?' He replied, 'Well, you'll never know if you don't play that card.' Not only did this boy have a theory about what was in my mind but he could also comment on my theory about what was in his mind. There is distinctive heterogeneity of ASD individuals; not all autistic children and adults have 'mind blindness' and this cannot be a necessary condition for diagnosis. High functioning autistic children and adults often pass tests of mentalising and individuals with autism can come to understand mental states. Similarly, mentalising problems are not entirely specific to autism. Deaf and blind individuals have been found to perform poorly on theory of mind tasks (Patterson & Siegal, 1995). Strong performance, however, on these tasks by deaf children of deaf parents has been reported (Peterson, Wellman, & Liu, 2005). It has been claimed, however, that mentalising ability in autistic subjects is not intuitive, and they must actively work out another's perspective (Frith, 2001). Mentalising difficulties, therefore, present differently in ASD individuals.

Alternatively, mentalising difficulties have been suggested as resulting from executive dysfunction (Russell, 1997). For example, deficits in self-monitoring and self-awareness may lead to a failure to develop an understanding of mental states. Equally, poor mentalising abilities could be a result of an inability to hold in mind and shift between arbitrary rules (Russell, 2002). There are other social impairments in autism, such as problems with face-recognition memory, control of emotion, imitation, attention to cues and heightened egocentrism, which are not *easily* explained by a problem of 'mind blindness' (White et al., 2009). Moreover, 'mind blindness' can explain little of the restricted, repetitive and stereotyped patterns of behaviour, interests, and activities or savant skill present in autism.

Without doubt since Baron-Cohen et al's (1985) original work, difficulties with mentalising and theory of mind have become a cornerstone of research into autism and into cognitive processes generally. Frith (2001) says that theory of mind makes sense of the core social and communication impairments common to individuals with ASD. Moreover, fMRI studies using a range of false belief tasks have yielded consistent findings. Functional underconnectivity between frontal lobe and parietal areas of the brain has been demonstrated consistently in subjects with ASD (Mason, Williams, Kana, Minshew, & Just, 2008).

Baron-Cohen's empathising/systemising (E/S) theory and ASD

Baron-Cohen (2003a, 2006) has developed a theory of autism based on some earlier work he undertook on the extreme male brain. Exposure to abnormally high levels of testosterone *in utero* have been linked to autism. Some children with ASD were found to have very low digit ratios (the ratio of index to third finger length), suggestive of high levels of testosterone exposure. His research has shown that there are gender related differences to the way that males and females respond to emotions in others. Females have been found to be more sensitive to changes in facial expressions, while it is generally men who have been mathematicians, engineers, and physicists (Baron-Cohen, 2006). These differences were found to exist across cultures (a view that would not pass a feminist critique).

Using these findings, Baron-Cohen (2006) suggested that females are generally more empathetic and men are more typically systemisers. According to his theory, females are often person centred and intuitively aware of how someone else is feeling while men are better at investigating how underlying rules and structures operate (Baron-Cohen, 2006). Children with autism often show the same sort of preoccupation with understanding how systems work. They frequently enjoy ordering collections of objects or data; show interest in encyclopaedias; have preoccupations with such things as washing machines, catalogues, timetables, technical manuals, and schedules. The classic savant skills, all attest to specific interests with systems and structures (Baron-Cohen, 2006). An extreme male brain may account for some of the classic diagnostic features of ASD. Baron-Cohen (2003b, para 2), stated in *The Guardian* that:

> Empathising is the drive to identify another person's emotions and thoughts and to respond to these with an appropriate emotion. The empathiser intuitively figures out how people are feeling, and how to treat people with care and sensitivity. Systemising is the drive to analyse and explore a system, to extract underlying rules that govern the behaviour of a system and the drive to construct systems. The systemiser intuitively figures out how things work, or what the underlying rules are controlling a system.

Baron-Cohen (2003b) continues by claiming that the female brain is predominantly hardwired for empathy and the male brain is predominantly hardwired for understanding and building systems. This is termed the empathising/systemising theory (E/S theory). The obsessional interests that people with ASD often show focus on a system with an underlying structured pattern (Baron-Cohen, 2006). The child may be focusing on the details of a system in order to work out the underlying rules that govern it. The characteristic approach of the person with ASD is to become obsessed with the minutiae of a subject, such as those noted above. Their learning style is to prefer a narrow, obsessional interest explored in depth. The child with ASD may have strengths with systemising but they usually have impaired empathising. Baron-Cohen et al. (2009) have also turned their attention to savant syndrome and suggest that the special skills, such as calendar calculation, musical ability, drawing in linear perspective, are all particular examples of systemising in action. These special skills require the application of involved rules and predictable structures. This is reminiscent of Treffert's (1989) notion of the 'unconscious acquisition of algorithms'.

Weak central coherence theory

Following on the development of theory of mind as being one of the central deficits in ASD, other theorists have suggested that autistic individuals have weak central coherence (Frith, 1989). Central coherence is a term, developed by Frith, that describes the tendency for non-autistic individuals to process information in its context in order to access higher level meaning. This was described by Plaisted, Swettenham, and Rees (1999), among others, as a 'global advantage'. In contrast, Frith suggested that autistic individuals demonstrate local processing, whereby details and parts are the focus; global, contextualised meaning is thereby somewhat neglected or disregarded. For example, in Nadia's drawing and that of other savants, particularly Stephen Wiltshire, the child commences by drawing small details of the object before attempting a general outline. (This is demonstrated by the stills of Nadia's drawing of a horse in Figure 2.5.) Normal children proceed in exactly the opposite manner in their drawing technique, moving from a global or general outline to incidental detail. Another example is the approach of autistic children to a jigsaw puzzle. Their focus of interest is on the individual pieces, this appears to give them a particular facility in completing the whole. Happé and Vital (2009) also suggest that detail-focused processing bias accounts for why absolute pitch seems more common in autistic savants than in comparable groups. In terms of linguistic skills, it had been noted that autistic children could recite fragments of a story or narrative with precision but were unable to explain the gist of the story. They cannot integrate the fragments easily into a coherent narrative, which is a relatively easy task for normally developing matched controls.

Previous theories had tended to focus on deficits in ASD such as poor social interaction and problems with a theory of mind. But weak central coherence theory can also account for some special abilities displayed by ASD individuals. (Shah & Frith, 1983, 1993). Children with ASD were found to be faster than matched controls in identifying a hidden figure in a picture in an embedded figure task. Shah and Frith (1983, 1993) suggested that autistic children can be shown to attend to detail better than normally developing children. In an experiment autistic individuals and matched controls performed a task assembling patterns from separated constituent blocks where attention to the small constituent parts is required. Participants with autism completed the task more quickly and with fewer mistakes. While typically developing children benefited from seeing the target design broken into its constituent parts, those with autism performed well whether the design was pre-segmented or unsegmented. Shah and Frith (1993) suggested that autistic children could apprehend elements of the stimulus even when presented unsegmented. Happé (1999) argued that ASD subjects can perceive segments and detail with less interference from the intrusive perception of the whole array.

Weak central coherence: deficit or strength?

Happé (1999) suggested that in tasks that require specific attention to detail (or a local processing bias), weak central coherence theory predicts enhanced performance. For example, autistic individuals are less likely to succumb to standard visual illusions, conjuring tricks and other events that might bemuse a normal child. Autistic samples have been presented with a series of visual illusions, such as the Titchener circles (see Figure 4.1 below; Happé, 1996). In non-autistic individuals the presence of the surrounding circles affects the ability to judge whether the two inner circles are really the same size. Autistic subjects appear to perceive such figures in a less unified, more piecemeal way and are, therefore, less likely to succumb to this illusion (Happé, 1999). In comparison, in tasks that require a grasp of the global meaning or integration of stimuli in context, weak central coherence theory predicts that performance will be limited. Individuals with autism have been found to perform poorly on tasks where preceding sentence context can be used to derive meaning and determine pronunciation of homographs (Frith & Snowling, 1983; Happé, 1997). An autistic sample were presented with sentences containing homographs, e.g., 'In her eye there was a big tear'; 'In her dress there was a big tear'. The sample failed to use preceding sentence context to determine the correct pronunciation of these homographs. This suggests that those with autism might read sentences like a list of unconnected words and disregard the overall meaning.

This theory may explain the remarkable ability of some autistic subjects in computation, music, and perspective drawing who otherwise show severe

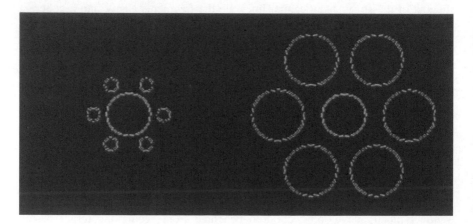

Figure 4.1 Titchener circles. This is a visual illusion whereby the centre circle on the left appears to be larger than the centre circle on the right. Both centre circles are exactly the same size.

impairments in global processing skills particularly with language, communication, and social understanding (Happé & Frith, 2006). Pring, Hermelin, and Heavey (1995) suggested that autistic individuals have a propensity for seeing wholes in terms of their parts rather than as 'unified gestalts' and this ability might be a general characteristic of individuals with or without autism, with an aptitude for drawing. Mottron and Belleville (1993) reported on an artist with autism who was able to describe and demonstrate the fact that he drew contiguous details slowly building up an object rather than sketching an outline first. This is described as 'local proximity strategy'.

Points of criticism

Other studies, however, particularly those of Mottron et al. (1999) and Ozonoff et al. (1994), have reported disconfirming findings. Ozonoff et al. failed to find the predicted local processing bias using a version of the Navon figures (Figure 4.2). Navon (1977) presented subjects with letters composed of a series of small letters. The stimulus figure is shown briefly and the child is asked to select which letter is being shown. The child can make the selection on the basis of the global configuration or on the basis of the individual letters that make up the overall pattern. Navon predicted that typically developing children will respond to the global configuration and this was confirmed but children with ASD also showed no preference for local detail (Ozonoff et al., 1994).

Similar to non-autistic controls, autistic participants were subject to the same bias towards global processing. Mottron et al. (1999, 2003) stated that the notions of local bias and global impairments as part of weak central coherence theory 'may need to be re-examined'. They suggested that the weak coherence effects can be best understood in terms of attention to detail and enhanced perception of subjects with ASD (as will be discussed in detail in Chapter 6).

It has been noted by other researchers such as Jolliffe and Baron-Cohen (1997), that children with ASD display problems in processing language in which sentences contain potential ambiguities (such as result from the inclusion of homographs as described above). However, Happé (1999) found that differences between ASD and non-ASD subjects faced with this problem disappear when the

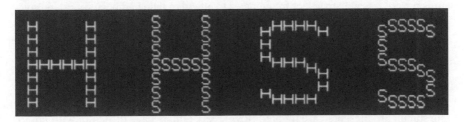

Figure 4.2 Navon figures. Navon (1977) suggested that there is a preference, in normal perception, for processing the whole field initially rather than detail. Typically developing children respond globally as Navon predicted.

children are asked to read for meaning. This led her to the view that children with ASD have a different cognitive style, rather than a cognitive deficit. They were able to process globally (i.e., comprehend the whole sentence and its meaning), but merely had a preference for local processing (that is, reading the homograph) regardless of whether it made sense in the sentence.

Baron-Cohen et al. (2009) suggest that there are differences between weak central coherence theory and that of hyper-systemising theory. They state that:

> WCC theory [weak central coherence theory] sees people with ASC as drawn to detailed information (sometimes called local processing bias) either for negative reasons (an inability to integrate was posited) or because of stronger local processing (in a later version of the theory). Hyper-systemising theory sees the same quality (excellent attention to detail) as being highly purposeful; it exists to understand a system.
>
> (p. 1378)

Another difference they note is that hyper-systemising theory predicts that over time the person may achieve an understanding of a whole system whereas, weak central coherence theory predicts that given any amount of time, the autistic individual will be always lost in the detail.

Plaisted, Saksida, Alcantara, and Weisblatt (2003) investigated the weak central coherence hypothesis noting the abnormal performance of individuals with ASD on tasks that involve local and global processing. They used a series of tests where autistic children and matched controls had to respond either to the array (block designs or dot patterns) as a complete configuration or to a constituent part of the array (what they term 'feature processing'). They found that while children with ASD were generally better at responding to the constituent parts, there was no difference in the response of these subjects and the response of normal subjects to the whole array.

Plaisted and colleagues (2003; Plaisted, Grant, & Davis, 2009) claimed that in ASD individuals visual perception operates to enhance the representation of individual local perceptual features but that this did not impact adversely on representation that involved the integration of these features. However, in the same series of experiments they investigated auditory sensitivity and found that individuals with autism were less able to select frequencies to attend to than had been found in typically developing subjects. Plaisted and colleagues speculated whether their findings are modality specific and subjects with ASD may show enhanced ability to attend to detail in visually presented materials only. They also distinguished between low level weak central coherence (in relation to perception, learning and attention) and high level processing in linguistic and semantic processes. Some ASD individuals perform well on embedded figure and block design tasks where the context in which the stimuli are presented are ignored (low level). Others have difficulty with homographs in sentences and other semantic and contextual processing tasks (high level).

The authors note that research involving people with autism has produced mixed results regarding the differences in response hypothesised by weak central coherence theory. But some findings have been replicated by researchers, such as Mottron et al. (2003). Plaisted et al. (2003) found that individuals with autism can respond at the global level, where participants are required to respond to the overall form of the stimulus. Also, under some circumstances, some people with autism show faster and more accurate responding to the local level (where the participants are asked to respond to the constituent parts of a block design task) than comparison individuals. This suggests attentional deficits related to global processing are not deficient in autism and cannot be the locus for low level weak central coherence.

The weak central coherence theory is therefore brought under scrutiny by the fact that autistic people can show enhanced local processing as well as normal global processing. Plaisted et al. (2003, 2009) conclude that a local level processing bias may not therefore result from a deficit in global-level processing. They were interested in outcomes of the perceptual processing resulting in abnormally acute representation of feature information. Also, they wished to identify the mechanisms underlying the abnormalities in stimulus processing associated with ASD. They concluded that enhanced feature processing in autism may be a consequence of abnormal cortical arousal systems that increases feature detectability, suggesting new avenues of future investigation.

Central coherence theory offers a great deal of evidence for a difference in cognitive style related to ASD and points to a facility with processing detail, possibly at the expense of context, particularly in visually presented materials but also demonstrable in processing language. Happé (1999) has linked these findings to suggest that the effects may indicate diffuse brain mechanisms and relates this to the finding that some people with ASD appear to have larger brains than normal with increased cell packing in some areas. She speculates that processing with excess neurons may lead to attention to detail rather than a more economical grasp of the gist.

Executive function theory and ASD

Interest in executive functioning and ASD has developed in parallel to weak central coherence theory. It attempts to account for cognitive deficits and to link this closely to underlying neurology. Ozonoff and Miller (1996) were one of the first research teams to investigate executive functioning in relation to ASD. Executive functions are the high level cognitive processes that facilitate new ways of behaving, and optimise one's reactions to unfamiliar circumstances. We engage in such processes when we switch from one activity to another or when we make a plan or change our mind about a situation (Gilbert & Burgess, 2008). Insofar as those with ASD show grave impairments in their ability to plan or to encompass change, especially in unfamiliar surroundings or in new social situations, they could be said to have deficits in executive functioning.

At the heart of most theories about executive functioning is the distinction between what we do automatically, as a well-learned routine, and what we do in a non-routine way when we have to consciously control our behaviour. Routine processing is behaviour that is overlearned and stimulus/response led. Whereas, non-routine behaviour is the processing we have to do when the situation is novel or when our usual responses are not appropriate. At an abstract level of functioning are the flexible representations of goals and intentions, such as planning to visit a friend. Such higher-level representations are often contrasted with lower-level cognitive processes involved in, for example, analysing specific visual stimuli such as seeing a familiar face and waving one's hand.

Ozonoff, Pennington, and Rogers (1991) used activities such as the Wisconsin Card Sorting Task to investigate executive functioning. In this task the subject is required to sort cards where the cards can be grouped along a number of possible dimensions (such as number, shape, colour, etc.). The subject is given feedback on the basis of a rule that can be changed at random and the subject has to discover which attribute constitutes the rule. The Stockings of Cambridge task (Hughes, Russell, & Robbins, 1994) was also devised to investigate executive functioning and requires the subject to move discs on pegs to match a sequence in as few moves as possible. Both these tasks require planning and processing of a higher order than automatic responding and autistic children were found to perform less well than normally functioning children matched for mental age. However, Liss, Fein, Allen, Dunn, Feinstein, Morris, et al. (2001) suggested that the results on studies of executive functioning deficits and autism indicated that only certain executive functions are affected in autism and the most robust finding is that individuals with ASD tend to make perseverative errors on such tasks. They point out that one of the diagnostic markers of autism is narrow focus, attention to detail and perseveration. They also point out that intelligence may be a major factor affecting performance on the tasks used to judge executive functioning.

Gilbert and Burgess (2008) suggest that executive functioning entails the modulation of lower level processes by those at a higher level (for example, deciding to go over and initiate a conversation). Executive functioning allows us to behave appropriately and flexibly, rather than being slaves to stimulus and response behaviours. The modulation of various cognitive, perceptual, and motor responses according to abstract aims and goals is commonly referred to as 'top–down control'. Although, as Gilbert and Burgess point out, this need not be unidirectional; at times we may be distracted from our goals or are led to respond before thinking. Higher level processes are commonly triggered in everyday life resulting from conflicts between representations at lower levels as, for instance, when something unexpected occurs.

Research on executive functioning and the brain

Over the last 30 years great advances have been made in our understanding of the function of the brain and the discrete areas of the brain involved in higher level executive function. It had been established that injury to the prefrontal cortex could disrupt executive functioning. Technological advances in scanning have enabled researchers to look into the working brain and to map functions. Studies using MRI scanning and other methods of neuroimaging have been able to map the link between demands made using tasks of executive function and the operation of the prefrontal cortex.

Activities such as the Wisconsin Card Sorting Task require planning and processing of a higher order than automatic responding. Gilbert and Burgess (2008) suggest that higher order tasks require the following:

- Inhibition: overcoming the tendency to respond in a stimulus response fashion when this is not appropriate.
- Working memory: remembering and manipulating information over time.
- Flexibility: switching between two or more stimulus response alternatives.
- Initiation: self-initiated behaviour in the absence of external cues.
- Strategy application: the development of a novel strategy or approach.
- Multitasking: control of novel behavioural sequences over a long period of time.

Researchers suggest that the dynamics of this paradigm are complex and that many other brain regions as well as the prefrontal cortex are found to be involved during executive function tasks. Much of our understanding of executive functioning is based on studies of patients with frontal lobe damage. Many of these individuals are found to be impulsive and unable to pursue goals over a long period or defer gratification. In other patients with frontal lobe damage the problem is that they perseverate over simple tasks and appear unable to stop an activity and pursue another.

Norman and Shallice (1986) put forward an influential framework for understanding executive functioning that accounted for what was seen in patients with frontal lobe damage. They suggested that normal behaviour is governed by sets of thought or 'action schemas'. A schema is defined as a set of actions or cognitions that have become closely associated through experience or practice. People operate with a repertoire of such schemas and Norman and Shallice propose that a second, higher order system is required to modulate these schemas so that the individual can select an appropriate schema or change schemas when necessary. Norman and Shallice label this the 'supervisory system' and suggest that this is the primary function of the frontal lobes. Damage to the supervisory system could explain both the excessive rigidity seen in perseveration in patients with frontal lobe damage as well as excessive distractibility and impulsivity.

Other theorists such as Duncan (2001) have suggested that the prefrontal cortex is involved in organising changes in responses and emphasised the remarkable ability of the human being to multitask and to be flexible. Executive function involves higher level processes and modulating lower level ones according to the current task demands so that human behaviour is very adaptable and is not driven by immediate goals. Gilbert and Burgess (2008) suggest, therefore, that executive function is an umbrella term referring to those higher level processes that control and organise other mental processes. They go on to claim that neuroscience is beginning to map features of executive functioning derived from batteries of tests that tap distinct areas in the frontal cortex. They conclude that we are beginning to have an understanding that a particular region in the prefrontal cortex supports a particular executive ability but not necessarily how it does this.

Non-verbal communication and ASD

In his book intriguingly entitled, *Can the World Afford Autistic Spectrum Disorder?* (2009), Tantam has reminded researchers that one of the most devastating and pervasive problems suffered by all children with ASD is their failure to read body language, facial expression and all the subtle ways we communicate without language via non-verbal communication. Although this deficit is generally well recognised as key in ASD, its significance and importance has been underestimated in recent years. Non-verbal communication is essential in expressing emotion in the service of mediating social relationships with others and there are specialised communicative channels to facilitate this. Touch, for example, is an important channel for mediating affection. Mimicry and mirroring posture are other ways in which we communicate our engagement with others (Tantam, 2009). Human beings deliberately show things to each other. The absence of being able to make eye contact as in blindness seems to have a substantial effect on social development. However, blind children learn from auditory and tactile input to be social beings. Non-verbal communication is pivotal in building and maintaining social relationships and the function is to facilitate collaboration between human beings. Tantam (2009) makes the point that social interaction is dependent on two or more people focusing on a task or issue that requires joint attention.

The interbrain

From this analysis Tantam (2009) develops a controversial but compelling notion of what he terms 'the interbrain'. Non-verbal communication is a special sort of automatic, non-intentional connectedness that has its roots in our social nature as evidenced by our social interactions. This theory draws upon sociological concepts from Durkheim and Merleau-Ponty's notion of intersubjectivity to support this position. The interbrain is his metaphysical construct of the unconscious shared knowledge and understanding all human beings require in interacting and conducting social activities. Imitation and joint attention in infancy are the precursors of social interaction and both are absent or impaired in infants with ASD. The behaviour of severely autistic people can be similar to people who are kept in social isolation. Such people do not have access to the interbrain and normal social interaction and feedback from others (Tantam, 2009). Romanian orphans are an example of autistic-like behaviour that result from extreme isolation and neglect. Tantam (2009) states that 'The explanation for their [people with ASD] social impairment is not that they have particular and specifiable problems with social processes but that they are, as people with ASD sometimes say, ' "cut off from other people" ' (p. 105). Tantam concludes: 'To make a case for the existence of the interbrain, I will need to establish that this kind of automatic networking actually does occur; I will need to establish that non-verbal communication will actually mediate it and I will need to deal with some of the obvious objections' (p. 101).

The remainder of his book develops his argument. Joint attention and imitation are important in primate behaviour, which has given impetus to research on imitation as a fundamental social process (Hadjikhani, Joseph, Manoach, Naik, Snyder, Dominick, et al., 2007). He argues that impairment in non-verbal communication represents impairment in connectivity to other people, which leads to many of the symptoms seen in ASD (Tantam, 2009).

Conclusions

It can be seen that there are a number of overlapping and interrelated theories about the central cognitive deficits in autism all of which have emerged since my original study of Nadia and all of which contribute to our understanding of this perplexing and distressing condition. Along with the difficulties posed by the lack of homogeneity in ASD, it is not one single condition; we also have different theories to explain the presenting symptoms. However, all these theories can coexist, especially since this is a heterogeneous group of children and young people, and as Tantam (2009) has pointed out, some of the theories may be linked by considering them as pertaining to different ages and stages of development. Non-verbal difficulties, such as failing to give eye contact, or failing to imitate can be demonstrated at a very early stage of development before the infant has any expressive language. A theory of mind involves understanding language and instructions and can only be demonstrated after the age of 2. Central coherence theory and executive functioning can also be seen as intimately related. Not being able to see the wood for the trees or grasping the general picture must lead to difficulties with decision making, planning, and executive functioning, for instance. That is to say, a person who cannot grasp the central issues of social interaction or the wider picture may have difficulties in making sense of the social world. There are other theories that apply specifically to subgroups and particularly to autistic children with savant syndrome but this will be considered in Chapter 6 when there is a closer look at research on savant syndrome and autism.

Research over the last 35 years, since Nadia was first diagnosed, has grown exponentially along with our knowledge and our understanding of ASD. The inclusion of high-functioning children with Asperger's syndrome has given us a group of people who can tell us what it feels like to be asocial and autistic. However, along with broadening the 'spectrum' has come concerns about both the diagnosis of autism and about the heterogeneity of the condition. The DSM–IV is currently being revised and it is expected that the new diagnostic framework will reflect functional differences as well as differences in intelligence, aetiology, and severity. Currently, behavioural checklists are the only diagnostic instruments, including the very best ones, like the Autism Diagnostic Interview Revised (Rutter et al., 2004) and the Diagnostic Interview for Social and Communication Disorders (Wing & Gould, 1991). These are used with parents who may be unreliable or even biased reporters. In addition, there are misgivings among practitioners and clinicians about diagnosis without performing an in-depth cognitive profiling of the child.

This is not to diminish or deny that there are central essential diagnostic features of autism but what is now advocated is a very careful assessment of children with ASD and the recognition of different syndromes requiring different educational treatments currently subsumed under the same umbrella. There is a need for very careful diagnosis over a longer period of time making use of a battery of tests and procedures in order to determine the appropriate educational programme. This would necessarily involve a longer assessment that could not be completed until the child was at least 4 or 5 years of age. A totally objective way of assessing ASD through a brain scan is now on the horizon but not yet readily available.

It is widely recognised that most parents want an answer to the dilemma that their child poses and want an early diagnosis. All parents believe, quite rightly, that the educational intervention should start as soon as possible, but in the rush to diagnose we are seriously in danger of overlooking and sacrificing an intensive investigation of the child and of the treatment.

Without a doubt, over the next 30 years, research into the range of disorders that currently make up ASD will elucidate distinct subtypes and the way forward in such research will be led by MRI scanning and genetic and chromosome analysis. Different syndromes currently subsumed under the ASD umbrella are already emerging. It is my view as a practitioner, that if we did a more detailed and objective assessment of children referred for the possibility of ASD, including genetic screening and brain scanning, we would discover that interventions for children who are currently labelled as ASD would need to be radically different. I share the view of a number of researchers who are now suggesting that the search for one cause or one treatment is doomed because of this heterogeneity of children currently categorised as ASD (Happé et al., 2006; Klin, 2009).

5   Savant syndrome

Introduction

The term 'savant' is beset by complex issues of definition. It has a long history that reflects outmoded notions of classification and ability. At the same time there are many aspects of the phenomenon about which no definitive answers have yet been obtained. It is presumed that there have always been cases of extraordinary talents in people with learning disabilities, but psychologists and others in related fields have only categorised such people since the end of the nineteenth century. Dr John Langdon Down (who also originated the term Down's syndrome to describe other children he treated with shared specific characteristics) is considered to be the first to use the description 'idiot savant' (Treffert, 1989). He used the term to describe those with extraordinary talents in music, art, or memory, but who were otherwise learning disabled. Down was Medical Superintendent of the Earlswood Asylum for the Mentally Deficient in Redhill, Surrey until 1868 and he described some patients with exceptional skills he had encountered there (hospital records data base). In the late nineteenth and early twentieth century doctors and psychologists used the word 'idiot' to describe a person with very severe intellectual disability according to the classification system used then.

The classification system for learning difficulties also described 'imbeciles' as those adults who had a mental age of 3 to 7 years and 'morons', who had a mental age of 7 to 10 years. These terms were abolished in Britain by 1959. In their place the label 'mental deficiency' was used to describe those 'whose general personality is so severely subnormal that the patient is incapable of living an independent life' (Royal Commission Report, 1957, as cited by Hermelin, 2001). It was not until 1981, following the Warnock Report, that the term 'learning difficulty' and the concept of special needs was brought into legislation and common usage.

The term 'savant' is from the French verb savoir, 'to know', so the term implies people with learning difficulty who have special knowledge or skill. There has been debate as to how best to translate the word savant. Some have used the description 'wise one'; Howe (1989) noted that 'savant' (whether prefixed by 'idiot', 'autistic', or 'retarded'), is best considered to be 'person who has knowledge'; someone with exceptional talent despite limited education or 'mental handicap'.

The French psychologist Alfred Binet (1857–1911), was one of the first to devise tests to measure intelligence. Intelligence was assumed to be distributed like other physical attributes (such as height and weight) following a normal distribution curve where most individuals cluster around an average point (100) but a few are gifted (above 130) and a few have severe difficulties (below 70). Individuals with the lowest scores (below 30 on standardised tests) were identified as 'idiots'. Hermelin (2001) indicates that Binet used the term 'idiot savant' to describe 'those people who had great learning difficulties and could not cope with life on their own but yet showed outstanding ability in a specific area' (p. 16).

In his book *Fragments of Genius* (1989), Howe examines the various other terminologies used at this time and decides that none is entirely satisfactory as a descriptive term. Hermelin (2001), too, notes the range of labels that have been (and in some cases still are) used. They include mental deficiency, mental retardation, mental impairment, learning difficulty, mentally handicapped, learning disability, as well as idiot savant, autistic savant, and retarded savant.

Miller noted (1998), that the term 'idiot savant' uses an archaic and pejorative terminology and may also mislead in the understanding of the skill. Hence the emergence of more neutral terms that include those of 'monosavant' (Charness, Clifton, & MacDonald, 1988) and 'savant syndrome' (Treffert, 1989) as alternatives to traditional terminology. The term 'savant syndrome' was suggested by Treffert (1989) to replace all earlier terminology. Treffert, based in the USA, has specialised in the subject, advising on films such as 'Rain Man'. He trained as a psychiatrist and he has become the acknowledged expert in the field.

Happé and Frith (2009) prefer the term 'intellectually impaired individuals' to describe savants and this coincides with proposals for changes in DSM–IV. To summarise, there have been difficulties in categorising children and adults with abnormal intellectual profiles and definitions of savant syndrome have been subject to changes over time in our understanding of intelligence and autism. In general terms it is a condition characterised by an exceptional talent or skill that any observer would recognise as being above the individual's generally accepted level of ability and beyond the normally expected level of skill in the population without a diagnosis of autistic spectrum disorder (ASD). These talents are discovered in children or in people who obtain scores in tests of intelligence that place them well below average.

Characteristics of savant syndrome

The talents identified are normally outstanding, especially in view of perceived intellectual deficit. The skills savants perform would be remarkable in the normal population (those who appear to have no significant intellectual deficits) and in those who are well above average in measured ability. The reason why the talent has emerged is subject to a wide range of different theories and these will be discussed in the next chapter. A feature common to most savants is a special memory (Pring, 2008). Some of those who can achieve remarkable feats in mathematics, for example, cannot necessarily do the simplest calculations, nor can they put their feat to significant use. Savant syndrome appears to be about six times more frequent in males than females (Treffert, 1989).

Different types of savant have been identified. Treffert (2009, p. 1353) distinguishes between three groups of savant as follows:

- **Prodigious savants**: a rare occurrence in which the talent is widely acknowledged to be spectacular, beyond the capabilities of anyone in the normal population. One estimate is that there have been no more than 100 such cases reported in all the literature and Nadia is one of these.
- **Talented savants**: those who perform above the expected level of their measured intelligence; but may not be especially spectacular compared with the normal population.
- **Splinter skills**: the most common in which the savant displays unusual abilities that may have no special function for them but which they practise endlessly, such as spinning coins, having great memory for sporting events, retaining car numbers and obscure historical facts.

Incidence of savant syndrome

Savant syndrome is extremely rare and is necessarily limited to those individuals with intellectual impairment. Approximately 1 in 1000 people have severe learning difficulties. The incidence of savant syndrome has been estimated as about 1:1000 in the population of individuals with severe learning difficulties (including those with ASD) (Howlin et al., 2009). The incidence of savant syndrome is, therefore, likely to be around 1:1,000,000 in the total population although this statistic is hypothetical and prevalence rates vary according to definition. An area of unresolved debate is the extent to which savant skills are associated with ASD. Treffert (2009) reported that although savant syndrome is rare about half of the known cases of savant syndrome occur in people with an ASD diagnosis. (The other 50% have some other diagnosed disability, mental disorder, or brain injury.) This figure was also noted by O'Connor and Hermelin (1987a, 1987b). However, Howlin et al. (2009) found a lower figure of almost 30% of those with special skills who also had a diagnosis of ASD (p. 1364). My own experience as a clinician, leads me to wonder if the incidence of autistic savants is higher since diagnosis was difficult to obtain at earlier periods. Many individuals described in the literature have many features associated with autism although they are not described as being autistic. The diagnosis simply did not exist before 1940. (See, for example, the case of 'Richard' described by Howe, 1989, p. 19.) There are problems in defining what is meant by ASD as discussed in the previous chapter. Some people may be at a very mild end and able to function perfectly well in the normal world; others may appear to be extremely disabled and dependent upon others. As discussed in Chapter 4 the procedures for the diagnosis pose some problems.

The recent work of Howlin et al. (reported in 2009, p. 1364) concludes that 'unusual talents are found in at least a third of individuals with autism'. In Miller's study (1998) almost one-third of males and one-fifth of females (19%) showed some form of savant skill. Howlin et al. conclude that conflicting statistics suggest several problems in definition and data collection. However, it is certainly true that not all individuals with savant syndrome have ASD. There are also some labelled as having savant syndrome who have no apparent neurological disorder apart from being learning disabled.

All those who display savant skill have some degree of intellectual impairment, but are not necessarily on the autistic spectrum. There are two distinct groups under the label savant syndrome:

- non-autistic savants (50–70% of cases);
- autistic savants (30–50% of cases).

Additionally savants can be categorised according to their level of skill and regardless of the nature of their disability, as described above.

Some problems of definition and reporting

Treffert (1989) is of the view that no model of brain functioning can be complete without incorporating an explanation of the 'rare but spectacular' condition of savant syndrome. Howe (1989, p. ix) comments that:

> Unusual individuals are always interesting but their strangeness often conceals surprising similarities with people who are not at all abnormal. One's first reaction to witnessing a person who is undoubtedly mentally handicapped but nonetheless capable of formidable intellectual feats is to be intrigued by the sheer weirdness of someone whose behaviour contradicts deep-rooted assumptions about mental abilities and human intelligence. These people can do things which it seems, ought not to be possible.

It is his view that savant syndrome is important in revealing human potential. He suggests that we may be underestimating the talents latent in ordinary people because of our deep-rooted and limiting assumptions about the nature of intelligence. He concludes too, that the feats of those with savant skills may help in focusing more attention on aspects of the abilities of those with normal functioning that are regarded as exceptional but who tend to be overlooked. Some typically developing child artists will be described and considered later in this book.

As has been touched on above, there are problems in defining what is savant skill; how outstanding does it have to be for such designation? An ability to read a book, but not be able to explain its meaning may be contrasted with an ability to spin a coin for hours on end. Howlin et al. (2009), note that definitions of what constitutes exceptional talent in terms of population norms are variable. This leads to the question of on whose judgement is the label provided and on what criteria?

This leads to a further question, considered by Happé and Vital (2009), namely, why are the special skills of savants more common in those diagnosed as autistic than in any other group? A question leading Heaton and Wallace (2004) to suggest that it is within an understanding of the cognitive strengths and weaknesses in autism that the possible solution to the puzzle of savant syndrome lies.

An alternative perspective is raised by Snyder (2009). He asks how are those with savant skills and without intellectual disabilities explained? He proposes that savant skills may be latent within everyone. Hermelin (2001) raised a similar question: 'Is talent independent of intelligence and of mental impairments such as are seen in autism?' (p. 19).

There is another issue that arises from questions about our selection of skills for attention in relation to savant syndrome. Why do there appear to be many more reports of savants with various mathematical, artistic, and musical skills rather than with 'splinter' talents, such as accurate time keeping without access to a watch or feats of orientation and directional skill?

There is a further concern that is voiced by Howe (1989). He reports cases of intellectually impaired savants who appear to have astounding abilities, such as being able to recall all the telephone numbers on the first three pages of a directory; to read and reproduce any word seen once; and to correct the spelling errors of others. However, he reminds his readers importantly that much of the evidence is anecdotal and possibly unreliable. Many reports are second hand; some are based on parental reports or memories; some of the accounts could be from very old sources that may not be easy to verify. He states that: 'To be entirely convincing, evidence in support of the claim that there exists memory capacities that are fundamentally different from those of ordinary individuals would have to be collected under closely controlled conditions, in which the amount of exposure to the information could be manipulated, and recall carefully measured' (pp. 44–45).

He suggests that in cases where this has been done results have not always sustained the assertion that certain individuals can retain huge quantities of information in their memory. With such issues in mind, it is interesting to review a range of cases that are frequently cited in publications dealing with autism and savants.

The areas in which savants most frequently display extraordinary ability

Treffert (1989, 2009) summarised the past and present literature, reviewed research data and concluded that there are probably no more than 100 cases of reported prodigious savant talent in the world at that time. He reviews research studies and those he cites are among the most outstanding. He describes a spectrum of savant skills, which range from the phenomenal to the extraordinarily bizarre. In addition to these, notably Rimland (1978), Howe (1989) and Hermelin (2001) as well as other authors and researchers, have uncovered examples of people with savant abilities. Phenomenal memory ability has been implicated in many savant skills.

The areas of expertise in general fall into a few categories relating to the following.

1   **Mathematics**: there are examples of people who can compute highly compli-
    cated calculations with rapidity and accuracy, even out-pacing hand held
    calculators. Some are described as calendar calculators because they can
    provide details of dates on which birthdays fall both backwards and forwards
    in time over, in some cases, a relatively short period, but in others over
    centuries.

2   **Music**: there are examples of people who, without any formal musical
    training, can listen to a complex piece of music on one occasion and repeat it,
    with variations, on request; others who have perfect pitch.

3   **Language, verbal, and literacy abilities**: there are examples of savants who
    can master foreign languages with ease, or read fluently at a young age
    complex texts about which they may have no clear understanding.

4   **Spatial skills**: some have mechanical and spatial skills and can measure
    distances with great precision without aids or show great ability in direction
    finding. Others display knowledge of passing time without reference to a
    clock.

5   **Drawing and art**: there are examples of people who can produce artwork
    and especially drawing, which is of a quality beyond their years or intellec-
    tual ability. Some can draw or paint, sculpt, produce architectural drawings,
    or carve in wood and make models, in ways that even specialist art critics
    concede are phenomenal.

6   **Multiple savant skills**: there are examples of savants who display savant
    skills in two or more areas.

Who are some of the most extraordinary savants?

Since the work of Nadia was published in 1977 there have been many more
discoveries of savants, most of whom are individuals with ASD. The publication
of Nadia appeared to reawaken interest in savant syndrome and single case studies.
The climate in psychology in the early 1970s was rigorously empiricist and behaviourism still held sway, so that single case studies were out of fashion. Treffert's
work appeared in the 1990s along with a renewed interest in the value of single
case studies and a more humanistic approach to the study of psychology. He
reviewed individual cases and researched extensively on this topic. His case
studies fall into each of the dominant categories. The information he provides
forms the basis of much that follows. Naturally, other academic researchers have
also assisted in throwing light on those with prodigious talent and savant syndrome
and it is from this range of researchers that the prodigious savants described
below, derive.

Mathematical skills

Calculation skills are the most common of the reported prodigious savant
skills. They impress and astound for many reasons. They are clearly outside any
normal or even, most gifted, mathematicians' skills. Perhaps, too, the fact that no

materials (keyboard or paper and pencil), apart from the savant's brain, are involved in the demonstrable talent. The skill is portable and immediately evident.

Treffert (1989) notes that in 1783 a report appeared in a German psychology journal of a lightning calculator named Jedediah Buxton, who also had an extraordinary memory. He appears to have been a phenomenal calculator despite having had little formal education and none that could have given him the skills he demonstrated. He was apparently able to answer accurately questions requiring calculations that would defeat the most competent mathematician today, being able to calculate numbers, it was said, up to 39 figures. In 1789 Benjamin Rush described the phenomenal ability of another calculator, Thomas Fuller, 'who could comprehend scarcely anything more complex than counting'.

O'Connor, Hermelin and their research team (Heavey, 1997, Heavey, 2003; Heavey, Pring, & Hermelin, 1999; Hermelin & O'Connor, 1986) have probably contributed the most to our understanding of what is entailed in calendar calculation. Many of the cases that they investigated provide further examples of savants with astounding arithmetical skills. Howe (1989) comments that while some of the skills of savants are ones that are also possessed by ordinary people, calendar calculating is different. Such skills are not found in typically developing children and it is not a talent that is normally practised. This is because the ability to know which day of the week was 15th April 1927, or in what years between 1905 and 1948 did 9th August fall on a Monday, is not considered to be a valuable kind of knowledge. Howe gives examples of people who have been able to make such calculations. They include the case, reported in 1920, of a man who if told the month, day and year for a date between 1901 and 1924 could supply the correct day of the week, without hesitation and accurately. He describes a man in 1909 who was said to be able to give the correct day of the week for any given date between the years 1000 and 2000. In 1965 a case was reported of a blind girl, aged 10, who had developed skills of calendar calculating. She was asked to undertake tests that provided a success rate of over 90% (some of her errors resulted from her failure to take account of leap years).

Howe (1989) also gives further examples of exceptional mathematicians, including that of a blind Frenchman, living in an asylum, who could supply the cube root of any six-digit number in 4 seconds. He could calculate the number of grains in 64 boxes, given that one piece of grain was placed in the first box, two in the second, four in the third, eight in the fourth and so on. He gave correct answers to the numbers in the eighteenth, twenty-fourth and forty-eighth box, taking 45 seconds to calculate the total number of grains in all 64 boxes.

Miller (1998) found that there were more than twice as many reports of calendar calculators than of musical or artistically skilled savants. Hermelin (2001) reminds us that structuring time has always been a human preoccupation and calendar calculators merely take this to extremes. She describes several fascinating cases. In one, a subject of research refused to assist until he had been provided with the dates of the birthdays of all the family members of the researcher. He was then able to provide relevant days of birth and recall them on subsequent visits over several years. Hermelin described meeting a calendar calculator in the 1970s who was, 'a low functioning 13 year old boy whose reasoning ability was that of a four year old' (2001, p. 17). He was instantly able to calculate accurately the day of the week that corresponded to her birthday on two dates 64 years apart. She reports that in her studies seven of the eight participants in the group of calendar calculators had been diagnosed as being autistic and the other one showed marked autistic features in behaviour. Their intelligence quotients (IQs) ranged from 38 to 88. She notes that outstanding arithmetic abilities in people who were otherwise 'mentally impaired' have been reported since the eighteenth century and gives the following example: 'One such early account tells of a mentally retarded man who, when 80 years old, could still answer questions such as how many seconds a man had lived when aged 70 years 17 days and 12 hours' (2001, p. 107). He gave a correct answer that even took leap years into account.

Horwitz, Kestenbaum, Person, and Jarvik (1965) described identical, intellectually disabled twins who could both name the day of the week for a given date in any year. They seemed able to subtract multiples of a 400-year calendar cycle from any given year and could compute 20 digit prime numbers. Yet both were inept at basic arithmetic.

Sacks (1985) describes his encounters with autistic twins aged 26 who had remarkable arithmetical skills with an ability to estimate accurately the number of matches that had been spilt on to the floor and instantly know the factor of the number. A similar ability was reported by Park (1967) who gives an example of a young autistic man's astounding skill. When asked whether there was anything special about the following numbers:

1   4875: the young man replied, 'It is divisible by 13 and 25';
2   7241: he said, 'It is divisible by 13 and 557'; and
3   8741: he said, 'It's a prime number'.

Sacks (1985, p. 203) notes Park's comment that: 'No one in his family reinforces his primes, they are a solitary pleasure'.

Savants with musical ability

It is interesting to note that in his study Kanner (1943) found that six of his ten cases of early infantile autism had specific musical abilities. Research into musical savants has noted that music is typically highly regular and rigidly structured (Heaton, 2003: Ockelford & Pring, 2005; Pring, 2008). Pring (2008) adds that, 'By constructing, storing and recalling the use of the rules and patterns that govern music, musicians are able to build up cognitive representations of musical structure and thus process musical information more effectively than non-musicians' (p. 218).

It has been observed that savants have shown the ability to transpose music across keys, imitate styles, and show exceptional memory for the pieces they play. It is suggested that their remarkable skills result from having absolute pitch, the ability to 'recognise, label and remember pitch information without reference to an external standard' (Pring, 2008, p. 218). She notes that this is an extremely rare ability, only 1:10,000 in the normal Western population possess it (Beethoven, Bach, and Mozart were reputed to have it). However, she states that it is possessed by all musical savants. A leading expert in the psychology of music, Ockelford, has noted that children with profound visual impairment appear to show a potential to develop the ability as well as having excellent pitch memory (Ockelford, 1988; Ockelford & Pring, 2006).

In a BBC radio programme (November 2009), the composer Matthew King discussed the extraordinary abilities of a musical savant, Derek Paravicini (Figure 5.1). He was born totally blind, with severe developmental and learning disabilities. His remarkable talent has been monitored throughout his life by Ockelford (Ockelford & Pring, 2006). Derek requires 24-hour care and support but his ability as a musician transcends his disabilities. His talent is such that he can perform a piece of music on request and change the style in which it is played, as jazz, swing, syncopation, classical, or other suggested forms. He has played with great success in clubs and concert halls in Britain and the USA.

In a longitudinal study Ockelford and Pring (2006), asked Derek to learn a specially composed piece of music over an 18-month period. The learning and

Figure 5.1 Derek Paravacini. Reprinted with kind permission: © 2008, Dr Evangelos Himonides (www.sonustech.com).

memory phases were monitored on a regular basis and the creative developments recorded. Derek knows from memory thousands of pieces in many different styles. The experiment involved comparative processes with a non-savant musician of exceptional ability who also had absolute pitch. They were asked to reproduce chords varying in size from four to nine notes played on an electronic keyboard. They heard only once, twenty different examples of chords from each level of difficulty (120 chords). The number of notes correctly reproduced was the measure of accuracy. Derek produced remarkable results with 97% accuracy overall, which outperformed the comparison talented undergraduate music student. The authors indicate that this is effectively at ceiling. Pring (2005) suggests that the particularly detailed way of processing information in people with ASD together with their specific interests may develop 'complex knowledge structures in long term memory' (p. 501). It may also be the case that such people display enhanced perceptual processing in achieving their talent (Mottron et al., 2003).

Treffert and Wallace (2002) met Tony Deblois in 1989 and have observed his development since. He is a prodigious musical savant, particularly talented in jazz improvisation who, unusually, has the ability to play a large number of instruments to a high standard. His mother reports that he was born weighing 1 lb ¾ oz. She says of him, that this was only the first obstacle that Tony had to overcome. Despite the fact that he suffers from visual impairment and is autistic, he has been playing the piano since age 2; for Tony there are no 'roadblocks' but mere obstacles to be cast aside or skirted, Treffert said of him that his favourite phrase seems to be 'I haven't learned that yet.' Such is his musical skill that he attended Berklee College of Music in Boston and successfully completed his studies there in 1996.

Treffert (1989) also described another musical savant, born in 1952, Leslie Lemke. He was premature and adopted at birth. He developed serious problems that resulted in blindness and brain damage. His new carer taught him survival skills and introduced him to music at a young age by placing his hands over hers as she played simple tunes on a piano. These were the only lessons he received; yet he developed a seemingly limitless repertoire, demonstrating the ability of repeating tunes after a single hearing. It was apparent that he had a remarkable memory; apart from recalling musical pieces he had heard, he was also able to repeat verbatim all the conversation that he had overheard in the course of the day. One evening when he was aged 14 he was heard playing perfectly a piece he had heard earlier in a film that he watched on television. It was Tchaikovsky's Piano Concerto No. 1. As his talent became more widely known he played to local audiences in churches and schools. Following one such concert a report was carried on television by the renowned broadcaster Walter Cronkite, who said, 'It's the story of a young man, a piano, and a miracle'. (Interestingly, Cronkite had already visited Britain to film Nadia, in 1980.) Leslie has given concerts throughout the USA and has toured Japan, to acclaim. Treffert (1989) states that music is Leslie's 'language', for whom it has been a channel toward normalisation. As a result of his musical skill and the enjoyment he gets from playing, he appears to have become more sociable and better socialised, acquiring many of the skills of interaction commonplace in the normal population.

Another case discussed by Treffert (1989) is that of Matt Savage. He was born in 1992. He is reported to have learned to walk very early and to read by age 18 months although exact details of this are not recorded. He was subsequently shown to be hyperlexic and was diagnosed at the age of 3 as having 'pervasive developmental disorder, not specified'. It is likely that he has high-functioning autism or possibly Asperger's syndrome. At a young age Matt had poor communication skill and was averse to loud noise. He was given a programme of social and medical treatment, received various therapies and by the age of 6 his musical talents began to emerge in remarkable ways. He learnt to read music and moved from classical music to jazz, although he is able to perform and compose in both idioms. He began studying at the New England Conservatory of Music in Boston in 1999. He has subsequently won many awards; he has toured widely and appeared on television. He has undertaken further studies at the Berklee College of Music.

Treffert (1989) further considers the case of Ellen Boudreaux who was born prematurely in 1957. She is blind, (retrolental fibroplasia) but has an astonishing musical ability, superior spatial sense and remarkable memory. She has an extraordinary facility to calculate time without reference to a clock. She was aged 4 before she walked but once ambulant, she seemed to be aware of hazardous objects, such as walls and buildings and was able to avoid bumping into them. She was heard to make constant chirping noises almost as if she had developed her own form of radar. At the age of 4½ psychological testing provided a score of 40 on the Vineland Social Maturity Scale (Watson, 1951), which suggested an estimated IQ, of between 30–50. Nonetheless, she proceeded through a series of steps in a special education programme, underwent speech therapy and began to develop language skills, 'with no sacrifice of her artistic skill'. Ellen's musical skill and memory were regarded as prodigious. She was able, for example, to construct complicated chords to accompany melodies she heard and transpose the orchestra and chorus of *Evita* to the piano. She can happily improvise and can transpose a piece into various styles, jazz, classical, or ragtime. Ellen, like other of the cases investigated by Treffert (1989), is seen as another example of a special skill being used as a 'conduit' toward increased socialisation and better language acquisition. In some savants it is thought that this could affect their special skill. In her case, she both retained her talent and became more verbal and sociable. One report commented that 'She instantly processes melodies and complex rhythms, intonations and lyrics. She can hear a song once on the radio, store it in her vast database, and recall it years later. Play it with absolute fidelity and technical precision' (p. 154). Treffert suggests that her obsession with rhythm and her ability to calculate passing time suggests some connection between them.

Howe (1989) quotes the work of a psychiatrist, Viscott (1970), who worked with a woman named Harriet with whom he came into contact when she was aged 40. Her IQ was measured at 73 (well below average); her performance was weaker on verbal than non-verbal items. She was poor at word definitions and at perceiving the non-literal meanings of metaphors. She was much better at visual patterns and knowledge of spatial orientation. He found she was a competent calendar calculator but her knowledge of music was described as breathtaking. She showed evidence of having powers of abstraction and an ability to express feelings, (the music was 'sweet', 'sad', 'scary') both absent from other spheres of her life (p. 510). She knew composers, the keys of classical pieces, could state the date of first performance and the correct key and opus number. In addition she knew the plots of operas and the motives of characters. Viscott (1970) noted that her talent for music carried 'not merely her feelings but her language as well'. Yet as a child she had a difficult upbringing. Harriet was the sixth of seven children but became socially isolated and displayed some of the features of autism; rocking and head banging. In her first year her father detected that she may have some musical ability, 'she was humming in perfect pitch tempo and phrasing the Caro Nome from Rigoletto' (p. 510); she was able to imitate perfectly the sounds she heard. When she was 2 years old it was observed that her banging and rocking followed rhythmic tempo; she could detect a singer who was off pitch or a pianist that played a wrong note, to which she reacted with anger and distress. By the age of 3 she could play the piano competently and other instruments that she found (including violin, French horn, trumpet, and clarinet). She also displayed other savant skills associated with memory and recall but as an adult was regarded as having severe learning difficulties. She worked as a kitchen assistant.

Ockelford and Pring (2006) have indicated that some specialised schools have emerged in recent years to cater for people with unique skills. For example, Soundscape Centre in London, which is described as a specialised educational facility dedicated to the needs of people with sight loss and special musical abilities including musical savants. There are institutions in the USA, especially in California, that cater for students with savant syndrome and special needs.

Fitzgerald, who wrote *The Genesis of Artistic Creativity: Asperger's Syndrome and the Arts* (2005), a psychiatrist at Trinity College, Dublin, goes so far as to argue that some exceptionally gifted individuals may have actually been suffering from undiagnosed Asperger's syndrome. He contends that this can be seen in cases of prodigiously talented people in the past. He considers the case of Mozart who showed prodigious musical ability from an early age. Hermelin (2001) provides an anecdote about the composer who it is said once heard a choral piece in the Sistine Chapel as a young boy and on returning to his lodgings wrote out the full score. He returned to hear it played the following day and found he had made few mistakes in his transcription. He is also reported to have had unusual personality traits, all of which suggest that he may have had Asperger's syndrome. Although not a view held by me, Fitzgerald (2005) suggests that Asperger's syndrome and creativity are closely related and those who are very creative are likely to have this diagnosis.

Other exceptionally musical people who might also be considered to meet the criteria include Glenn Gould, the outstanding Canadian pianist. He was noted to be obsessive about routines in his performances, for example controlling the room temperature with precision; using the same piano seat until it required repair.

(This was an adjustable-height chair, which he used throughout his life. It was specially designed to facilitate his style of playing.) He was noted for the fact that he hummed and rocked forward and back as he played. He had many idiosyncrasies, showing signs of hypochondria. He did not enjoy face-to-face interactions, preferring to use the telephone or other means of communication.

Other eminent musicians who displayed odd characteristics of behaviour in their day-to-day lives which might, today, lead to a diagnosis of Asperger's syndrome, include both Eric Satie and Beethoven. However, this is a view dismissed by some critics who suggest that there are many reasons for someone to have eccentric patterns of behaviour, especially great artists, who may well have their mind distracted by their need to focus on things less mundane and of more significance to them (Draaisma, 2009; Hacking, 2009). It is apparent that it is difficult to assess such people retrospectively, especially in view of the fact that even today there are no definitive tests for autism or Asperger's syndrome. There is no evidence, for example, to suggest that Felix Mendelssohn (1809–1848) displayed such characteristics. He became a creative and prolific composer from a young age having made his first public concert appearance at about the age of 9. Between the ages of 12 and 14, he wrote 5 operas, 11 symphonies for strings and his first published work, a piano quartet. At the age of 15, in 1824, he wrote his first symphony for full orchestra. At the age of 16 he wrote his *String Octet* in E-flat major, now an acknowledged masterpiece. It was said of him that he appeared to have an intuitive grasp of form, harmony, counterpoint, colour, and the compositional technique of Beethoven (who was also a prodigy, having given his inaugural debut at the age of 7). He died at the age of 38 and is regarded as one of the greatest composers of the romantic period. The question remains (as with all prodigies), whether he had some innate talent or whether his culturally rich home environment nurtured his early skill enabling him to produce so many great works in his short life.

Savants with language and verbal abilities

Treffert (1989) recounts the phenomenal ability of a man, Kim Peek (1951–2009) with severe brain damage who had read and memorised over a thousand books. He was the inspiration for the film 'Rain Man'. He had an IQ of less than 80; he had problems with basic motor skills, walking, doing up buttons, catching, throwing, and writing. But he is reported to have had an encyclopaedic knowledge of geography, music, literature, sports, and several other areas of expertise. It was claimed that he could read two pages at once, simultaneously scanning one page with his left eye and the other page with his right and could recall the content of the vast number of books he had read. In 2008 a study concluded that he had a rare genetic syndrome that resulted in the physical anomalies he displayed including low muscle tone and an abnormally large head.

Hermelin (2001) describes Christopher, who was, as a child, in a school for disabled children and subsequently was unable to lead an independent life. His mother had contacted rubella in pregnancy and was over 40 when Christopher was born. By the age of 37 he could understand, talk, write, and translate from 16 languages. While at 14 his verbal IQ score was in the average range (just below 100) it was well below that for perceptual, spatial abilities. From the age of 3 he showed interest in language, picking up some French from his sister's text-books. He was not diagnosed as autistic, although he showed some of the qualities associated with the syndrome. He could not understand jokes or other people's states of mind. His case illustrates the problems of diagnosis.

Hermelin (2001) describes how Christopher's language skills were uncovered, largely by chance. He was able to absorb new languages from many different sources, both in informal ways (by overhearing conversations, from the radio and foreign newspapers) and more formally by receiving instruction. Hermelin was able to test his ability in German and French; which he could switch between with great delight. However, Hermelin notes that what Christopher said in any of these languages was very limited (as it was in English). Hermelin makes the important point that the accuracy of reports of people being able to speak large numbers of foreign languages in the past must be viewed with some scepticism. However, he did show ability in translating passages of texts in 16 languages and could answer questions in a range of foreign languages that included Russian, Hindi, and Modern Greek. This ability was beyond the capability of most professional linguists. The experimenter reports that he did not notice or care whether what he said made any sense and so did not notice mistranslations; 'he translated the text word by word as if each stood not in a context but on its own' (p. 71). It was found that his linguistic strength lay primarily in the speedy and correct acquisition of apparently unlimited vocabulary items. Hermelin (2001) concludes that the tests conducted on Christopher show that his aim in acquiring new languages is simply their acquisition. It is this which gives him satisfaction.

The ability that some children have to read fluently words considered beyond their reading age and chronological age, and that of their peers, without understanding the meaning of the words, is termed hyperlexia. This appears to be another skill that such savants can achieve which is beyond the ability of any typically developing child with even superior intelligence. Some hyperlexic children, at very young ages, can even read text accurately upside down. Aram and Healy (1988) claim that their skill seems to be based on an ability to memorise letter sound correspondences. However, in my experience such children also read phonically irregular words with equal facility. What is especially dramatic is that these children frequently have no under-standing or even fleeting acquaintance with the words they are able to read. This apparently useful ability to read well may also, ironically, be used as evidence for the fact that the child is on the autistic spectrum. Some assessments include savant skills as a positive indicator for an ASD diagnosis. Further tests should be undertaken to ascertain if the hyperlexic child has other difficulties with social relationships and other communication skills including non-verbal communication.

Savants with spatial skills

As discussed, Treffert (1989) describes the case of Ellen. She was blind and, in addition to her other savant skills as a musician, was able to tell what time it was without having been exposed to a clock with Braille hands. This skill developed at about the age of 8 when she listened to the 'talking clock' on the telephone. She mimicked what she had heard and thereafter developed a full appreciation of accurate time keeping.

Langdon Down (1887) reported a case of an intellectually impaired 17-year-old boy who also appeared to have a perfect appreciation of time passing, being able to tell the time to a minute at any time of the day. Treffert (1989) discusses the case of an 18-year-old autistic boy who had memorised the highway atlas of the entire USA. He could describe with detailed precision, the routes to be taken from one city or town to another many hundreds of miles apart. The numbers of reported cases of savants who have a precise sense of direction appear to be rare.

It may be that there are more savants with skills in assessing time or distance whose feats are either not recorded or held in less regard than the more spectacular abilities that other savants possess. It is likely that any of the savants who possess astounding memories for numbers, dates, or texts could, if so inclined, absorb the information that would enable them to recall timetable data or the road routes of a country. Many savants are reported to be able to reproduce a learned sequence in a rigid, automatic way.

Howe (1989) makes the point that it is likely that the majority of people who develop such skills do so for the same reasons as anyone who has a fascination with some specialist area, which is presumably because we all find some things more worth remembering than others. He says that individuals, including those with intellectual disabilities, are likely to gain an unusual degree of competence in a skill 'if they become sufficiently interested in it to devote a substantial proportion of their time towards it, giving it their undivided attention' (p. 165).

Savants with special skills in drawing and artwork

Paine (editor of *Six Children Draw*, 1981, and author of *Artists Emerging*, 2000) states that 'Beliefs about art (and drawing) in educational practice present a series of dramatic conflicts: is it play or work, is it a gift or something that can be mastered, can it be learned but not taught, is it meaningful or irrelevant to life . . .?' (Paine, 1981, p. 2). She raises the question of how child art is to be appraised. What are the significant features that allow a child to be labelled as a prodigy? What are the special skills that distinguish a prodigy from the merely talented or average child artist? Another issue that arises is at what point will prodigious talent become less remarkable and is the perceived skill simply a matter of age?

Paine (2000) suggests that special skills might include those that are not normally observed in children under the age of 7 years. Such abilities, she suggests, might include the following:

- To show the ability to portray spatial relationships and depth and to convey a sense of space using a projection system (perspective).
- To be able to foreshorten the limbs and trunks of, for example, horses or people.

- To display an awareness of the relationship between edges and spaces between them with relevant tonal contrasts. (Tonal difference can produce variations in the impact of the artwork and the impression the picture creates.)
- To be able to use occlusion effectively (to show a rider astride rather on top of his horse).
- To provide a sense of movement and atmosphere from subtle lines and contours and variations in tone.
- To show aesthetic selectivity in the use of shading and colour.
- To show a capacity to build on experience and to invent or adapt from earlier images or generate new images and project them into a coherent and meaningful pictorial representation.
- To show the ability to go beyond mere reproduction of what had been seen or remembered as having been seen.
- To show a facility for the use of various idioms (drawing, painting, printmaking) and to display a wide artistic vocabulary.

With such comments in mind it is interesting to examine the drawings and paintings of some prodigiously talented savants and consider the comments made about them.

Gottfried Mind

The work of Swiss born Gottfried Mind (1768–1814) has been cited (Tredgold, 1914) as an early example of a child savant who had remarkable gifts as an artist (Figure 5.2). His drawings, mainly of animals, some of which hang in important European galleries, do indicate the skill and talent he possessed. His reputation as a

Figure 5.2 Gottfried Mind's (1768–1814) watercolour of cats.

savant with apparently low intelligence comes from reports of the period. An account appears in *The Mirror of Literature, Amusement, and Instruction* (Anon, 1828) that in turn may have been obtained from the account in the Economic Society of Bern (1778). The report states, 'Mind's special talent for representing cats was discovered and awakened by chance' (p. 201). It was not till after the death of the lady in whose home he was living, that Mind fully developed his talent. It was said of him in a publication of 1828 (Anon, p. 201) that for the remainder of his life:

> He applied himself with such special affection, and which, accordingly, he succeeded in representing with such fidelity and truth. . . . He learnt his art of drawing, and colouring with water-colours, etc. but nothing more; in all the other branches of human knowledge he remained at the lowest grade; for he could with difficulty be made to write his name, and he had not the slightest idea of arithmetic.

Again, while the information is of great value it remains important to bear in mind the words of Howe (1989, p. 44), 'like most anecdotal descriptions it is reported at second hand; and some aspects cannot be verified'. Whether or not Mind was an autistic savant is not possible to say with certainty. He sounds to have been an unusual child with an obsession for drawing animals.

> While he sat painting, a cat might generally be seen sitting on his back or on his shoulder; and many times he kept, for hours, the most awkward postures, that he might not disturb it. Frequently there was a second cat sitting by him on the table, watching how the work went on; sometimes a kitten or two lay in his lap under the table. Frogs (in bottle) floated beside his easel; and with all these creatures he kept up a most playful, loving style of conversation; though, often enough, any human beings about him, or such even as came to see him, were growled or grunted at in no social fashion.
>
> (Anon, 1828, p. 201)

All this suggests that he lacked normal social skills and had unusual patterns of behaviour. A description of him adds to a view that he was seen as someone out of the ordinary; but there is no way of knowing how accurate it is:

> His countenance, especially in latter years, was a mixture of the bear's, the lion's, and the human, for most part of a dull brick-colour; so that many people, particularly children, were afraid to look at him. In figure he was very small, and bent; but, at the same time, had hands and fingers of extraordinary size and coarseness, with which, nevertheless, he produced the cleanest and prettiest drawings.
>
> (Anon, 1828, p. 201)

Tredgold (1914), described Mind as a 'cretin imbecile'. Mind died at the age of 46. If Tredgold is right in his assessment, then Gottfried Mind was a savant with remarkable artistic talent but it is not clear at what age Mind was when he first drew his animals or whether accurate records were kept of his development. The truly outstanding savants produce their extraordinary work at a very young age. As the person gets older, their skills become less remarkable in so far as their work could be achieved by normally trained artists.

James Henry Pullen

James Henry Pullen (1835–1916) was, at the age of 15, placed in the Earlswood Asylum (later called Royal Earlswood Hospital). The superintendent was Langdon Down from whose reports some of the details about Pullen derive. Later, Tredgold (1914), also had contact with Pullen and noted that: 'His powers of observation, attention, memory, will and pertinacity are extraordinary; and yet he is obviously too childish, and at the same time too emotional, unstable, and lacking in mental balance to make any headway, or even hold his own, in the outside world' (cited in Treffert, 1989, p. 35).

It is always difficult to attribute a syndrome retrospectively, since the diagnosis relies on information derived from clinicians operating with quite different forms of knowledge and understanding in an earlier period. From such reports it appears that James and his brother William were regarded as 'mentally handicapped' (Tredgold, 1914). As a child James is reputed to have had very limited vocabulary and could not read or write but could communicate through gestures. Both brothers had artistic skills and it was the policy of the hospital to encourage handicrafts among the patients. As a result James Pullen became a skilled carpenter and his drawing abilities developed. He enjoyed drawing the corridors of the hospital. Interestingly, this focus of interest has been noted in other autistic savant artists (Selfe, 1983). Such were his talents that Queen Victoria and other members of the royal family accepted some of his drawings and constructions. His mood swings were reported to be severe and his behaviour not always predictable made more problematic by his limited speech. Nonetheless, he produced a range of fascinating and bizarre artwork. Among the remarkable pieces he created in wood was a model ship, *The Great Eastern*, that he built over a 7-year period and which was duly exhibited at the Crystal Palace Exhibition of 1851. Another well-recorded piece was described as the *Mystic Representation of the World as a Ship*, and was built by Pullen in 1866 (Figure 5.3).

In addition he made elaborate and decorative collages from cigar bands and a carefully drawn representation of events from his life (Figures 5.4–5.8).

After his death his workshop became an exhibition room of his work. Some items have been on permanent display in a shopping centre in Redhill, close to where the asylum once stood. On his death a post-mortem examination of Pullen's brain took place in an attempt to find some explanation for his talents. It showed only hardening of the arteries of his brain, arteriosclerosis (which was not unusual at Pullen's age). Langdon Down (1887) described 10 cases of people he had encountered in the course of his work with patients in the mental asylum as having special faculties similar to those recorded more recently and described as having savant syndrome. One patient was reputed to have memorised *The Rise and Fall of the Roman Empire*, and could recite it backwards or forwards. Tredgold (1914), described at least 20 more cases.

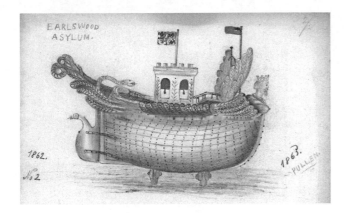

Figure 5.3 A carved ship made by Pullen in Earlswood Asylum, known as the Mystic Representation of the World. Reprinted with kind permission of the Surrey History Centre, UK.

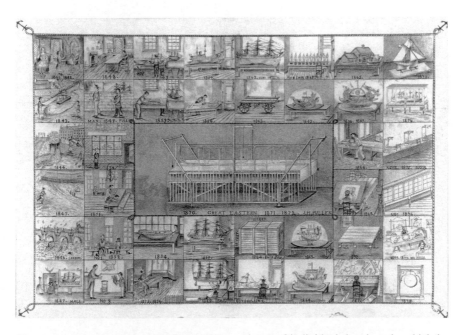

Figure 5.4 Representation of Pullen's life, made up of individual drawings in which he recorded important incidents. Some of these can be best seen as separate illustrations (Figures 5.5–5.8). Reprinted with the kind permission of the Surrey History Centre, UK.

Figure 5.5
A happy memory of Pullen's schooldays.
Reprinted with the kind permission of the
Surrey History Centre, UK.

Figure 5.6
Pullen recalls sailing a boat on a pond.
Reprinted with the kind permission of the
Surrey History Centre, UK.

Figure 5.7
Pullen observes a bridge across the
Thames. Reprinted with the kind permis-
sion of the Surrey History Centre, UK.

Figure 5.8
Pullen draws a sad memory of his days in a
classroom. Reprinted with the kind permission of the Surrey History Centre, UK.

Ping Lian Yeak

Writing of the Malaysian savant, Ping Lian Yeak, Treffert says: 'Such artistic prowess demonstrates, in addition to providing us with beautiful art, serves as a source of satisfaction, development and growth for him, eventually to minimise whatever limitations might spring from his disabilities' (www.pinglian.com, para. 3).

Ping Lian was born in Malaysia in November 1993. He is described as being initially hyperactive as a growing child, living in his own world, not showing affection or an awareness of danger, unable to hold a pencil to write or use scissors to cut. Ping Lian's mother decided to strengthen his fine motor skills by focusing on tracing and colouring activities. These encouraged him to occupy his time more fruitfully. Ultimately, tracing became a catalyst for discovering his exceptional art talent. He still has limited communication and social skills, but he has become a prolific and successful artist (Figures 5.9 and 5.10).

He uses charcoal, acrylic, water colour, ink, and oil pastels and his works have been exhibited throughout the world. Art expert Dr Rosa Martinez (2009), said of his work: 'His paintings tend to encompass hidden aspects of forms, not initially noticed on first view . . . each stroke appeared effortlessly calculated' (personal communication). One may make similar comments about the work of Nadia and other savants with exceptional ability. They all operate with a speed and fluency

Figure 5.9 The Capitol Building. Painted by Ping Lian Yeak at the age of 11. Reprinted with the kind permission of Mrs Sarah S. H. Lee.

Figure 5.10   Cockerel. Painted by Ping Lian Yeak at the age of 11. It is interesting to note that the cockerel was one of Nadia's favourite images to draw. Reprinted with the kind permission of Mrs Sarah S. H. Lee.

often denied non-savant artist. It is also apparent that his architectural drawings have some similarities to those of Stephen Wiltshire.

Stephen Wiltshire

The remarkable work of Stephen Wiltshire, which has been monitored over a long period of time from his earliest years, undoubtedly places him within the category of autistic savant but this may not do justice to his development as an artist. Stephen Wiltshire was born in London to West Indian parents in 1974. In his early childhood he had no language and did not interact with others. At the age of 3 he was diagnosed as being autistic. Two years later he entered a school (Queensmill) where his drawing skills were first observed and encouraged. His earliest subjects were animals, buses, and buildings. By the time he was 8 years old, he was drawing complex city views of buildings, roads, and traffic. He had mastered perspective in a dramatic way and his memory for detail after comparatively brief periods of observation enabled him to produce drawings of exceptional realism. He was also able to show an ability to invent scenes such as the effects of an earthquake on a city (based on pictures he must have seen in school or on television). But they were not copies but created from his imagination. He did not learn to speak until the age of 9 following interventions in his school to encourage him in this necessary social skill.

O'Connor and Hermelin (1987a) studied Stephen when he was 15 years old and they recorded his history and development. Later he was promoted and encouraged by Margaret Hewson who publicised his work, secured commissions and wrote about Stephen in his book of beautiful architectural drawings

(Wiltshire, 1991). Sacks (cited in Wiltshire, 1991, p. 7) met Stephen when he was still a boy and wrote 'I found him somewhat "strange", clearly autistic, but a charming and friendly boy with a wonderful gift for drawing'. Sacks explained that one would expect such a person to be lacking the normal human qualities of sociability. He says that the autistic person is classically 'intensely alone, incapable of relationships with others, incapable of perceiving others' feelings or perspectives, incapable of humour, playfulness, spontaneity, creativity – mere "intelligent automata", in Asperger's terms' (cited in Wiltshire, 1991, p. 7).

Margaret Hewson (cited in Wiltshire, 1991, p. 12) said of him that: 'conversation is factual although he responds enthusiastically to nonsense. His hearing is extremely acute but he is selective in what he chooses to hear. It is possible to discuss the concrete but abstract concepts do not appear to exist for him'. While some of Stephen's behaviour patterns fitted the description of autistic, Sacks (1995b) notes that others did not. He displayed good social responses leading Sacks to the view that he was 'a real person, a friendly one, not like an automaton at all' (p. 55). Sacks accompanied Stephen on drawing projects abroad. When he went into the streets of Moscow to see the buildings he was to draw, he is described as being, 'actively curious, taking photographs, peering, struck by all the novelty . . . he is very ready to smile if people smile at him first' (Sacks cited in Wiltshire, 1991, p. 8). At the end of the day he completed a range of drawings of the buildings he had seen with great accuracy and artistic interpretation (Figure 5.11).

Figure 5.11 A view of Moscow drawn by Stephen Wiltshire at the age of 15. Reprinted with the kind permission of Stephen Wiltshire, The Stephen Wiltshire Gallery, London. © Stephen's Gallery.

Sacks concluded that: 'It was at this point that I stopped seeing him as a "prodigy" and saw him as an artist through and through. Immense powers of perceiving detail, of spatial sense, of draughtsmanship, of memory, had gone into his lordly drawings . . . this was pure joy, playfulness, aesthetic delight, art' (cited in Wiltshire, 1991, p. 9).

Yet at that time Stephen was incapable of independent existence and in need of special support and care. Sacks does, however raise the interesting question as to how much Stephen's art can change in character; whether it can only develop technically or become 'charged with moral and human depth' (cited in Wiltshire, 1991, p. 10). Sacks is clear that this depends 'on Stephen's human development – on how much he can develop as a genuine human being, despite being (as he always will be) an autistic person' (cited in Wiltshire, 1991, p. 10).

When Hermelin and O'Connor studied Stephen Wiltshire, Hermelin (2001) remarked that: 'We had been especially impressed by his vivid and dynamic style of line drawing and his superb intuitive ability to portray spatial relationships and depth' (p. 142). Figures 5.12 and 5.13 show Wiltshire's drawings of St Pancras Station. In his drawings of cities he is able to use lines and variations in tones that indicated the movement of water, the presence of trees, and a sense of energy (Figure 5.14).

In relation to the question posed by Sacks as to Stephen's future development, after the age of 15, it seems that he has progressed and is fulfilling the early potential he

Figure 5.12 St Pancras Station by Stephen Wiltshire, drawn before the age of 12. Reprinted with the kind permission of Stephen Wiltshire, The Stephen Wiltshire Gallery, London. © Stephen's Gallery.

Figure 5.13 St Pancras Station by Stephen Wiltshire with photograph (inset top right) that shows the accuracy with which Stephen recalled the scene, however, it is also evident that Stephen's drawing is a reconstruction rather than a copy. Notice the small differences between the drawing and the photograph. Drawn before the age of 12 years. Reprinted with the kind permission of Stephen Wiltshire, The Stephen Wiltshire Gallery, London. © Stephen's Gallery.

Figure 5.14 View of Amsterdam railway station by Stephen Wiltshire. This was drawn at the age of 15. Reprinted with the kind permission of Stephen Wiltshire, The Stephen Wiltshire Gallery, London. © Stephen's Gallery.

showed. In 1987 Sir Hugh Casson former President of the Royal Academy described him as 'the best child artist in Britain'. He said, in the introduction to Stephen's book, *Drawings* (1987): 'Every now and then, a rocket of young talent explodes and continues to shower us with its sparks. Stephen Wiltshire – who was born with severe speech difficulties – is one of these rockets ... These drawings show a masterful perspective, a whimsical line, and reveal a natural innate artistry' (p. 5).

Hermelin (2001) states that when her team first tested his intelligence at the age of 15 he had a verbal reasoning ability of a 7- to 8-year-old. However, his visuo-spatial intelligence was near the average for his age. Interestingly, Hermelin (2001) reported that Stephen had a 'temporary loss of personal style' during early art school training. She continued that 'it is often only later that a student develops the ability to use his acquired pictorial vocabulary for his own purposes and intentions' (p. 145). She reports that his teachers observed that he did not love colour for its own sake. She concluded that as a trained artist, then in his twenties, Stephen remains: 'A predominantly graphic artist, most at home with the linear style by which he is able to express his own temperament, his preferences and his particular skill. His artistic talent thus remains most evident in the idiom that he originally and spontaneously selected' (p. 148).

She says it seemed likely that Stephen will retain his initial artistic identity. Stephen Wiltshire was awarded the MBE in 2006. Stephen's drawings are highly valued and are exhibited in his own gallery near Pall Mall. In interviews (such as one in *The Independent*; Philby, 2009) he describes his life in London in his thirties. He speaks of his delight in strolling around the streets, especially the city of London, observing the futuristic buildings, making up new ideas, buying magazines and drawing. He describes his favourite shops, celebrities, style icons, books that inspire him, favourite works of art (anything from Richard Estes) and his favourite clothes. He explains that he can sing well and play the piano and recognises that he has an unusual talent for art and music. Interestingly, he describes his favourite film, as 'Rain Man', and enjoys the character of Raymond whom Stephen describes accurately as 'an autistic savant'. He hopes in the future to have his own penthouse where he would be living with his friends in good company. It would require the comments of an art expert to answer the question posed by Sacks (cited in Wiltshire, 1991), as to whether his art has subsequently become charged with 'moral and human depth'. But there is evidence that his most recent work remains extraordinary since he is producing drawings of cities and their buildings in ways that even a mature and well-trained artist could not achieve. For example, a report in October 2009 described how he produced an 18 ft drawing of the New York skyline having spent only 20 minutes in a helicopter to view the scene. He went on to reproduce it in a public display with details of every building sketched in to scale (Figure 5.15). He has achieved similar feats in Tokyo and Rome.

Multiple savant skills

It is evident from the examples of savants with mathematical, musical skills, and drawing abilities that they exhibit extraordinary memory ability (Pring, 2008). This was observed by Kanner (1943) when he first published his account of autism. He noted, too, that such children have restricted pattern of interests. Howe (1989) suggested that powers of memory and restricted obsessive interest accounts

Figure 5.15 Stephen Wiltshire in front of his huge canvas on which he is drawing his recollections of the scene of New York viewed from a helicopter. Reprinted with the kind permission of The Stephen Wiltshire Gallery, London. © Stephen's Gallery.

for savant abilities although he did not link this to autism. There are some remarkable individuals who show a number of savant skills and they frequently have a diagnosis of Asperger's syndrome.

Daniel Tammet (2006) has described himself as an autistic savant in his biographical account *Born on a Blue Day: A Memoir of Aspergers and an Extraordinary Mind*, at the age of 25 he received a diagnosis of Asperger's syndrome. He experienced epilepsy as a child, which he believes brought on his synaesthesia (the ability to see numbers in colours and shapes and textures). He has the ability to describe what it is like to be a high-functioning autistic person although introspection is extremely rare among savants. His skills at computing and memorising numbers are phenomenal. For example, he can be shown a long numerical sequence and he can recite it backwards or forwards. His most remarkable achievement was to recite pi from memory to 22,514 digits in just over 5 hours. (Pi, being the number used to calculate the dimensions of a circle, usually rounded off to 3.142. In fact its numbers actually go on to infinity.) He also has the facility to learn new languages quickly. He mastered Icelandic as a television challenge in one week sufficiently well to be interviewed in the language. He claims to be able to speak more than 10 others. His mother says of him that as a child he was constantly counting things. He still finds some environments difficult, such as a visit to the beach, where he becomes obsessed with counting the pebbles around him. Although he cannot drive and lives a relatively secluded lifestyle, he has learned some basic social skills. He knows that it is helpful to give eye contact and not to infringe the personal space of others. These are ways of behaving that many autistic people fail to achieve. Such is his ability that he has set up a business website that offers a variety of educational courses with strategies for learning languages and maths. He has also written books on what it means to be autistic and has appeared in television and radio programmes to demonstrate his talents and explain his skills.

A report in 1970 described the wide-ranging savant skills of a disabled child named Harriet (whose IQ was 73). She had a phenomenal memory in addition to other savant skills described by Howe (1989). He says: 'She could remember every single one of the weather reports she had heard on the radio; on being told a date by someone . . . she would recite the appropriate report. She could recall on request any of about 300 telephone numbers that had been told to her' (p. 33). This child had multi-talents, also having ability as a musical performer and as a calendar calculator. She could provide the correct day of the week for any date between 1925 and 1970.

Howe (1989) also describes the case of Richard (from the work of Scheerer and colleagues, 1945). His IQ was measured at about 50 (when tested at the ages of 11 and 15), yet again he was found to have an extraordinary memory. He successfully memorised Lincoln's Gettysburg address without error, but without understanding its content. He was unable to cope easily with basic day-to-day tasks, unless they followed a very well-defined pattern of action. His dressing, eating, and social activities are described 'as fixed and unvarying ceremonies that left no room for flexibility' (Howe, 1989, p. 24). He had no idea of the concepts of cause and effect; he did not appreciate the work of a conjuror in making things appear and disappear. The tricks that were performed appeared to him 'no more and no less surprising than the routine happenings of everyday life' (Howe, 1989, p. 25). His savant skills related to his ability to memorise items of written information and repeat them in parrot-like fashion, to recall dates of meetings with people over intervals of many years, and calendar calculating.

Dr Langdon Down (1887) famously presented ten cases from his 30 years experience. He considered all the subjects to be 'mentally retarded' while demonstrating special faculties that included having prodigious memory.

Conclusion

The remarkable savant talents, which have been observed in children with known pathology, have intrigued the general public and have caused psychologists, psychiatrists, and neuroscientists to search for explanations. These range from those that invoke neurological dysfunction, while others consider possible environmental influences that drive a child to narrow repetitive interests. Some research has considered the development of such skills as compensation for lack of language; other work has focused on possible genetic factors. The apparent inability of the savant to conceptualise or be able to use abstract thought has been presented as a possible explanation. Recently, researchers have favoured explanations that have highlighted the role of the enhanced perception that savants seem to display. All these explanations are considered in the next chapter.

While acknowledging the truly remarkable skills of a few of the most exceptional savants, it has been noted by some commentators that many of the skills demonstrated could be performed at an impressive level by those of normal intelligence with the desire to achieve them and to learn through constant practice. Returning to the point made by Howe (1999), non-autistic individuals of average intelligence can show phenomenal special skills. We will look at some child prodigies in the field of art in Chapter 7. But consider, too, the astounding feats of athletes and acrobats. Outstanding musicians are very rarely autistic and it is important to remember that intelligence and skill acquisition usually go hand in glove. Savants are the exceptions to the general rule. A New Zealand mathematician, Alexander Aitken (1895–1967), is regarded as the greatest mathematician/calculator of recent times; he was able to achieve results in his calculations that today could only be matched by a computer (Hunter, 1977). He was a non-autistic, highly intelligent man who was also a linguist and musician. It was noted of him that he could recite Pi to 707 decimal places. He became a professor in Edinburgh University. According to Hunter (1977) his abilities made him the greatest mental calculator for whom there is any reliable record. He was, for example, able to multiply accurately two nine-digit numbers in his head in 30 seconds.

Pring (2008) suggests that there appears to be sound evidence to show that both savants and non-autistic prodigies share important qualities. Implicit (unconscious) learning and the organisation of 'proceduralised knowledge' plays an important part in the manifestation and development of remarkable talent. All those who have studied savant syndrome have noted the significance of the extraordinary memory (variously described as eidetic, photographic, or enhanced) that the savants appear to have for pattern recognition and for having access to the underlying rules or structures of the areas in which they display special interest. While memory can be improved in most people, there are some skills beyond even the most enthusiastic typically developing learner. Howe (1989) accepts that there are some cases, such as Nadia, where explanations in terms of practice or memory cannot be sufficient. Any thoroughgoing theory needs to be able to explain the anomalies as well as the more averagely talented savants. Consequently, there is not yet any single explanatory theory for the savant phenomenon.

6   Theories of savant syndrome

How do they do it?

Happé and Frith (2009) ask why, of all the features of autism, none is so widely admired as the remarkable talent sometimes found with this condition, known as savant syndrome: 'Yet these are still less researched and understood than other features of autism. Extraordinary talents of past geniuses such as Mozart, Einstein or Newton are sometimes considered in this light, although these authors regard the personification of the association of autism and talent to misrepresent both' (p. 1345).

Happé and Frith also note that O'Connor and Hermelin (1989a) moved research from the descriptive case study through innovative experimental design and the use of control groups. They paved the way for modern cognitive psychological studies that considered the question, how can individuals with substantial intellectual impairment and very poor social adaptation show skills that outstrip the most intelligent neurotypical (non-autistic) individuals?

Hermelin and O'Connor (1964) also pioneered research with children with autistic spectrum disorder (ASD). Their initial hypothesis suggested that children with autism favoured sensory modalities of touch and smell over vision and hearing. This gave way to accounts centred on the nature of the resulting representations in the mind of the autistic child. It was their notion that sensory information was stored seemingly true to fact, but less adaptively, due to lack of recoding for meaning. In O'Connor and Hermelin's book *Seeing and Hearing and Space and Time* (1978) they suggested that there were modality specific memory systems and that children with autism had difficulties in relating information across modalities. If they were presented with pictures they did not code them as words and vice versa. This view pre-dates some contemporary theories.

The issues that arise from the foregoing are as follows:

- Does autism predispose to special talents? If so, why?
- Why do people with ASD appear to show striking isolated talents at such a high rate and more often than any other neurologically impaired group?

Theories to account for savant syndrome

A range of theories and suggestions have been proposed. There is no single theory to account for how all savants achieve their extraordinary talents. The research focuses on such issues as:

- deficits in abstract thought and conceptualising;
- compensation and reinforcement;
- eidetic imagery;
- extraordinary memory;
- the role of practice;
- genetic factors;
- brain dysfunction and neurological factors;
- privileged access to lower level, less processed information.

Theories specific to savants who are autistic include:

- sensory deprivation;
- enhanced perception;
- weak central coherence;
- hypersystemising and hypersensitivity.

Cognitive theories of savant syndrome

Deficits in abstract thought and conceptualising

At the most basic level cognitive development involves the acquisition of words and icons as internalised representations for objects, characters, figures, colours, and properties in the external world used to order, structure, and codify experience. Manipulating these allows us to engage in abstract thought and form concepts. Howe (1989) states that defining abstract thought is not easy and he suggests that the explanatory power is limited due to our meagre understanding of cognitive mechanisms. But he also says, 'There is little doubt that deficiencies in the ability to think abstractly have a central place in the limitations we find in retarded savants' (p. 64).

Howe (1989) refers to research that suggests that the absence of symbolic abilities in a savant or learning disabled child (such as the ability for 'pretend play', or very limited or absent language development) may have advantages (Lindsley, 1965). For example, it might become easier for the child to focus more directly on underlying features of a task without the distractions of the various meanings or possible interpretations a typically developing child may use. Howe (1989, p. 60) states 'A savant artist's concentration on shapes and the physical dimensions of objects may be assisted by the decreased likelihood, compared with other people, of attention shifting away from the physical dimensions of seen objects and towards their meaning'. In the savant there seems to be an absence of normal cognitive processing and an inability to reason abstractly, being much more limited to concrete thinking.

The very limited ability to understand language or abstract ideas or indulge in the full range of symbolic activities from play to mathematics, has led some to view savants as having developed the unusual skills they possess because of the concentration, practice, and repetition that has taken place as a means of coping with the world that is otherwise beyond their comprehension (Howe, 1989). This theory of impairment of abstract ability leads to the view that the savants have achieved their skills not in spite of a disability, but because of a disability. In some cases, for example, they have developed an amazing rote memory in which the savant accumulates vast amounts of often trivial information without comprehending its meaning or significance (Pring, 2005). The savant appears to lack the rational options open to those in the normal population to widen their range of interests. The theory has been used to explain the ability of calendar and other calculators (Hermelin, 2001). But Treffert (1989) concludes that the limitations in abstract thinking is best seen as a symptom rather than a cause of savantism. The concentration on the concrete describes the typical savant; it does not necessarily explain the behaviour associated with the syndrome.

Arnheim (1980) speculates on the possibility that Nadia's ability to draw in such a remarkable way was the result of her inability to conceptualise the subjects that she drew. This was close to my own view at this time.

As Howe (1989, p. 138) comments: 'It is possible to state with certainty that there is no conceivable way in which any normal child of the same age could have equalled Nadia's achievements. With almost all the other savants' feats they can be done by at least a few people of normal intelligence or, intelligent people could perform them if they were willing to devote a very large proportion of their time to . . . tasks of learning or remembering'.

My original explanation for Nadia's prodigious ability and her subsequent loss of it was in terms of her initial lack of language and her subsequent linguistic development (which was always minimal) (Selfe, 1977, 1983). As discussed in Chapter 3, it has frequently been stated that in drawing, typically developing young children are dominated by the need to set down their conceptual under-standing of an object (Goodenough, 1926; Harris, 1963). This has been referred to as a symbolic activity (Luquet, 1927/2001) or canonical representation (Freeman, 1980) or the search for equivalents (Arnheim, 1970; Golomb, 1992) or invariant structures (Willats, 1987). The child represents the characteristics rather than the idiosyncratic features of an object. This conceptual domination arises mainly from the central activity of generalisation and categorisation in thinking processes (Bruner et al., 1966). Language, too, is seen as pre-eminently a categorising and symbolising activity whereby multivarious experience is organised, codified, and reduced. The single word 'chair', for example, can stand for all objects that are for sitting purposes, and all possible relevant visual and tactile experience is hence organised and reduced by the use of this one single verbal label. Willats (2005) makes a parallel between the work of Chomsky on language acquisition and that of Marr on visual perception seeing both essentially as the formation of internal representations.

Willats (2005) would maintain that much the same symbolising activity characterises the drawings of very young children. Children represent those objects that have functional significance for them (people, animals, houses, vehicles). The production of a characterising and meaningful symbolic representation appears to be more important than attention to idiosyncratic detail or to a single viewpoint representation of an object (Light, 1985). However, the autistic children in the group that I studied (Selfe, 1983, p. 189) were better able to record a single viewpoint, static spatial configuration. I suggested that this may be due to their symbolic representational abilities being very limited. Using the work of O'Connor and Hermelin (1978), I also speculated on the possibility of this being related to problems with transpositions between cognitive modalities in autistic individuals.

> It can be seen that restricted transposition and inflexible use of one representational code may help to account for the fact that their drawings are much more photographically realistic and spatial information is more accurately portrayed. Presumably the autistic children are using the visual/spatial modality without the interaction or contamination of the temporal/verbal mode as may normally occur.
>
> (Selfe, 1983, p. 197)

Nadia did not develop language properly. As described in Chapter 1, the few words she had acquired around 12 months disappeared. At the age of 6 she had extremely limited vocabulary of about 10 words. Testing showed that Nadia had profound difficulties not only with verbal expression but also with comprehension. She appeared to lack many of the prerequisites of language development. She could not imitate. She could repeat monosyllables but not two syllables of different sounds and she was never seen to engage in symbolic play. She was clumsy and poorly coordinated. She could not hop, nor walk up stairs one tread at a time. She did show average-for-her-age ability with some visual matching tasks and jigsaw puzzles. She could match quite difficult items that had the same perceptual quality although she failed to match items in the same conceptual class. She could match a picture of an object to a picture of its silhouette but not pictures of chairs as a class (an armchair, kitchen chair, and a deckchair).

It could be argued that the fact that Nadia was more concerned or better able to record single fixed views of static spatial configurations was due to the fact that her symbolic and verbal abilities were severely retarded. In the absence of the usual domination of conceptual understanding of the world around her, Nadia was better able to attend to and record her purely visual experience (Selfe, 1983).

O'Connor and Hermelin (1978) had shown that autistic children have difficulty in transposing information received in one mode (visual, tactile, or auditory) to another internal cognitive system. They appear to be inflexible in transposing between modalities in a range of tasks where auditory or spatial stimuli were presented but responses had to be given in an alternative mode. For such children, the visual image did not invoke the spoken word, and the written or spoken word did not appear to invoke matching visual images as compared with matched controls (Hermelin & O'Connor, 1970). It can be conjectured that Nadia, as an autistic child, may have had reasonably well-developed imagery and spatial abilities but that her verbal and discursive thought processes were defective. All that we know of her behaviour and intellectual development supports this speculation. Since, presumably normal drawing development results from the normal integration of the various modes of thinking, and verbal and discursive processes are believed to influence the nature of early drawing, it was reasoned that autism and its attributed cognitive deficits accounted for the special spatial, photographic characteristics of Nadia's drawings. These drawings were seen as a symptom of her autism and of an underlying pathological condition taken in conjunction with her other severe deficits in other areas of functioning. This is not, of course, a necessary symptom of autism; it is in fact a very rare occurrence (Selfe, 1983).

In my second book (Selfe, 1983) I reported on several children with special drawing ability all of whom had learning difficulties and were autistic. I was influenced by Gibson's view of perception in *The Ecological Approach to Visual Perception* (1979), and the notion of perception being dynamic where the viewer is afforded information from the 'optic array'. I argued that when these anomalous children represented, through drawing, those aspects of their optic array, such as lines, edges and occlusion, they are attending to non-symbolic aspects of their visual experience. I suggested that the drawing of autistic savants is far less symbolic; objects are partially occluded, truncated and represented without their object-defining characteristics or invariant structure (in Gibson's terms), as seen from one fixed viewpoint. Such a view is necessarily special and is autistic and asocial insofar as one fixed view is possible only to one single viewer at one fixed spot (Selfe, 1983).

The subjects in my study also represented spatial rather than symbolic aspects of the optic array. The space between objects and their position relative to other objects was more accurately represented and was therefore given more consideration than is evident in the drawings of normal children, where the depiction of the invariant structure of objects is paramount. I suggested that the drawings of these autistic savants was, in this sense, more detached and objective, but this was not the objectivity of mature intelligence. For most normal children, photographic realism in graphic depiction is a late accomplishment. For these anomalous children, with deviant language and deficient symbolic abilities, it is another symptom of their cognitive deficits.

It was hypothesised that in drawing, these anomalous children respond to objects in their optic array more as patterns, edges, contours, and shapes, rather than as representatives of classes or categories. It is further suggested that linear perspective drawing before the age of 6 years is as much a symptom of learning disability in these children as is their delayed language development. I suggested that it was perhaps coincidental that adult lay people generally value photographic realism in drawing and this feature is the hallmark of the drawings of the anomalous group (Selfe, 1983).

The question of whether photographic realism in drawing could be promoted in children at an earlier age remains open. What is suggested here, is that symbolic representations of objects predominate in normal children and this precludes the depiction of other spatial features. Young children do not have an interest in portraying these features, not so much because they lack the planning strategies to do so, but because they are dominated by other considerations, although this may in itself amount to an incapacity to do so.

As typically developing children grow older they eventually come to depict features related to linear perspective. They come to accept and require far less information in the recognition and depiction of an object. They learn to depict an object from one point of view where distortion of what is known about an object is tolerated and then preferred. For example, a car can have one wheel from one fixed viewpoint. Their understanding now incorporates spatial relationships as a worthwhile feature of depiction.

The drawings of the children I had studied were truly anomalous and if they were able to depict photographic realism and have an elaborate symbolic under-standing of their world to be mediated by complex language usage, they would be very gifted. But it was much more probable that the anomalous group depicted lines, occluding edges, and contours in their drawings because they could not symbolise or categorise their visual experience at anything like the level of complexity of typically developing children.

In relation to savant drawing O'Connor and Hermelin (1987a, p. 87) remarked that: 'One ingenious solution that has been suggested is that this is not so much a gift as a failure to be able to symbolise or imagine, perhaps because of the autistic child's tendency to what has been called "pathological concreteness" or lack of ability to construct, infer or think. In consequence, the child draws what he sees and not what other children think about'.

To explain Nadia's outstanding ability in terms of her deficits may seem disappointing or parsimonious. But I believe that such an explanation in no way detracts from her achievement because she demonstrates how rich, detailed, and imaginative visual experience translated as drawing can be, even in a child with very restricted cognitive abilities. In summary, it is an often repeated aphorism that children draw what they know rather than what they see. Nadia with her extreme impoverishment of both language and intellect drew what she perceived. She showed it was possible to draw without the usual domination of the canonical form. The ability to retain a visual image with high fidelity over a number of weeks must be part of the answer to explain Nadia's drawing ability. The current status of this general theory will be critically examined again in Chapter 8.

Compensation and reinforcement

Howe (1989) notes how everyone enjoys doing things that they do well. We get approval from others that acts as a reinforcement. The encouragement savants receive to develop their special skills can be seen as a driving force in their lives. There is also the effect of a compensatory drive in savants to develop a talent in one area to offset defects in another. This, together with positive reinforcement, increases the amount of practice and concentration that the savant devotes to the skill. The developed talent becomes a form of coping mechanism and wins approval from those around them, especially parents, who achieve satisfaction from the achievements of their child.

A more negative view is that the focus on the skill, which is of little social value, becomes a habit or compulsion that is increasingly difficult to break. This may result in the savant failing to develop other types of stimulation or interests that may have a more positive value (Hermelin & O'Connor, 1991).

On the other hand, there is wide agreement on the need to foster talent once it is seen to emerge. Heaton (2009) makes a strong case that learning a skill such as music has benefits for social integration and personal development for young people with autism. Her work suggests untapped potential special to ASD. It seems likely that parents or carers often discover an existing talent by accident. Grandin (2009) is an outstanding example of an autistic individual who is able to tell her own story. Her extraordinary accounts of her own development raises the possibility of life-long learning and the speculation that developmental periods of exceptional brain plasticity may be extended in ASD. Life-long learning may be of special importance in autism. Hacking (2009) considers the paradox and power of autobiographical accounts in shaping our concept of autism. This is not without dangers. It is not clear to what extent we can generalise from the experiences reported by a number of high-functioning people with ASD to the experience of others who may never be able to speak for themselves. He warns that we can never know precisely what it is like 'inside the autistic mind'.

There is also the concern that for some parents of autistic savants the special skill the child has developed may not be one that brings them pleasure. Whereas, those parents whose child has musical or artistic skills can be delighted, those parents whose children have obsessional abilities such as calendar calculating, spinning coins, or recording number plates sometimes say that they would have channelled their child's interest into a different direction if only they could.

Winner (1996) uses the phrase 'the rage to learn' and argues that this is what characterises extremely gifted children. For them, learning, practice, and performance are all rewarding in their own right and not a means to other rewards. Happé and Frith (2009), suggest that it remains a puzzle to know why repetitive practice in a narrow domain is so rewarding for individuals with ASD who develop savant skills. They note that most 'neurotypicals' do not enjoy trying to master savant skills. When volunteers are asked to learn calendar calculation they stop as soon as they can. Perhaps this can be understood through the notion of 'detailed focus'. They point out that repetition is not repetition if you have expert levels of discrimination. They give the example of how listening to various recordings of the same symphony can bring delight to an expert, but may not be appreciated by the lay person. They draw an analogy and suggest that the child with autism who spends hours watching clouds or water falling through fingers might be considered 'a connoisseur seeing minute differences between events that others regard as dull repetition' (p. 1348).

Happé and Frith (2009) continue their analysis by noting that in the natural environment it makes sense for animals to stay and exploit familiar surroundings. A well-adapted animal will move further afield and this will require exploring the unknown and finding reward in doing something different. They conclude, 'in autism the aversion to novelty suggests a different balance of reward value for exploiting versus exploring. Thus reward-learning paradigms might open new avenues for investigation of savant skills' (p. 1348). Hence, it is their view that understanding why the individual with savant skills chooses to practise intensively: 'May lead to a better understanding of the apparent meaningless repetition and insistence on sameness seen throughout the autism spectrum ... In this way the study of savant skills could, perhaps, lead to a better appreciation of the beautiful otherness of the autistic mind' (p. 1349).

However, it would seem unlikely that such factors as reinforcement, compensation drives, and parental encouragement account entirely for the savant skill, since the emergence of the skill must pre-date such reinforcement. Until the skill is obvious there would be no impetus to give it undue encouragement. In addition, not all disabled children develop savant skills despite the encouragement they may receive from parents and carers to develop a special talent. It appears also to be a condition more prevalent in males than females. Why do not all such children seek to compensate by developing talents? It seems that the processes of compensation and reinforcement may have some effects but there are other explanations to consider. Treffert's view (1989) that the concept of compensation must be treated with caution is one with which I concur. The problem here is that one might expect all such children with language impairment to show similar perceptual skills that manifest themselves in drawing ability or other visuospatial creative ability. It is clear that they do not. Children with language problems seldom develop any obvious compensation.

Eidetic imagery

Research on eidetic imagery had its heyday in the 1960s and 1970s. With the emergence of new theories of visual perception interest has waned. Eidetic imagery describes a specific memory function sometimes linked to neurological impairment, in which a person retains a very strong visual impression or image of an object or picture for at least 40 seconds after it is removed. The person with strong eidetic memory will be able to describe the object in great detail and with great accuracy (Haber, 1969). In experiments in which pictures are placed on an easel for a short time before being removed, those with eidetic memory will see the pictures as if on the easel; describing precisely what they can still 'see' with discernible eye movements as they scan the image although now invisible. Haber (1969) claimed that the images are not 'photographs' seen as a whole before the eyes but operate more as an after image. Eidetic imagery was, therefore, described as the ability to hold in the brain or 'mind's eye' an image that is an exact copy of what has just been seen. It was assumed that once lost, the image could not be recalled but Duckett (1977), was unable to confirm that such images differed from other forms of visual memory. Researchers (Gray & Gummerman, 1975) concluded that eidetic imagery is only quantitatively different from visual image memory in so far as the imagery is more vivid.

Treffert (1989) notes that the term 'eidetic imagery' is used generally to cover both phenomenon (after images and visual memory) and is taken to be a developmental stage that decreases in importance as a child grows. Whereas eidetic ability is almost universally present in young children, 'during the course of development the process of concrete visual perception expands to include the process of imagining, rather than just perceiving' (pp. 165–166). As the person grows and develops normally the ability to conceptualise and use abstract thought emerges and increasingly dominates. Eidetic imagery is therefore, seldom found in normally functioning adults.

Some studies (e.g., Duckett, 1977; Giray & Barclay, 1977; Siipola & Hayden, 1965) have found eidetic imagery to be associated with brain damage. It has been suggested that remembering calendars could account for calendar calculators. But it cannot account for those who can calculate into the future for which no calendars exist. Studies of a number of such calculators (including a girl who was blind from birth and presumably had never seen a calendar; Hermelin & Pring, 1998) have not shown conclusively that they are using eidetic memory and that they must have some other facility. Treffert (1989) summarises the findings of research that show that it does not appear to exist more frequently in savants than in a similarly retarded, but non-savant group. Where it exists Treffert says, it may be more an effect of brain dysfunction rather than a cause of the savant's special abilities.

In my original work (Selfe, 1977), I considered the possibility that Nadia had unusual eidetic memory and her drawings were produced by drawing around an image that she had remembered. I concluded that for several reasons eidetic theory did not hold for Nadia because she could clearly manipulate the images she had seen rotating and changing their orientation. During my second study, Gibson published his work (1979) on *The Ecological Approach to Visual Perception*. Gibson's analysis of visual perception dissolves any distinction between visual and eidetic imagery since perception is viewed as necessarily selective and dynamic and that the idea of an eidetic image as a 'passive photograph' of a scene, object, or picture is misconceived (Selfe, 1983).

Extraordinary memory in savant syndrome

Howe (1989) claimed that savants remember things for similar reasons that ordinary people sometimes remember well. He suggested that items are retained in memory because they have received sustained and concentrated attention. 'Savants, like people of normal intelligence, are most likely to keep concentrating on something if they find it especially interesting. What matters is that, for one reason or another, the information gains a person's close attention' (p. 46). He goes on to state that what is vital is that the attention of the savant is engaged, as it sometimes is for hours at a stretch. He suggests that research findings 'give ample support for the assertion that sustained attention leads to remembering even in the absence of any definite intention to remember' (p. 47).

Most authors who discuss the issues relating to savant syndrome emphasise the factor that is seen in them all, namely phenomenal memory. Treffert (1989), for example, says that it is seen in all savants no matter what particular individual skill they exhibit. Books are available to advise the ordinary reader with average intellectual abilities how to improve their short-term and long-term memories and human memory can hold an astonishing amount of information. In 1991 Dominic O'Brien was able to memorise the exact order of 1820 playing cards (35 packs) and could recall the order in one pack in 55 seconds. An actor playing Hamlet must memorise more than 1500 lines of speech, which are rehearsed in short-term memory and then committed to long-term memory. The key point that is emphasised in methods to improve memory is the application of techniques that need to be practised constantly. The aim is to find patterns to impose on the material to be recalled (grouping or categorising items for a shopping list, for example, according to types of goods) or to establish ways of linking related memories together to assist recall.

Such memories are assumed to involve electrical and structural changes in the brain. Brain activity is increasingly open to investigation through scanning processes, and pictures of brain activity can be obtained while a subject performs a range of mental tasks. Research on memory owes a great deal to studies of people who have suffered strokes or brain injuries that have affected their ability to recall or learn new tasks (Baddeley, 2004). For example, people can sustain damage to the visual cortex, which results in visual agnosia. This presents as a defect in visual memory where the patient is unable to recognise familiar faces or objects, a problem described by Sacks (1985) in *The Man Who Mistook His Wife for a Hat*.

The study of human memory is a major component of both developmental and cognitive psychology. In recent years the field has been dominated by the work of Baddeley (2004). In the 1960s it was proposed that there are essentially two types of memory (Atkinson & Shiffrin, 1968). Long-term memory is the memory used to recall things that happened to us days, weeks, and years before. It is assumed that structural changes have taken place within the brain so that memories in long-term store are permanent. Short-term memory is the memory needed for immediate action such as dialling a telephone number, but is subject to rapid decay. The validity of the distinction between these types of memory rested largely on observations of people with dementia or other forms of brain damage. People with cerebral dementia, for instance, frequently had intact long-term memories while failing to recall events that had just happened. Alternatively people with Alzheimer's syndrome have problems with long-term memory retrieval.

It had also been proposed that memories are encoded as words or as images (Baddeley, 1986). Baddeley suggested that memory could be auditory in form, such as memory of conversations, remembered facts, material that has been read; or visual in nature, such as memory for faces, locations, and spatial arrangements. In 1974, Baddeley and Hitch proposed that short-term memory be renamed as 'working memory'. They suggested that short-term memory was not a unitary entity but comprised three parts that they termed the central executive, the phonological loop, and the visuospatial sketch pad. The phonological loop allows us to hear and understand language and holds traces for a few seconds; the visuospatial sketchpad is assumed to allow for temporary storage and manipulation of visual information, and the central executive has a supervisory attentional role. More recently Baddeley has added a fourth dimension to his model and suggested that there is also an 'episodic buffer' that allows for information to be integrated between modalities and appears to interface with long-term store (Baddeley, 2004).

Long-term store has similarly been fractionated (to borrow Baddeley's term). Two functions operate in long-term store. The declarative function is accessible and allows us to recall events and facts learned in the past and the non-declarative function is inaccessible and consists of our habitual responses, skills, and memories of how to do things like riding a bike or mending an electric plug.

The question is then, from this complex model of memory, what type of memory is being invoked by researchers who work with savants; and do savants with drawing ability use the same memory mechanisms used by calendar calculators or savant musicians? The memory involved in drawing, which is likely to involve retrieval of long-term visual, spatial, and motor memories (graphic motor schemas), may be different from the memory involved in playing music, which is likely to be auditory in nature.

Studies have been conducted on savants to try to understand how their memories work (Pring, 2008). It would appear that they are applying some of the techniques that those of normal intellectual ability can adopt such as finding structures and relationships to aid memory. Studying a group of artistic savants, I found that they all possessed good recall of designs using the tests from the British Abilities Scale (Selfe, 1983) and this ability was in contrast to low scores on auditory short-term memory. However, according to published norms, their memory abilities were not out of the ordinary. O'Connor and Hermelin (1987a, 1987b) and later Hermelin and Pring (1998) undertook several experiments with the savant artists they encountered. O'Connor and Hermelin (1987b) compared the outcomes of results including tests of memory using a group of eight savant artists who had a diagnosis of autism (with intelligence quotient [IQ] levels between 38–78) and selected on the basis of their drawing ability with those of various control groups. They selected control groups from intellectually normal subjects with artistic ability; from another group who had no special drawing ability; from subjects with matched mental age and from subjects with ASD with no special abilities. The various experiments produced results that showed that savant capability was confined to the execution of that activity for which they were gifted, namely, to draw from memory. The degree of accuracy in drawings proved to be independent of their intelligence. The savants did not differ from the control subjects in their ability to draw objects accurately from memory in short-term memory tasks (visual recognition tasks) but they were superior when the task involved reproduction of a complex figure from long-term memory. The researchers concluded that only when they were drawing from memory did the savants do better than others with the same diagnosis of ASD and intelligence levels. As with savant calendar calculators, 'Better memory was related to the actual activity for which the savants had a specific ability' (Hermelin, 2001, p. 128). Hermelin notes the comment of Gombrich (1960), 'drawing is an activity, and therefore the artist tends to look more at what he does than at what he sees' (cited in Hermelin, 2001, p. 128). The research suggests 'this statement holds true for savants as it does for artists in general' (Hermelin, 2001, p. 128).

Hermelin and Pring (1998) went on to examine whether savants could use the pictorial devices central to Western art. These are the use of linear perspective (the gradual convergence of lines in a picture of parallels in the real world for creating the illusion of depth) and the ability to ignore perceptual size constancy with increasing distance (to indicate three-dimensional space and distance). This work confirmed earlier studies (Selfe, 1983) described in Chapter 3. They found that the 'pictorial rules were employed with equal efficiency by savant artists (aged between 17–29 years) and by those of higher intelligence who had a gift for drawing' (1998, p. 1000).

Their particularly remarkable finding was that the artistically gifted autistic individuals could examine a scene (using small models of a horse, a tree, and two people), and reproduce it, not only as they themselves observed it, from one viewpoint, but they could also reproduce it from the perspective of another viewer (Figures 6.1 and 6.2). They performed as well as the normally functioning artistically gifted subjects on this task. Hermelin (2001) comments that her ASD subjects might be 'mind blind' but were by no means 'view blind' and that 'The drawings by the autistic savants were by no means restricted to what they saw or had seen, but demonstrated as much artistic freedom as those by the control participants' (p. 137). Presumably visual memory would be an important component in this task.

Figure 6.1 Model shown to an autistic savant. He was asked to draw what he thought the view would be like from another angle (Figure 6.2). From Hermelin (2001). *Bright splinters of the mind: Pictorial strategies*. London and Philadelphia: Jessica Kingsley Publishers. Reprinted with kind permission of Jessica Kingsley Publishers.

Figure 6.2 Drawing produced by an autistic savant who has looked at the model in
Figure 6.1 and was asked to draw what he thought the view would be like
from another angle. It shows how well he could imagine another's viewpoint and reproduce the scene. From Hermelin (2001). *Bright splinters of
the mind: Pictorial strategies*. London and Philadelphia: Jessica Kingsley
Publishers. Reprinted with kind permission of Jessica Kingsley Publishers.

Linda Pring (2008) in a chapter entitled 'Memory Characteristics in Individuals
with Savant Skills', usefully examines the significance of memory performance in
a range of savants who have been studied by her and her colleagues and by others.
She provides a theoretical interpretation that gives a convincing account of the
development of savant memory abilities. She describes the effects of the uneven
intelligence profile typically found in autism characterised by unexpectedly
high scores in tests requiring local rather than global processing, as evidence
for 'weak central coherence theory' (Frith, 1989). People with autism have difficulty drawing together information in order to construct higher-level meaning in
context. In their perceptual performance the cognitive strategies displayed signify
weak central coherence underlying exceptional skills. Pring (2008) suggests that
this may play a significant role in predisposing certain individuals to develop their
talents to savant level. Furthermore, the effects of focusing on detail rather than
the whole (as displayed in the block design tests) may not only apply to people
with ASD but may help explain some of the characteristics seen in gifted individuals drawn from the typical population, such as artists or mathematicians
(Pring et al., 1995, p. 1065).

Some researchers have discussed the concept of 'rote memory' in connection
with savant performance (Howe, 1989). This implies the unorganised absorption
of facts. But evidence based on group studies suggests that information involved
in calculation or musical performance is far from inflexible but is instead reliant

on highly organised, flexible knowledge structures capable of being used for creative production (Heavey et al., 1999).

Pring (2008) also indicates how implicit learning and long-term memory factors can be examined in the cases of remarkable calculators (such as those described in Chapter 5). In some cases they work at remarkable speed; in others it is the extraordinary memory involved that has been noted. She suggests, 'a complex hierarchical associative network of number concepts and related numerical material may characterise the knowledge of these savants' (p. 215). Again, there can be an explanation in terms of attention to detail that seems to help focus on the specific information; whether number factors or details of days, months, and years. Regularities are observed in the material as well as the associations and internal relationships among numbers, which form discernible patterns over time, allowing, for example, the recognition of prime numbers. Calendar calculators are also able to work with great speed. Pring explains how analysis of a calendar shows that it conforms to certain regularities. The work of researchers (Ho, Tsang, & Ho, 1991; Hermelin & O'Connor, 1986; Young & Nettlebeck, 1995) has shown that such calculators are aware of certain predictable formulations, such as dates falling in years with identical structures. There is a rule where, in the Gregorian calendar, the day–date configuration repeats itself every 28 years; or the corresponding month rule, where certain month pairs share the same day–date structure within a given year. O'Connor, Hermelin and their associates conducted a series of studies and were able to show that the memory performance of savants is sensitive to the structure of the calendar material and reflects its organisation (Heavey et al., 1999; Hermelin & O'Connor, 1986, 1990, 1991; Pring & Hermelin, 1997, 2002).

Pring (2008) concluded from her studies that the calculators must encode date information unusually effectively, rather than having increased memory capacity. Another study (Heavey et al., 1999) also showed that active practice and processing by savants produced more accessible memories compared with passive learning conditions suggesting that the savants make use of the underlying rules and structure of date information rather than having phenomenal memory capacity.

The memory processes with which musical savants develop their amazing performances are also considered by Ockelford and Pring (2005). They argue that music is rule-governed and structured in specific ways and conforms to the traditions of a society in which the performer is a member. The exceptional skills that have been uncovered (as discussed in Chapter 5) appear to result from the following:

• The structural knowledge they possess, which influences memory performance. Although it was found that they experienced difficulty memorising music written in unfamiliar styles (Sloboda, Hermelin, & O'Connor 1985; Young & Nettlebeck, 1995).
• Absolute pitch abilities (Heaton, 2003; Hermelin & Pring, 1998; Miller, 1989; Treffert & Wallace, 2002). This is a very rare ability. It is estimated that only 1 in 10,000 in the normal population possess it (Takeuchi & Hulse, 1993).

Its acquisition is unconscious and automatic and likened to the acquisition of language (Deutsch, Henthorn, & Dolson, 2004). It is the ability to recognise, label, and remember pitch information without reference to an external standard. It is a skill supposedly possessed by Mozart, Beethoven, and Bach but by no means by all musicians; whereas all savants with musical talent appear to have absolute pitch. Their ability is dependent on or linked to weak central coherence. Children with profound visual impairment also appear to show a potential to develop absolute pitch ability (Ockelford, 1988). They also have excellent pitch memory (Pring & Painter, 2002).

Pring (2008) also reviews the explanations for savant artistic ability and the role played by memory (Hill, 1975; LaFontaine, 1974). She says that the capacity of savant artists to produce visually correct, complex artistic outputs, sometimes months after seeing the initial image are clearly feats of outstanding memory (Sacks, 1985; Selfe, 1977). But that the visual knowledge and perceptual comprehension that must underlie the ability to draw in linear perspective, taking account of size constancy and achieving rotational transformations is not well understood. In reviewing the work the artists have produced, Pring comments: 'The sense that the image has been reproduced on a piecemeal basis, without regard to the holistic impression, is hard to miss in such drawing behaviour and seems to support the weak perceptual coherence theory described with the cognitive style seen in autism' (p. 223).

Pring (2008) also describes the experiments conducted with Hermelin (2001) which demonstrated that while savant artists demonstrated size constancy and diminishing size with distance in line with the rules of linear perspective in their drawings, this skill did not transfer to the placement of model cars and planes of varying sizes in a display. Their ability is therefore highly specific. Pring (2008), drawing on the work she conducted in association with O'Connor and Hermelin (1987a, 1987b), concluded that there was some implicit specific mechanism involving long-term memory components in savant performance, rather than short-term memory capacity. She links this to weak perceptual coherence and the model of 'enhanced perceptual function' (Mottron et al., 2006). Pring concludes that savants may have a particular facility with long-term visual memory and make use of what she terms 'long-term memory schemas'.

The role of practice

Pring (2008) notes that individuals with autism typically display repetitive and obsessional interests. 'Practice with the subject matter may be something that comes easily both to individuals with high motivational levels and interest and to individuals with autism' (p. 213). Several other researchers have emphasised the role of practice in savant skills (Davidson & Sloboda, 1998; Howe, 1989).

Pring (2008) notes that there is a problem in the use of the term 'practice' in that it implies the use of explicitly determined cognitive strategies, whereas in the case of savants, reports seem to describe implicit processes based on simple exposure to the material as the basis for learning in long-term memory.

The work of Anderson (1990) throws more light on the significance of practice for savant performance. Pring (2008) explains that he argues that 'expertise is best understood as being based on a knowledge system which is developed piecemeal, dependent on the accrual and tuning of small units, which can be combined to produce complex cognition' (p. 214). Again, this view relates to studies that have shown that autistic people perform better than expected from their intelligence levels on tasks requiring the study of small parts of a task (such as block design) in order to build the design of the larger whole (Mottron et al., 2006).

There is an extraordinary range of information that is retained by savants calculators/mathematicians, musicians, linguists, and others with splinter skills that focus on specialist areas such as geographical information, timetables, weather reports, sporting events, accurate transcriptions of conversations heard as described in Chapter 5. It is often related to the savant's obsessions. Howe (1989) notes how: 'It is hard to understand how certain of the topics could ever capture someone's attention. For instance, one autistic seven year old boy remembered the English and Latin names of eighteen different varieties of deer despite the fact that he was quite ignorant of the Latin language and would not have recognised a single one of the animals if it had presented itself in front of him' (p. 41).

I recently encountered a boy with ASD who had memorised all the details of the Travelodge hotels up and down the country and if given a number could match it to details and location of the hotel in the catalogue from his memory.

Howe (1989) goes on to warn about the problems of verifying exaggerated claims about savant abilities. However, he points out that there does not seem to be evidence from research under controlled conditions to support the view that there exist memory capacities in savants that are fundamentally different from those of ordinary individuals. It is only when the subject has had the opportunity to study certain kinds of information to be recalled for some time, that the person's memory is seen to be more effective. What research has shown to be most important is that the person gives full attention to the material to be recalled. Howe says that this is true of everyone, whether a savant or not. People can remember things when they are sufficiently motivated to concentrate (Craik & Tulving, 1975).

Howe (1989) claims that whenever people are interested enough in something to give it their full attention they are able to remember a striking number of detailed facts. For example, once the football results have been given, the enthusiastic listener can easily recall many with accuracy (Morris, Gruneberg, Sykes, & Merrick, 1981); details of a weather forecast may be recalled by someone going on holiday; the lyrics of songs may be quickly learnt by someone who is a fan of a singer. Waiters and waitresses in restaurants may develop considerable memory for the orders they have received (Bennett, 1983). In the same way while some deliberate intention to learn may occur, a savant's success at remembering vast amounts of apparently bizarre information may not necessarily depend on such attempts; the factor of interest could be sufficient. There is also the factor of the extent to which the individual is already knowledgeable or interested in the subject matter. Howe (1989) places emphasis on the lengthy exposure and practice that may be required leading to gradual improvement over a period of years. There may be the added advantage for savants that they may be largely free from the responsibilities and personal involvements that distract others from pursuing a skill single-mindedly. Experiments have been conducted to see if memory can be effectively improved in non-savants and these included one that involved paying a young man to spend 1 hour a day remembering digits (Chase & Ericsson, 1981). After 2 years his span increased from 8 to 70 items. He developed techniques for recalling the digits by associating numbers with running times, one of his hobbies. Howe suggests that such information as to how a person can deliberately improve his memory helps to demystify the skill of the savant. The question then arises, what is it that drives them to spend long periods of time concentrating on and practising tasks that many would see as pointless? Among the answers suggested by Howe are the following:

•   The savant's restricted range of interests and occupations may be an advantage in sustaining attention to detail and enhance the enjoyment of endless practice.
•   Intellectual limitation combined with personality characteristics that limit their social life may result in more inward contemplation, which promotes concentration.
•   The activities do not necessitate the child entering a threatening social environment of others or having social interaction with people. The areas of special ability are neutral and safe and areas of great enjoyment (Cain, 1969).
•   There are social rewards obtained in that the savants often achieve approval and praise for their special skills, with minimal costs. This encourages further concentration on such tasks.
•   The process of specialisation on the part of a savant is likely to result in increased competence (Nurcombe & Parker, 1964).
•   Special abilities in a savant may have a role in exacerbating certain aspects of the child's intellectual limitations or autism. The child becomes obsessed with repetitive or stereotyped patterns of behaviour. The suggestion is that this may induce the patterns of inward concentration that promote further attitudes of isolation and 'otherworldliness' (Happé & Frith, 2009).

Howe (1989) concludes that there are many circumstances in which being learning disabled can, paradoxically, provide advantages for the person. 'Certain memory achievements are facilitated by an absence of distracting thoughts that impede a person's concentration on some kinds of detailed information' (p. 61). He suggests that perhaps Nadia's drawing skill may have been a result of her failure to have any understanding of the meaning of the objects she drew. From Howe's perspective outstanding talent is due almost entirely to concentrated practice, as opposed to innate talents.

The view that much of the exceptional talent that is observed in people (both those with ASD and those without) is due to practice and endless effort is often opposed by the belief in innate talent. Howe argues strongly for the former point of view. He notes, for example, how the eminent British explorer and soldier

Richard Burton mastered at least 40 languages. He refers to his journals that make it apparent that he did not find this easy; rather, he had a prodigious capacity for hard work; it was not a matter of special mental capabilities. He grew up in a family that enjoyed travel, he was gregarious and wished to communicate; he was encouraged by early success and his family's delight in his linguistic development. Howe accepts that there are cases, such as that of Nadia, where practice does not seem to be the answer. Although she did spend long periods of time drawing at the expense of any other activity, as do others who have unusual talents.

However, an interesting comment is raised by Woollett, Spiersw, and Maguire (2009) who studied the skills developed by London taxi drivers in mastering the complexities of London streets. They found that approximately two-thirds of those who began the 3-year training dropped out before acquiring the 'knowledge' (that is the layout of 25,000 streets in London and the location of thousands of places of interest). Taxi drivers need to pass stringent exams to obtain their operating licence. In their comments Happé and Frith (2009, p. 1347) conclude that the large drop-out rate may indicate that future taxi drivers who stay the course 'have a pre-existing talent and it is in the context of this self selected sample that years of practice translates into the highest level of expertise'. Perhaps the message from this is that talent requires practice but that without talent the case may be bleak. Talent has to exist before practice enhances it.

Genetic and neurological theories

Inherited skills: evolutionary and genetic explanations

Humphrey (1998) wrote an intriguing article about Nadia in 1998 linking her abilities to the evolution of man, the evolution of art from Neolithic times and the development of language as our principal means of communication. Humphrey discusses the debate as to the possible effects of the acquisition of language to account for Nadia's loss of drawing skill. He noted that by the age of 6 she had still failed to develop any spoken language. He also pointed out that some of Nadia's drawings bear astonishing parallels to cave art of the upper Palaeolithic period. He states that there are several features of similarity. There is the striking naturalism and realism of the individual animals. In both cases the graphic techniques used are similar. Linear contour is used to model the body of animals; there is foreshortening and hidden line occlusion to give depth and perspective. There is a preference for side-on views; salient parts such as faces and feet are emphasised. There are similar idiosyncratic features to be observed. There is overlay and overlap as if the artist has not noticed what had already been drawn.

Humphrey (1998) notes that at the age of 6 Nadia's vocabulary consisted of only 10 single word utterances that she used rarely. Humphrey suggests that the hypothesis that without the domination of language and verbal mediation in the early years when graphic competence was being acquired, Nadia was able to attend to the spatial characteristics of their experience. They were not so strongly contaminated by the usual designating and naming properties of normal children's drawings. Cave drawings appear to have emerged about 30,000 years ago. Humphrey asks whether the artistic ability of cave artists was due to the fact that they, too, had little if any language so their drawings were uncontaminated by designating and naming. Language evolved later in man and Humphrey speculates that the earliest cave artists can be seen as having been, not the first artists of the age of symbolism, but the 'last of the innocents'. He disputes the theory that the cave artists of the Upper Palaeolithic period had essentially 'modern' minds. Humphrey offers evidence that language is a relatively late development in mankind and he states, strikingly, that human beings could have cave paintings or the oral tradition of poetry, but they could not have both. Mitner's work quoted by Hermelin (2001) suggests that humans had not developed a theory of mind before BC 30,000 years.

His conclusion for supposing that cave artists shared some of Nadia's cognitive limitations looks surprisingly strong. At the end of the last Ice Age, about 11,000 years ago, naturalistic cave art of this type appears to have ceased. A new tradition of painting emerged in Assyria and Egypt, quite different from the earlier naturalism of cave art. Nothing to equal cave art realism was seen again in Europe until the Italian renaissance when life-like perspective drawing was reinvented.

Humphrey prefaces his conclusions by acknowledging the problems with his thesis and noting that we should not be too quick to see a significant pattern where there is none: 'resemblances do not prove identity'. He speculates that: 'Suppose it was the case that a person not only does not need a modern mind to draw like that but must not have a typical modern mind to draw like that. The cave paintings might be taken as proof that cave artists' minds were essentially pre-modern' (p. 171).

I have argued in Chapter 4 that what we currently refer to as ASD may be a catch-all description for many yet unknown conditions with different genetic and/or environmental aetiologies. This would appear to make the effort to find a genetic model for autism a lot more difficult, and perhaps even pointless. Nevertheless, a number of genetic models have been proposed to try to explain the results of twin and sibling studies (Ronald, Happé, Bolton, Butcher, Price, Wheelwright, et al., 2006). Studies on the degree to which inheritance can account for characteristics in human beings has traditionally focused on twin studies. If the characteristic (eye colour, autistic behaviour) is found in both identical twins then the cause is likely to be genetic. Early research on concordance rates in monozygotic autistic twins gave low rates. Less than half of twin monozygotic pairs were both autistic. Later studies with larger samples reported much higher rates but currently it is agreed that heritability forms part of the cause of ASD but not all of it. Environmental factors also play a part.

Other authors have looked at the role of genetics and inheritance in savant syndrome. Treffert (1989) quotes data from a study undertaken by two zoologists who examined many cases of savant ability (Rife & Snyder, 1931). They concluded that special abilities can develop in the presence of severe learning difficulties in the absence of training or instruction. They added that where special abilities do occur 'they seem to be definitely due to heredity since they appear frequently in relatives of the patients' (cited in Treffert, 1989, p. 171). Treffert also notes that Rife and Snyder claimed that 'special abilities are inherited quite independently of general intelligence and that it is merely coincidence when a person inherits both' (cited in Treffert, 1989, p. 171).

Treffert (1989) refers to the work of the Austrian born psychiatrist Abraham Brill with a mathematically skilled savant named Jungreis (Brill, 1949). Brill reported that the lineage of the child included at least one brilliant mathematician and others who had been educationally talented for many generations and he assumed that the skill had been inherited. His skills emerged suddenly at the age of 6 and disappeared as suddenly at the age of 9. However, Brill's explanation for the disappearance of the skill was in terms of the psychosexual development of the child. His talent was said to have been awakened by the death of his mother and sister and extinguished on the death of his father. Both genetic and environmental explanations are invoked.

Research published in 2003 on savant syndrome and genetics found a common genetic abnormality (duplications on chromosome 15) in affected individuals but the commonality of this finding to savant syndrome is unclear (Nurmi, Dowd, Tadevosyan-Leyfer, Haines, Folstein, & Sutcliffe, 2003).

One fundamental question that arises is whether inheritance through genetic processes includes more than the usually accepted aspects of traits and physical attributes such as the colour of hair and eyes, and height? Does it also include the transmission of remarkable talents, as are displayed by savants? Learning has to be experiential. How else can savants acquire the rules of musical structures, construction of calendars, the knowledge of a mature artist to produce a sense of three dimensions or the complex rules that govern mathematics? There are many examples in the literature of savants who both have and fail to have families in whom similar skills are found. Nadia has no other family members with either ASD or special artistic talents (personal communication). Critics of the genetic theory of the inheritance of skills and abilities argue that invoking inheritance may become a simple way of explaining phenomena that cannot otherwise be easily understood (Howe, 1989). The role of environmental influences, of parents teaching and encouraging a talent, is not taken into account in any genetic explanation. Severe learning disability can occur as a result of accident or disease; some examples of people developing savant skills late in life as a result of such factors have been noted (Miller, Boone, Cummings, & Mishkin, 2000). In such cases genetic explanations are not significant. With Treffert (1989, p. 264), one might agree that we must also take account of unique brain function and circuitry as well as psychological factors of motivation. The mechanisms of inheritance are as yet poorly understood and the role of epigenetics is an emerging science. The notion that savants may have inherited talents is a difficult one compounded by the fact that there are also known environmental pathological factors involved in some cases.

The brain and neurological explanations

Over the last 30 years our understanding of the brain and the underlying neurology involved in cognition has gained significant ground. Some theorists have focused on the brain structure with respect to the specialisation of certain areas for carrying out specific tasks. At its simplest, distinctions have been made between left and right brain hemisphere functions. The two areas are connected anatomically and neurally by the corpus callosum, carrying a network of circuits transferring impulses from side to side. Treffert (1989, p. 187) referred to many studies that indicate that the typical savant has skills that suggest left hemisphere damage and intact right hemisphere functioning occurring together. Brink (1980, p. 250) states that: 'The left-brain generally governs the use of language, mathematical computation and other orderly conceptual or abstract analysis. The right-brain is generally superior in tasks involving spatial relationships, activities involving visualisation and movement skills such as mechanical ability'.

It was claimed that left brain function was primarily the processing of verbal, logical, rational information in essentially linear or sequential fashion. By contrast, the functions of the right hemisphere involved the processing of spatial, non-linear and intuitive information (Rimland, 1978). This view has persisted to the present (Tantam, 2009).

While there is evidence both to support and question the theory of lateralisation of functions, Treffert (1989) among others, accepts that any skill or ability as complex as language cannot be a function of only one brain area or hemisphere and in individuals with brain damage compensatory effects appear to develop in other areas of the brain. Treffert (1989, p. 191) acknowledged that it would be a mistake to assume that functions are entirely in the province of one hemisphere or the other. But he accepts the view that 'the right hemisphere can more easily derive meaning from concrete objects or events, while the left hemisphere is more involved, although not exclusively so, with symbolic language'. Along with notions of the lateralisation of cognitive functions including language, Treffert (1989) also pointed out that savant syndrome is much more common in males and links this to the possibility of exposure to testosterone in the developing foetus. He also points out that 'unusual cerebral dominance as seen in some brain disease or lesions, is not a cause of that disease . . . rather it is a symptom' (p. 192). Treffert and Wallace (2002) concluded that as research on brain function has progressed, it has made less sense to discuss savant syndrome as a right brain/left brain phenomenon.

Frith (2003) suggested that in autism early sensory processing areas of the brain are activated normally or even overactivated while later developing processing areas are underactivated. Frith reviewed evidence from neuroimaging studies that suggests differing ways for neural circuitry to occur affecting the progression of sensory analysis in savants. Greater brain size has also been observed in autism. It has also been linked to abnormalities in connectivity. Studies have found that some children with ASD have overconnectivity in some areas of the brain and underconnectivity in others. Parallels between these findings on brain morphology and weak central coherence theory have been drawn and have been linked to notions of perceptual enhancement and potentially more detailed percepts.

Casanova and Trippe (2009) have undertaken research into the brains of autistic savants. They review the anatomical findings to explain the pattern of preserved and superior abilities found in ASD. A hypothesis has emerged, which assumes that there is a developmental bias towards the formation of short-range neural connections. They claim that this results in excessive activity and overconnectivity within susceptible local networks. They speculate that these supposed areas might become partially isolated and acquire novel functional properties. Post-mortem studies of the brains of people with autism have shown characteristic differences in the morphometry of radial cell minicolumns, (multiples of neurons assumed to be working together in a concerted fashion) that add credence to the short-range connectivity hypothesis.

Current genetic research speculatively suggests that autism involves disruption of synapse development and function. Casanova and Trippe (2009) looked at the structures that involve multiples of neurons as minicolumns. They speculate that the pathological processes that lead to autism have distributed effects and reflect a disruption of multiple fundamental processes during the patterning and organisation of cortical cytoarchitecture compounding developmental disruptions in subsequently developing areas. They suggest that minicolumn peculiarities are seen in talented neurotypical scientists and are found in ASD individuals, regardless of savant status.

Wallace, Happé, and Giedd (2009) comment that 'cognitive and neural mechanisms underlying savant skill development and expression remain elusive' (p. 1425). In order to examine the issues they undertook an assessment of neuropsychological functioning and brain morphometry in a savant case, with ASD. He had high-level savant skills in two domains, an ability to calculate and he had artistic skills. These were quantified and compared with a small group of neurotypical controls. The cognitive profile of the savant subject, G. W., was characterised by a good memory and strengths with mental calculation and visuospatial processing. He appeared to have an implicit knowledge of calendar structure but he also had weak central coherence. They tested three neuropsychological domains hypothesised to be relevant to savant skill development. These were weak central coherence, implicit learning, and information processing speed. There is evidence to indicate that autistic people tend to favour local over global processing (which is different to the typical pattern). People with ASD perform well (often out performing controls) on tests that require an ability to perceive which parts make up a whole (as in a block design test). It was found that G. W. was prodigious in his talents; his verbal and non-verbal IQs fell in the average range yet he had phenomenal memory ability according to statistical norms.

The authors were then able to examine his brain. They examined cortical thickness from a structural magnetic resonance image. His cortex was found to be thinner in regions associated with social cognition and other domains impaired in ASD, but thicker in a bilateral segment of the superior parietal lobe which, according to the authors, has been connected with visuospatial functions including drawing, as well as calculation abilities. The authors speculate that this increased superior parietal thickness may have been acquired through practice of calendar and drawing skills. However, they conclude that without longitudinal imaging they cannot establish whether these anatomical differences played a part in the initial selection of G. W.'s talent domains or are the result of talent development and practice. Another difficulty with this research is the apparent confusion in the significance of the relative thickness of the cortex since some studies have suggested that brain pruning and thinning of the cortex indicates maturity and efficiency of neural transmission (Giedd, 2004).

The ability of autistic artistic savants to make use of perspective in drawing has been interpreted in terms of differential circuitry (Ropar & Mitchell, 2002). The authors conclude, 'Higher order knowledge can have an interfering rather than an advantageous effect' (p. 647). This analysis, Pring (2008) suggests, is also consistent with musical perception in autistic savants in whom 'pitch memory is characterised as retaining uniquely specified individual percepts/representations'. She concludes that: 'If the unusual neuronal circuitry indicated in autistic spectrum disorders . . . are confirmed, it could explain why savants build up differently structured memory stores that are accurate in perceptual terms and may mediate different styles of learning and behaviour' (p. 225).

Tantam (2009) lays great stress on the problems of non-verbal communication evident in ASD and he reviews studies on mirror neurons found in the brains of macaque monkeys that are activated when the monkey attends to the actions and behaviours of others. Although the research evidence for the existence of similar structures in the human brain is inconclusive this concept seems promising.

Belmonte et al. (2004) warn that the evidence from neuroscience resembles 'a fragmented tapestry' and that terms, such as connectivity, are defined differently in different studies. Tantam says that the output of research is staggering and keeping up with it and integrating all the findings, almost impossible. A central problem for research on savant syndrome is to decide which brain structures are abnormal (damaged or enhanced) from birth or which have developed from practice. While the significance of brain structure remains an important area of research the neuroimaging studies suggest that while practice may have altered brain structure or function, there is no clear evidence that unexpected or abnormal brain areas are present at birth.

Just as it is possible that Nadia was brain damaged and that her peculiar deficits and abilities could be explained physiologically, the science has not yet provided sufficient evidence to explain her strange talent. Treffert (1989) is optimistic and believes, however, that of all the theories put forward, neurophysiological explanations come closest to helping explain the phenomenon of savant syndrome. In this Treffert reveals his background as a medical man and he places greatest store on future developments in brain imaging and scanning.

Neurological dysfunction and privileged access to lower level, less processed information

Snyder (2004, 2009) proposes a controversial hypothesis, which he accepts is as yet unproven (although some preliminary evidence is supportive, it requires further replication by others). Snyder's ideas were based on some fascinating findings that some people with frontotemporal dementia developed an ability to draw and paint in the early stages of the disease. The ability flowered and then died as the disease progressed (Miller, 1998). Snyder's view is that savant skills are latent in everyone and can be switched on and off by special interventions including natural causes. He suggests (Snyder, 2009) that savants, as a result of atypical brain function, have privileged access to lower level, less processed information before it is 'packaged into holistic concepts and meaningful labels. They can tap into information that exists in all our brains but is normally beyond conscious awareness' (p. 1399). His work leads to the view that savant skills can arise spontaneously in otherwise normal people or can be induced by repetitive transcranial magnetic stimulation. The privileged access 'facilitates a distinct literal cognitive style in which a person thinks in detail, working from the parts to the whole' (De Clercq, 2003, cited by Snyder, 2009, p. 1399). What savants appear to be able to access, according to Snyder, is normally inaccessible in most normal people through introspection (Snyder & Thomas, 1999). While this process is not fully understood it may arise from 'hemispheric imbalance wherein concept networks are by-passed or inhibited' (Snyder, 2009, p. 1399). Snyder suggests that this supports the notion of a right hemispheric bias and left hemisphere dysfunction.

Snyder's work (2009) has suggested that savant-like skills can be induced artificially in normal people by inhibiting part of the brain (the left anterior temporal lobe). Other researchers, (Miller, Cummings, Mishkin, Boone, Prince, Ponton, et al., 1998; Sacks, 1995a; Treffert, 2009) have also suggested that autistic savants have atypical, left brain dysfunction, with right brain compensation. This leads to a predilection for literal, non-symbolic skills (Sacks, 1995a, pp. 314–315; Treffert, 2006, 2009). The implications arising from such findings are that everyone has the potential for savant skills but an 'atypical hemispheric imbalance' must be accessed to produce them. Creativity in a person might be artificially induced.

The fact that there are many reports that suggest that the savant skills have appeared apparently spontaneously and in some cases, such as that of Nadia, disappeared in the same mysterious way, leads Snyder to the view that such skills are acquired from a variety of causes. The list of possibilities he provides include:

- frontotemporal dementia (Miller et al., 1998);
- physical injury to the left temporal lobe (Snyder, 2009);
- left hemispheric strokes (Sacks, 1995a, p. 315);
- severe illness to the central nervous system (Treffert, 2006);
- the influence of hallucinogens (Sacks, 1995a).

Miller et al. (1998), reported on patients with frontotemporal dementia who displayed autistic savant like artistic skills where none (previously) existed along with other autistic traits such as preoccupation with visual details and a loss of semantic memory. The left anterior temporal lobe has been specifically implicated in savant syndrome both for autistic savants and for individuals who become savant at the onset of dementia (Miller et al., 1998, 2000). They say that a loss of function in the left anterior temporal lobe may lead to 'paradoxical functional facilitation of artistic and musical skills' (Miller et al., 2000, p. 458).

There is also some interesting research on the degradation of drawing skills in people with frontotemporal dementia (Patterson & Erzinclioglu, 2008). They gave patients with this form of dementia line drawings to copy directly and then after a short time delay (delayed copy drawing). Whereas subjects performed in the same way as normal controls on the first task, their drawings, after a short delay, showed substantial degradation. The researchers said that 'The nature of semantic deterioration in SD [semantic dementia] is, however, also a source of considerable insight into the structure and organisation of conceptual knowledge in the brain' (p. 282). They suggested that direct copying was essentially a perceptual/motor task whereas delayed copying involved memory reconstruction and conceptual knowledge. The resulting drawings in the delayed condition are striking in the loss of form and detail and resemble drawing development thrown into reverse. The authors concluded that with the progress of the disease, conceptual loss was partial and graded and that as detailed concepts were lost, as evidenced by their drawings, certain central features were retained. They also found that as defining conceptual details were lost, visual imagery as well as linguistic concepts were affected. The possibility that, if patients look at pictures of camels or pianos and are unable to name them, it is unlikely that they can still recognise what they are looking at. They found that the image of the object as well as the verbal label is degraded.

Snyder (2009) claimed that the effects of using repetitive transcranial magnetic stimulation have been to inhibit temporarily neural activity in a localised area of the cerebral cortex. Eleven right-handed healthy participants were subject to the effect. They were given one minute to draw a dog, a horse, or face from memory before, during, and after the treatment. The result showed enhanced skills emerged in the drawings of four of the subjects. Snyder reported that one subject 'could hardly recognise the drawings as his own even though he had watched himself render each image' (p. 1400). Two of the four also showed improvements in an experiment to test their proof-reading skills after the treatment (Osborne, 2003, p. 38). Improvements were also observed in an experiment to test the ability of subjects to estimate accurately a large number of objects observed with no time to count them. Out of 12 participants, 10 improved their ability to guess with accuracy the number immediately following magnetic pulse stimulation. Snyder claims that the problem for typically functioning people is that estimates of numbers of objects are based on prior experiences, not on the actual raw sensory input, whereas savants are literal in their perceptions and have less interference in reaching their estimates.

Snyder (2009) suggests that the effect of damage (through accident, disease, or other misfortune) to the left anterior temporal lobe is likely to give rise to savant-like skills. This may be because, whereas in the normal brain the conceptual networks that operate (concerned with semantics and giving context to objects) tend to inhibit networks concerned with fine detail, in the savant no such controls are at work. By inhibiting these networks through the use of repetitive transcranial magnetic stimulation in normal people access to the literal details observed by savants is facilitated. Snyder claimed, 'They see a more literal, less filtered view of the world . . . Their skill does not depend on active learning, but on an effortless reading off of this less-processed information' (p. 1402). Hence, his conclusions that the extraordinary skills of savants are latent in everyone and can be artificially induced by '*turning off*' parts of the brain.

Snyder (2004) speculated as to why savant skills are normally suppressed, although, according to his hypothesis we all have potential access to them. 'Perhaps they are deliberately inhibited as a principle of economy-object attributes are inhibited from conscious awareness once a label (concept) is formed' (p. 470). He considers, too, why all autistic people are not savants, suggesting that: 'Autistic savants typify and idealise, pure autism, most closely identified with Kanner's "infantile autism" – a mind in a protracted state of infancy, a pre-conceptual mind that thinks in detail, rather than through concepts' (Snyder, 2004, p. 470). He suggests that the state of pure autism is a failure in the process of concept formation. The function of concepts is to order the world and make it comprehensible in a shared language. Without such access order is imposed externally, hence the imposition of rigid routines that characterise infantile autism.

Snyder raises the interesting question as to whether truly creative people are able to free themselves from previous interpretations of the world. He notes that autistic savants are the antithesis of creative, being largely imitative. Hermelin (2001) stated 'There are no savant geniuses about. Their mental limitations disallow and preclude an awareness of innovative developments in the areas of their special abilities' (p. 177). But are there instances when privileged access facilitates the creative process? Snyder asks, 'are there radically different routes to creativity: normal and autistic?' (2009, p. 1401). He also speculates that it may be that some intellectual giants had autistic traits (as discussed by Fitzgerald, 2004).

Theories specific to savants who are autistic

Sensory deprivation and isolation

Rimland had a long and distinguished career in autism research in the USA. He suggested that the extreme social isolation, amounting to sensory deprivation, suffered by savants, including visual impairment, hearing or other loss, causes them to focus on unusual or bizarre preoccupations, such as counting, memorising, calculating or observing and recording specific features of the environment such as cloud formation, tall buildings, particular animals, etc. (Rimland, 1978). One of the essential diagnostic features of autism is impairment in social interaction leading to social isolation. Rimland suggested that the effects of this isolation are to alter the sensory pathways in the brain. According to Rimland (1978) autistic children lack the ability to access the pattern of memories and associations that enable the non-autistic person to make connections with past events, so that they have meaning within a context. One stimulus generalises to evoke a whole host of other associated meanings. Rimland suggests that the autistic person is unable to access such prior memories or experiences because of a biological defect with incoming stimuli locked into a narrow, closed loop. This results in a 'super-intense' concentration and, according to this theory, the result of this intense mental concentration is that the savant deals with minute details in great specificity, focusing on specific internal preoccupations. Rimland suggests that this accounts for how savants perform their extraordinary abilities. It is because they have a pathological inability to broaden attention. He acknowledges that at that time the precise site of the mechanisms that explain this faulty process had not been identified.

Treffert (1989) concludes that sensory deprivation theory may 'more describe savant behaviours and attributes than explain or account for them' (p. 177). It must be the case that while some savants have been socially isolated, others have not. However, he accepts that sensory deprivation may well be a causal factor in ASD but argues that some other factors must be independently at work in creating savant syndrome. He states this is an incomplete theory to explain all the savants.

Enhanced perceptual functioning in savant syndrome: patterns, structures, and creativity

Pring (2008) suggests that the theoretical model provided by Mottron et al. (1999, 2003, 2006), described as enhanced perceptual functioning in autism, usefully 'advances the ideas encapsulated in weak perceptual coherence and provides a convincing account of the development of savant abilities' (Pring, 2008, p. 224). Mottron, Dawson, and Soulieres (2009) present a theory that autistic perceptions are related to two mechanisms: enhanced perception and an ability to complete or fill in any missing information in perceived units or structures.

Hermelin and Pring (1998) examined the pictorial strategies used by their artistic savant subjects that linked an enhanced ability to segment a pattern into its constituent parts, to a talent for drawing. The experiments studied outcomes of performance on a block design test (in which a picture showing a total pattern has to be recreated from individual blocks showing part of the design). This is a test in which autistic people usually perform better than expected from their intelligence levels. However, it was found to be a skill that also existed in normally functioning artistically gifted individuals.

The enhanced perception model (EPF) proposes that autistic perception is characterised by enhanced perceptual skills in low-level cognitive operations (such as memory and visual imagery). In such tasks there is greater activation of the perceptual areas of the brain (Mottron et al., 2006). The authors propose that autistic people have enhanced detection of patterns available to them: they can locate both patterns and similarities within and among patterns (as in block design tasks). They claim that pattern detection is important for cognitive systemising and coding. Autistic individuals have a natural orientation towards material possessing the highest level of internal structure (Baron-Cohen, 2006).

This ability enables them to detect the internal structures in materials with which they are presented (such as in calendars, aurally presented music, and in pictures). They can also complete any missing information in these patterns and structures.

The authors examine the contribution of the two mechanisms of enhanced perception and pattern detection and that of the ability to complete missing information to the creativity evident in savant performance (Mottron et al., 2006). They argue that autism is characterised by this 'enhanced perceptual processing'. Autistic subjects are superior in low-level cognitive operations such as discriminating between musical pitch in memory tasks and in block design tasks. They see this as an integral part of the explanation of savant abilities (since they are also manifested in autistic behaviour, learning and intelligence; Mottron et al., 2006).

Mottron et al. (2009) discuss aspects of perception and pattern detection in savant syndrome. Structured codes (such as those of language, music, numbers) are subject to pattern recognition. They also claim that in drawing, artistic savants reconstruct remembered visual images (and not copied eidetic images). This variously coded information can be recalled as resemblances and identified at various levels of complexity. The authors contend that the type of perceptual and cognitive codes, as processed by autistic people, determines the key roles that the codes play in savant abilities. Mottron et al. (2009) claim that studies of autistic children have established that they notice structures (presence of repeating patterns) especially, and that this would explain the relationship between such repeating patterns and the perception processes in autism. This is true in both the auditory and the visual modalities. (This appears to be in line too with Baron-Cohen's systemising theory.) The detection of repeating patterns is essential in achieving a particular savant skill and a high level of performance. Savants may have the ability to detect patterns with a high density of similarity, which orients them towards areas of special interest (e.g., letters/digits with multiple recurrences and associated with non-arbitrary rules, such as the calendar 28 year repeating rule). This maximises their salience in stimuli (e.g., digits occupying consistent places in the structure of calendars).

The role of pattern detection in autistic savants is highly significant (that is, the capacity to detect organisation in the world experienced by the senses, by perceiving the relative properties and their similarities and symmetries). Mottron et al. (2009) argue that it would account for their heightened interest in codes and the rules of perspective. Savants are able to detect the structural similarities (the repeating patterns) between two series of elements corresponding in form: e.g. written/oral codes. They have mastered 'between code mapping'. However, the savant is generally unable to verbalise the strategies used to do so. An example of such pattern detection is the child who can estimate weights of objects below 500 grammes with precision (to 5%) by mentally comparing each object to a cereal bar weighing 35 grammes. Memory for tunes and transposition to musical styles is another example.

The individual savant with artistic/graphic skills is able to take his/her own internal rules of graphic construction based on enhanced pattern perception and apply them to any requirement in a wider setting (Mottron et al., 2009). Rules about linear perspective are applied to all buildings viewed. Equally, a musical savant can make use of his/her own special knowledge of pitch and musical structure and transpose and enhance the skill more widely. The special process displayed by autistic subjects detects regularities in underlying patterns in even very large structures. Ockelford and Pring (2005) showed that a non-autistic expert musician with absolute pitch is far more limited than an autistic savant musician in completing or filling in the pattern of the individual notes in large chords.

Mottron cites Miller's work (1999) showing that savant performance cannot be reduced to rote memory skills. Some can produce creative new material within the constraints of pattern generation. Miller noted how savants imposed structure in musical performances where none existed in the original.

A combination of multiple pattern completions by an autistic savant would explain aspects of their creativity. In the autistic person, subject to atypical cognitive processes, the parallel integration of patterns across multiple levels may occur without information being lost. They also display an ability to absorb new techniques more rapidly than non-autistic students demonstrating the versatility of the autistic brain (Mottron et al., 2009).

Among the areas about which more information would be useful, are the atypical ways in which autistic savants learn (and how best to teach them effectively); also the causes of the initial area of interest that begins to absorb many savants in an intense and all pervading way (Dawson, Mottron, & Gernsbacher, 2008). For example, Nadia's preoccupation with picture books and the positive emotional response that occurred may have been the result of an early experience with her mother. The interest of Stephen Wiltshire in drawing was developed by the art teacher in the school he attended as a young child in a more directive way. Also of interest is the nature of the expertise effects that autistic savants display. These include:

- a superior ability to detect anomalies and departures from patterns of similarity;
- an ability to suppress negative interference effects;
- the fact that they work with speed and ease.

Savant syndrome is identified by Mottron et al. (2009) as aptitude, material availability, and expertise combined with an autistic brain (characterised by enhanced perceptual functioning). They conclude that the fact that not all autistic people are savants is no more surprising than the fact that not all non-autistic people are experts. They concede that their proposals lack sufficient support from savant studies, but they refer to some which suggest brain function differences between autistic and non-autistic individuals when faced with specific tasks. They suggest future research should explore the role of enhanced perception in the range of abilities in savants and autistic subjects, especially those in which they perform with proficiency, flexibility and creativity.

The role of weak central coherence theory

As has been discussed in Chapter 4, weak central coherence theory (Frith, 1989) is hugely influential and has explanatory power about many aspects of cognitive performance in autistic subjects. It has also been used extensively to examine savant syndrome. Happé and Vital (2009) claim that special savant skills are far more common in association with ASD than in any other group examined to date. Allied to weak central coherence is an enhanced ability of children with ASD to show a detail focused, processing bias. They consider that this attention to detail rather than a focus on the whole, precisely characterises savant skills. They develop a compelling explanation for savant skills in terms of weak coherence and enhanced perceptual functioning allied to extreme attention to detail. They suggest that this appears to be 'the most promising predisposing characteristics, or "starting engine" for talent development' (p. 1369).

Skill in block design tests was notable in children with artistic abilities and in some children with autism (Pring et al., 1995). Happé and Vital (2009) suggest that in art the ability to attend to details, to break the gestalt into parts, is helpful in achieving realistic looking drawings.

The relationship between bias towards superior local processing and reduced global processing has been re-examined in recent accounts of weak central coherence (Happé & Booth, 2008). They suggest that individuals with ASD most likely to develop talents are those that show superior local processing without any impairment of global processing. Such individuals focus on detail but they can also integrate that information and understand the overall concept. Happé and Booth (2008) remark that this hypothesis needs to be tested.

Happé and Vital (2009) conclude that 'it is not autism per se that predisposes to talent but the detailed focused cognitive style (weak coherence) that is characteristic of but not confined to, ASD' (p. 1373). Consequently, attention to detail is the 'starting engine' for talent. Their prediction is that where savant-like talents are found, they will be linked to a detail focused cognitive style regardless of diagnostic group. These researchers also make the point made by Rimland (1978) that 'mind-blindness' may act to enhance talent; autistic people have reduced social influences and are less concerned about the views of others as well as having the time to devote themselves to their talent rather than socialising. These all contribute to the perfection of their skills.

Hyper-systemising; hyper-attention to detail

Simon Baron-Cohen et al. (2009), in their explanation of the link between talent and autism, argue that people with 'autistic spectrum condition (ASC)' have a way of perceiving, interpreting and remembering information that can be described as hyper-systemising. This theory has been described in detail in Chapter 4. It is the ability to be able to recognise repeating patterns in stimuli; it is a process that is directed towards detecting logical structures and can produce special talents especially in areas subject to systemising (such as mechanical, numerical, musical, motor, and graphic skills). Baron-Cohen and colleagues cite the work of Jolliffe and Baron-Cohen (1997), Mottron et al. (2003), and Shah and Frith (1993), to establish that subjects with ASD have particular ability to attend to detail. It is their view that such excellent attention to detail in autistic spectrum condition exists 'because of evolutionary forces positively selecting brains for strong systemising, a highly adaptive human ability' (Baron-Cohen et al., 2009, p. 1377). Baron-Cohen and colleagues (2009) also suggest that attention to detail is a consequence of sensory hypersensitivity. This could result from a processing difference at various sensory pathways.

In many respects this theory is similar to weak central coherence theory as discussed above and in Chapter 4, which suggests that the detailed, focused cognitive style (a processing bias) of the savant predisposes them to talent. But Baron-Cohen et al. (2009) argue that weak central coherence theory focuses too much on the negative aspects of attention to detail, which suggests that individuals will be overwhelmed by attention to minutiae and will remain unable to understand the whole system. They cite contrary evidence of instances of talented mathematicians with Asperger's syndrome who can integrate details to provide an understanding of the general system.

Baron-Cohen et al. (2009) define 'savantism' as prodigious talent irrespective of underlying intelligence. They have also renamed autistic spectrum disorders as 'autistic spectrum condition'. They see the excellent attention to detail and the recognition of regularities in repeating patterns as positive assets. The authors suggest that the process of systemising is the drive to construct rule-bound systems. As a result it is possible to become predictive about outcomes and this may help the person with ASD to make sense of the world. The areas in which savants have been especially remarkable in their skills are those that are susceptible to such systemising analysis, such as understanding the rules of the calendar, musical structures, use of numbers to calculate, ability to recall digits, and learning and remembering vast numbers of words.

The strong systemising theory also explains why those with ASD display a lack of enjoyment of social interaction and changes in routine, found in the normal population. Such changes interfere with the systemising of the world into understandable patterns achieved through repetition.

The various areas of social life in which the different types of systemising take place are described with examples by the authors who distinguish the resulting patterns of behaviour between those with classic autism and those with a diagnosis of Asperger's syndrome. For example, sensory systemising in classical autism, such as the acts of tapping surfaces and letting sand run through the fingers is contrasted with the insistence on having the same foods each day noted in some diagnosed with Asperger's syndrome. Motoric systemising, such as spinning round and round or rocking, in classic autism is contrasted with learning knitting patterns or a difficult tennis technique in Asperger's. In the same way they describe other types of systemising, which include collectible; mechanical; numerical; abstract; natural; social and motoric sytems that are characterised by being rule bound.

Baron-Cohen et al. (2009) suggest that attention to detail can be viewed as sensory hypersensitivity. They quote research that has established that sensory abnormalities are present in 90% of children with ASD. In their own studies, Baron-Cohen et al. (2009) found that thresholds for visual acuity were much higher for subjects with ASD. The hypersensitising process has a positive effect in the quest for understanding a system ('however small and specific that system might be'; p. 1378). People with ASD may be at a disadvantage in ordinary examination settings since, while they may have a deeper and more extensive knowledge than many others, they are slow to process the material. They may undertake to present every thing they know in response to a seemingly straight-forward question since it is all held as part of the systemising process. Baron-Cohen and colleagues use the example of the person with ASD who had extensive knowledge of beetles for whom there would be no simple answer to a question 'What is a beetle?' Every bit of related information would be relevant: 'For the hypersystemiser, getting these details correct matters, because the concept and the classification system linking concepts, is a system for predicting how this specific entity (this specific beetle) will behave or will differ from all other entities' (2009, p. 1380).

Hypersensitising theory can explain patterns of apparent mindless repetition (such as motoric systemising, spinning objects, or shaking a piece of string endlessly) as a positive sign that the individual recognises the patterns behind the movements being observed. The autistic person may gain emotional pleasure from a long sequence of sounds made, since it is precisely the same each time, in the same way that a mathematician, artist, or other talented person gains satisfaction from observing the outcome of a calculation or accurate drawing (Baron-Cohen et al., 2009).

They conclude that: 'The search for the association between autism and talent should start with the sensory hypersensitivity, which gives rise to the excellent attention to detail, and which is a prerequisite for hypersystemising. Consequently, it is at the sensory level that the origins of the association between autism and talent begins' (p. 1382).

Conclusion

Twelve explanations for savant syndrome have been reviewed in this chapter. Many have overlapping concepts such as weak central coherence theory; attention to detail; enhanced perception; the role of memory and practice. Findings from neurological research often parallel the work in cognitive psychology but such research is likely to hold most promise for the future. In addition there are intriguing theories offering further insights such as that of Humphrey's evolutionary theory and Snyder's privileged access theory. Miller's discovery of some individuals with prefrontal dementia who for a brief period flowered artistically also potentially throws light on savant syndrome. All the explanations have something to offer. The question arises, which of the twelve theories discussed best accounts for Nadia's extraordinary talent and her subsequent loss of ability? This question will be considered in the final chapter.

7 Gifted children: precocious artists

Introduction

Goodenough (1926) developed a test of intelligence or 'mental maturity' based on children's drawings of a man. This work was updated and extended by Harris (1963). It is still used in schools as a rapid assessment of the child's intellectual potential and indeed the Draw a Man test was part of the National Curriculum foundation stage assessment. A fundamental supposition is that children's ability to draw follows a well-documented developmental trajectory and the more intelligent the child, the faster milestones on that trajectory are accomplished. The significance of non-savant prodigious artists to the understanding of the development of drawing skills in savants has been considered by Drake and Winner (2009). They comment that the ability to draw realistically at an earlier age than average is a feature of those who go on to become established artists (in the Western artistic tradition). Cox (2005) has also reviewed cases of exceptional talent among typically developing young children. She says that very few cases have been reported and generally researchers (Golomb, 1995, and Pariser, 1995), have concluded that the drawing development of artistically talented children follows a normal path but at an accelerated rate. However, in one study the drawing styles of talented and less artistically talented children were studied and differences analysed (Milbrath, 1998). She suggested that the talented group had a heightened visual sensitivity. They were more visually aware. They used models to guide their drawing more effectively and produced more elements of view centred depiction such as foreshortening and hidden line elimination earlier.

Drake and Winner (2009) examined the cognitive characteristics of non-savant precocious realists to determine whether these are seen in autistic savants with artistic ability. The authors investigated whether young children with highly developed skill in realistic drawing display the same cognitive style and local processing bias that has been observed in the savants who have been tested. The ability to focus on detail, possibly at the expense of processing the whole (global processing) is thought to help explain the outstanding drawing ability found in some autistic savants.

Drake and Winner tested the abilities of a group of children in relation to their artistic skills. The authors used the ability to draw 'realistically' as their datum for giftedness. They were then able to select three groups: those who were gifted; a group who were moderately gifted; and an age-typical group. They asked the subjects to draw a still life picture; complete a version of the block design task and tested their memory for block design items. They were also given an intelligent quotient (IQ) test. The gifted artistic children were able to create life-like presentations that differed in many ways from the drawings of the typical children. Drake and Winner considered differences between their three groups and then considered differences between the performance of their gifted subjects and some of the cognitive and perceptual skills associated with those with a diagnosis of autistic spectrum disorder (ASD) and who had a talent for drawing.

Drake and Winner (2009) found that there was a relationship between precocious talent for drawing and intelligence, and not just performance IQ but also verbal IQ. (This is unsurprising given the work of Goodenough, 1926, and Harris, 1963, who established scales for 'cognitive maturity' based solely on drawing ability.) Their gifted group showed global processing strengths over local processing, which meant they were able to recall cohesive items in the block designs better than fragmented ones. They did not show heightened memory for segmented items. None started with detail in drawing but sketched an outline first. The gifted children showed superior visual memory and strong visual analysis, 'With visual analysis perhaps the stronger of these two skills' (p. 1457). The authors suggest that heightened visual analysis is especially implicated in precocious talent for realism. Unlike autistic savants, 'Precocious realists do not store fragmented designs in memory at a superior level, they do not use local drawing strategy and they do not have below average IQs' (Drake & Winner, 2009, p. 1457).

They conclude that precocious realists are in many ways, unlike savant artists (although there are some resemblances). Unlike savants they showed a global advantage in the visual memory tasks (but not for fragmented items) and their graphic realism was correlated with verbal IQ as well as full scale IQ. Their findings can be summarised as follows.

Autistic savants with exceptional drawing ability have the following characteristics:

- IQs well below average (below 100). Their talent is independent of their IQ level;
- superior visual memory and heightened visual analysis;
- weak central coherence (Frith, 2003) and enhanced perception (Mottron et al., 2006);
- a focus on detail (a local drawing strategy) rather than on the global layout of the drawing (drawings could finish off the edge of the page, for example);
- local proximity strategy (a drawing starts with a detail, and then another detail, or another section of it nearby is added. They then add other sections until the whole emerges);

- they can apparently spontaneously mentally segment a whole into its parts. For example, the analysis of a design (such as that on a block design) into its relation to a whole pattern;
- ability to recall fragmented designs at a superior level.

Gifted child artists have the following characteristics:

- IQs generally above average;
- exceptional scores on ability tests involving visual perception but also high verbal IQ scores;
- superior visual memory and heightened visual analysis;
- good central coherence, executive functioning, and enhanced perception evident;
- a global advantage rather than focus on detail;
- no special ability to segment designs (no local processing advantage);
- no local proximity strategy – drawing commences with outline sketch;
- possess a high level of skill, drive and technical ability as valued by their culture at an early age (Pariser, 1995).

Examples of non-savant artistic prodigies

It is necessary to bear in mind that savant syndrome is described by Treffert (2009) as a rare condition in which people with developmental disorders (including ASD) have one or more areas of extraordinary talent that contrasts markedly with the individual's intellectual limitations. It is apparent that there are many examples of people with extraordinary talents (in art, calculation, music) who do not appear to have a developmental disorder that disadvantages them in the social world. It would not be accurate, therefore, to describe such a person as a 'savant'. Those without intellectual impairment and with precocious talent may be better described as prodigies. Most gifted artists have been people of at least average intelligence and who have often been polymaths. As in any sphere of life, highly successful artists have been able to demonstrate a range of skills including having good social skills and a good head for business. Some artists have appeared to lead difficult lives sometimes due to poverty and the single-minded pursuit of their vision. Some artists have seemed fixed and determined to pursue their art, in the face of poverty and rejection and some artists have been genuinely eccentric. As in any profession the range of personality and life history is too wide to draw anything that is meaningfully 'typical' of them. However, Fitzgerald (2004) has controversially claimed that L. S. Lowry, Vincent Van Gogh, and Andy Warhol may have suffered from Asperger's syndrome evident in their eccentric or unusual social behaviour.

As with all the creative arts, artists have a talent and are driven to learn and improve. It has always been notoriously difficult to make a living as an artist so that embarking on painting or drawing as a career is not an easy option. One must believe in one's ability and one's vision. Most of the population do not have the talent or the determination. Richard Thompson (1981, p. 38) makes the point 'Most of us as children gave up drawing when our brain's ability to analyse the world as we saw it became more advanced than the aptitude of our hand to draw that world'. Those with extraordinary abilities seem not to be so deterred.

Who are the artists who would make a valid comparison group for the savant artist? A search has been conducted. The search has not been exhaustive but it has been conducted over many years. Selection for a meaningful comparison with savant artists was based on the following criteria:

- Artists who showed exceptional talent in depiction under the age of 12 years. This being the age cited for the stage of formal operations (Piaget & Inhelder, 1956) and the age when children spontaneously use more advanced projection systems.
- Childhood drawings have survived and there is some reliable evidence of the age of the artist when the drawing was made.
- Drawings exhibit the features of realistic depiction (diminishing size with distance, correct proportions, hidden line elimination, and linear perspective).

Unfortunately, the list meeting these criteria is not long. The childhood drawings of most of the major artists have not survived. In his *Lives of the Artists*, Giorgio Vasari (1568) relates that Giotto was discovered at the age of 10 by the great Florentine painter Cimabue drawing pictures of his sheep on a rock. They were so life-like that Cimabue approached Giotto's father and asked if he could take the boy as an apprentice. Vasari wrote about many of the Italian Renaissance artists and we are given tantalising glimpses of their early years and precocious skills but unfortunately the evidence of their childhood drawings does not survive. The question is of course, were they prodigious as children but their drawings not valued because they were children, or were the early drawings simply unremarkable?

Among the artists who showed prodigious skill as children and whose drawings survive are well-known artists such as Picasso, Toulouse-Lautrec, Millais, and Landseer and neglected artists such as Jan Lievens, John Scarlett Davis, and Brian Hatton. There is also a contemporary artist David Downes and one child artist, Kieron Williamson (aged 8 years). What unites all these artists is their ability to master one or more of the culture's norms of visual representation (perspective drawing or visual realism) at an early age.

The question is contentious as to whether there are more great artists whose talent began to fully develop later in life than ones who showed prodigious talent at an early age. There are examples of both. It may be that great art comes with experiences and knowledge that age brings (as in the case of Cezanne, Matisse, and Francis Bacon). On the other hand, early remarkable draughtsmanship and apparent technical ability may in some cases develop into a mature and critically agreed talent (such as Picasso and Toulouse-Lautrec) but not in others, as in the case of Landseer who, although successful, is often regarded as a sentimental and second-grade artist.

Do the childhood works of renowned artists reveal traces of their future genius? Is realistic depiction at an early age the appropriate measure for later success as an artist? Leading on from this are larger questions about the nature of art. Fineberg (1997), a scholar of contemporary art, has raised the question of how child art is best perceived. Is the criterion the imposition of an adult eye? He suggested that Picasso's childhood drawing 'Bull Fight and Pigeons' (see Figure 7.10), features realistic-looking birds and shows that even as a 9-year-old he drew with confidence. But he also concludes, 'It's not about skill, but about unique qualities of seeing. Art is about a novel way of looking at the world' (cited in Camhi, 2006, para. 6).

Another question relates to the status of the remarkable work produced by child prodigies. In short, what is art? Who can legitimately be called an artist? There is no single simple valid definition of 'art'. It has been variously defined by eminent authors and critics as follows:

- The philosopher Wollheim discusses the complexities of understanding what art is and he is sceptical that a definitive answer can be given. He writes, 'Art is the sum or totality of works of art. What is a work of art? A work of art is a poem, a painting, a piece of music, a sculpture, a novel' (Wollheim, 1980, p. 1).
- For Ruskin, above all else, art should communicate truth that rested on the artist's moral values. He laid much emphasis on the moral, social and spiritual purposes of art. But on the judgement of what is good or bad art, he said 'Public opinion is no criterion of excellence except over a long period of time' (Ruskin, 1843, p. 1).
- For the art historian Gombrich there could be no valid definition of art; there are only individual artists producing pictorial representations of the world; drawing or painting what they see influenced by what they know (cited in Hermelin, 2001, pp. 120–121).
- The philosopher Schopenhauer said that all arts aspire to the condition of music; which he believed was the only art form 'that did not merely copy ideas, but actually embodied the will itself' (cited in Albright, 2004, p. 39).
- Benedetto Croce, in his philosophical writing said art is a vehicle for the expression of emotions and ideas. His contention is that all creative literature and all art consists in the production of an image. This is the whole work, conceived as a single picture that brings together many details into a complex unit (Orsini, 1961, p. 24).
- The critic Collingwood said, 'Art is not contemplation, it is action ... it is pursued by an artist who constitutes himself a mere spectator of the world around him ... the artist should participate in his public's emotion and the activities with which these emotions are bound up' (Collingwood, 1938, p. 332).
- Tolstoy (1896) defined art as the creative presentation of ideas communicated to others. He opposed the view that art should belong to any particular social class. It can disseminate moral values and express any human experience. Good art is that which is intelligible to its audience and so judged by the majority; bad art is incomprehensible. A great work of art is one that can be understood by every human being; it has a universality which expresses emotions and concerns that can be experienced by everyone (Tolstoy, 1896/1960, pp. 96–110).

- The critic Herbert Read defined art in terms of something that expressed ideas that stimulated thoughts and emotions to others. 'The work of art is shown to be essentially formal: it is the shaping of material into forms which have a sensuous or intellectual appeal to the average human being' (Read, 1938, p. 7).
- The French author Baudelaire said 'Art is an infinitely precious good, a draught both refreshing and cheering which restores the stomach and the mind to the natural equilibrium of the ideal' (Baudelaire, 1846/1955, p. 43).
- Oscar Wilde famously said 'All art is quite useless' (Wilde, 1891/1992, p. 4).

The nature of art has been described by the philosopher Wollheim as 'one of the most elusive of the traditional problems of human culture' (Wollheim, 1980, p. 1). His view is that the artist is someone who consciously sets out to create something, from his or her own mind, which has never been seen as such before, to communicate something to the audience who views it.

It has long been a debate as to whether random events such as throwing paint at a canvas or finding objects and giving them special presentational qualities can be said to produce a work of art. A contestant for the prestigious Saatchi prize in 2009 found a tree trunk embedded in some park railings, exhibited it and won. This leads to the optimistic view that everything has the potential of being art and everyone is an artist; it is just that some people are more talented than others at seeing aesthetic qualities and revealing them to others. The more traditional view would be that art cannot be produced unintentionally without the conscious rational mind of the artist organising the material to achieve some desired end. This may be why no savants have been identified who produce expressionist abstract art.

A press report in *The New York Times* (York, 2004) described the work of a 4-year-old girl in New York whose paintings were prompting comparisons with Pollock and Kandinsky. Marla Olmstead had been painting since just before she was 2 years old. It was stated that she used brushes, spatulas, her fingers, and even ketchup bottles to create large canvases and had sold about 25 paintings, raising $40,000. Drake and Winner (2009) have noted how unusual it is to find true abstract prodigies. They suggest:

> Every domain in which child prodigies have been noted has been a fairly formal structured rule governed domain, whether this be classical music, mathematics or realistic drawing. We do not see prodigies in philosophy or novel writing and we do not find them in the domain of abstract art. It appears that the kinds of domains that attract young prodigies are those with a formal set of rules to master.

> (p. 1453)

The art prodigy debate

The problem of assessing the childhood work and development of non-savant artists is considerable. This is especially the case when considering their work retrospectively. For artists who have a reputation of having been prodigies such assessment rests on anecdotal evidence and references that lack certainty as to the dates when artwork was produced. Picasso is widely regarded as one of the greatest artist of the last century. Fineberg (1997) notes his possibly self-mythologising claims that he was an artistically brilliant child in light of the comments of his biographer Richardson (1991). He indicates that Picasso believed he was frightened by his artistic ability at the age of 7, since he lacked the normal naivety of a child artist. Yet his bullring sketch, despite his precocity, is the drawing of a child. The truly significant thing about defining a child as a prodigy is the age at which exceptional drawings were first produced and the extent to which it shows evidence of skills that normal children of the same age do not possess.

Some critics have argued that since the construction of a work of art requires rational thought and mature analysis of content so that ideas are expressed through reflective experiences and the emotions of the maker, there can be no youthful prodigies in art. The view would be that it seems unlikely that young children can ever be sufficiently aware in terms of emotional maturity, ideas, concepts, use of line or colour for special effects, to give their drawings real depth and power. Yet the work of Kieron Williamson shows a maturity of perception and feeling for the landscape that would seem well beyond his years. In the same way a musical prodigy such as Mozart was able, almost intuitively, to understand the rules governing key change, harmony, and dissonance, some young children seem able to comprehend the rules of perspective and composition to produce what can be described as works of art such that they can command critical review as well as high prices.

The matter of assessing any piece of art is a complex matter and open to debate. As discussed, abstract art has always been open to the accusation that 'anyone could do it'. This view has been fuelled by some very accomplished artists such as Jackson Pollock who dribbled paint over canvas or William Green who rode a bike over one. Most abstract art, however, is highly structured and rule bound as their creators can make abundantly clear. Artists such as Rothko, Kandinsky, and Mondrian, for example, were all able to explain their masterpieces and the effects they strived for in detail.

Visual realism in art is much more accessible to lay judgements as well as that of informed critics, especially in cases where the young artist continues to develop and in due course become an established artist. Nonetheless, the question remains, at what point in the child's artistic development can the word 'artist' be attached to them in a meaningful way? On the other hand, while children with a prodigious talent may not appear to have been intellectually old enough to have developed the emotional sensitivity and perceptions normally thought to be required for the production of art, some seem to have done so. They can use light and shadow, perspective, and a fluency of line that is well beyond their years.

The prodigies selected and described below all display such qualities. In this comparison with savant artists an attempt is also made to consider what all these artists had in common in order to understand more about what makes for prodigious talent. All these child prodigies shared features in common. They each had a home background in which drawing and painting was encouraged and valued from a very young age. They all had parents who were either themselves talented artists or who recognised the emergence of such ability. They all had parents who went out of their way to encourage the talent. It could be the case that having interested parents is the reason why their early work has survived.

The theory of Drake and Winner (2009) would predict that each prodigy displayed some qualities of the autistic savants (such as sharing superior visual memory, enhanced perception, and heightened visual analysis) but also others that were different. They would be more likely to have a global advantage, with less focus on the smaller detail at the expense of the whole, and be less likely to use a local drawing strategy, placing their work in a wider context and aware of the placement of objects on the page. They are also all likely to have a high verbal and general intelligence level.

Jan Lievens (1607–1674)

Jan Lievens was born in Leyden in Holland where he served his first apprenticeship. He later became a friend and associate of Rembrandt. He was described as a precocious child in terms of his artistic ability (Wheelock, 2008). By his early teens he was regarded as a phenomenal painter and draughtsman showing technical skill and emotional intelligence in his work, such that, some of his teenage work was acquired by wealthy patrons. Critics talk of his verve for deft line and his exhaustive attention to detail both of costumes and objects. Evidence for his precocity is from reports and anecdotes about his childhood but the painting done when he was just 15 admits him for inclusion here (Figure 7.1). The picture is also

Figure 7.1 Jan Lievens' Allegory of the Five Senses (1622), painted when he was 15 years old. Reprinted with the kind permission of Private Collections, image courtesy of the Board of Trustees, National Gallery of Art, Washington, D.C., USA.

remarkable in the context of this book because it depicts the social communication between the revellers and between the revellers and the viewer.

However, despite this meteoric start to his career, he did not develop into the phenomenal artist that Rembrandt became; rather he followed a variety of styles, perhaps to ensure a steady income. It is not clear whether this diversity hindered his development as a major artist. There has been speculation that he suffered a personality disorder. He is described as 'brilliant, ambitious, and self-confident' and 'by the time Lievens returned home at the age of twelve the precocious boy was so self-assured that he began painting on his own . . . grandiose allegorical scenes' (Wheelock, 2008, pp. 1–2). For whatever reason he did not fulfil his early promise. Exhibitions of his work throughout the world in recent years have begun to remind people of his outstanding talent.

Edwin Landseer (1802–1873)

Edwin Landseer was the youngest son in a large family. He showed talent as a young child, which was fostered and encouraged by his father, who was an engraver (Figure 7.2). The household had several animals that became the subject of Edwin's earliest sketches. A report in *The New York Times* (Anon, March 1874) notes that sketches of Landseer's, on display in the museum at South Kensington, had been drawn when he was aged between 5 and 6 years of age.

He was 7 or 8 years old when he engraved the heads of horses (Figure 7.3), donkeys, sheep, lions, and tigers. From a young age he was taught by Haydon who gave him lessons in anatomy, providing him with the carcass of a lion to dissect in order to learn more about the animal's anatomy.

Figure 7.2 A fox in profile produced when Landseer was 5 years of age in 1807. Reprinted with the kind permission of the Royal Academy of Arts, London. Photograph by John Hammond.

Figure 7.3 Head of a horse with nosebag (circa 1810–1812), drawn by Landseer at the age of 8–10. Reprinted with the kind permission of the Royal Academy of Arts, London.

It has been suggested (Ormond, 1981) that he worked rapidly and was ambidextrous, being able to paint with each hand simultaneously, painting the head of a horse with one hand whilst simultaneously painting its tail with the other. Figure 7.4 shows a cockerel he drew at 10–12 years of age.

Figure 7.4 A cockerel, drawn by Landseer at about the age of 8–10 (1810–1812). Reprinted with the kind permission of the Royal Academy of Arts, London.

The New York Times (Anon, March 1874) reported that at the age of 13 he exhibited the portrait of a pointer and puppy in the Royal Academy. In that year (1815) he received a silver medal from the Society of Arts for his drawing of a hunter. By 1822, aged 20, he was a recognised artist, being made an Associate of the Royal Academy in 1826 at the age of 23. Thereafter, he became increasingly popular and financially very successful, painting mainly animals. The best known of his works include the sculptures of the lions in Trafalgar Square in central London, The Monarch of the Glenn, and several portraits of Queen Victoria. One of his most important patrons was the Duke of Bedford. He was elected as an Academician in 1831. In 1850 he received a knighthood and was elected president of the Royal Academy in 1866, which he did not accept through ill health. He had suffered a nervous breakdown in his thirties and the remainder of his life was affected by depression and mental instability, becoming increasingly serious in later life. Reports of the time note that on his death flags flew at half-staff, his bronze lions at the base of Nelson's column were hung with wreaths, and large crowds lined the streets to watch his funeral cortege pass.

It is generally agreed among critics that while he remained a very talented artist with regard to technique, his later, mature work was often sentimental and he anthropomorphised the animals he painted. Ormond (1981) said that Landseer's Scottish paintings in particular, have become irretrievably linked to a mawkish sentimental vision of Scotland. He is an artist who influenced many other land-scape painters of the nineteenth century, many of whom went on to produce work that is perpetuated on innumerable tourist brochures and biscuit tins. He concludes that Landseer was producing a potent image of Scotland for an English audience. Many of his major early works were purchased by English aristocrats. His work is now to be seen in the British Library, the Fitzwilliam Museum, the Victoria and Albert Museum, and the Royal Academy of Arts.

It is interesting to note that the youngest ever exhibitor at the Royal Academy (beating two earlier prodigies, John Millais and Edwin Landseer) was Eileen Soper (1905–1990). Her speciality was in portraying children in an unsentimental way and she became an eminent illustrator of children's books. She was 13 when her work was hung there, whereas the more famous male artists had to wait until they were over 16 before they achieved the same status.

John Scarlett Davis (1804–1845)

In his biography of John Scarlett Davis, Hobbs (2004) provides evidence from John's brother that he was regarded as a child prodigy. He wrote of him: 'From early infancy he began to admire pictures and at five years of age astonished his school master and parents with innumerable examples of truth of imitation, combined with beauty and taste. When he was about seven years of age he made a drawing of a cart and etched it all in one sitting' (p. 3).

It is believed he received some tuition from an eminent artist, David Cox (1783–1859), who was a drawing master in a school in Hereford near to the market town in which Davis lived.

By the age of ten he was invited by his family doctor to see some anatomical engravings, which he copied. This won him a prestigious award and he duly travelled to London to collect it. An announcement in the *Hereford Journal* (5 June 1816) stated, 'It was with pleasure that we observe the name master John Scarlett Davis, a young self taught genius, eleven years of age, from the borough of Leominster, son of James Davis, as a successful candidate in anatomical engravings' (cited in Hobbs, 2004, pp. 6–7). His prize was presented to him by the Duke of Sussex, who commented that he was so much younger and smaller than any of the other candidates that although he did not see him immediately, his talent marked him out. Figure 7.5 is a painting by Davis at the age of 10–12 years.

He began to develop his skills producing drawings of the human figure as a child and was encouraged to take up art as a profession (Figure 7.6). At the age of 13 he travelled to London to study in Paul de la Pierre's Academy in Hackney. He was awarded another prize by the Society of Arts, for his drawing of the Coronation of Henry VI, which they initially did not believe could have been completed by a boy of 13. At the age of 15 he was accepted as a probationary student in the Royal Academy and became a fully qualified student at 16. In 1821 he obtained his third major prize for his head of William Blake in pen and ink. He became a highly proficient painter of portraits in oils and was employed under

Figure 7.5 Childhood painting by John Scarlett Davis, aged between 12 and 14 years, of a street in Leominster painted on a wooden panel in his bedroom. Note the use of perspective. Reprinted with the kind permission of Hereford Museum, Herefordshire Heritage Services, UK.

Figure 7.6 The Head of Michelangelo by John Scarlett Davis, drawn when aged 12.
Reprinted with the kind permission of Hereford Museum, Herefordshire
Heritage Services, UK.

George IV at Charlton House where he painted the portrait of the Lord Mayor of
London and other eminent men of the time. Thereafter, his talents developed,
especially for architectural drawings; which can be seen in the record of his travels
in Europe. He died a relatively poor man in 1845 of a lung disease.

John Everett Millais (1829–1896)

Despite his extraordinary talent as a child, there is no suggestion that Millais was
anything other than a normal bright boy. Malcolm Warner (1981) records evidence
to show that John Everett Millais was a prodigiously talented artist as a child
(Figure 7.7). He recounts how at the age of 6 some army officers had a bet on
whether such a young child could have produced the drawings of soldiers that he
appeared to have made. It transpired that he had, and the young Millais was called
into the dinner given by those who had lost the wager and toasted by them. At the
same age he had duly impressed the colonel of the regiment in Dinan, when he
drew him smoking a cigar.

Millais came from a background in which his father was an amateur musician
and interested in the fine arts. His mother educated him at home (having been
expelled from school after the first day when he bit the teacher's hand). Warner
suggests that he probably acquired his technical skills of draughtsmanship from
constant practice in copying engravings and drawings. He makes the point that he
was never encouraged as a child to draw from nature and as a result his childhood
work is dominated by figure drawing made indoors (Figure 7.8). By the age of 8

Figure 7.7 A cavalryman on horseback (circa 1837) by John Everett Millais, drawn at the age of 7. Reprinted with the kind permission of the Royal Academy of Arts, London. Photograph by John Hammond.

Figure 7.8 A man carrying a sack by John Everett Millais (1837), drawn at the age of 7. Reprinted with the kind permission of the Royal Academy of Arts, London. Photograph by John Hammond.

he had left his home in Jersey (where he had been taught to draw by copying anatomical studies) to live in London where he received more professional training in art. Millais was winning prestigious medals, awards and prize money from the age of 9 years from various important bodies. He was admitted to the Royal

Academy at the age of 11 as a probationer, and became the youngest ever to achieve full student status 6 months later. He won first prize in the annual students' competition at the age of 14. He had his first painting hung in the Academy's annual exhibition at the age of 17.

Some of his drawings bear some similarities to those of Nadia, but she was much younger when executing them. Millais was aged 7 when he drew his horse and rider (Figure 7.7); Nadia was 5 years old (see Figure 2.7).

When he was 19 he had met Holman Hunt and his circle and became a founding member of the Pre-Raphaelite Brotherhood. They set out a new creed for painting influenced by the critic Ruskin centred on truth to nature in all its detail, arguing that in future 'artists need to go to an observation of nature' (Gaunt, 1942, p. 187). He observed that nature was built to certain beautiful workable structural laws, as was society itself. In this way he and his acolytes were led to a critique and opposition of Victorian society in favour of that of a more perfect one, pre-Raphael.

Holman Hunt claimed that Millais recognised the decline in quality of his later works, admitting to an acquaintance that 'I'm not ashamed of avowing that I have so far failed in my maturity to fulfil the full forecast of my youth' (cited in Gaunt, 1942, p. 169). However, at his death he had a substantial annual income and a large house in Palace Gate, London, having become one of the most successful English portrait painters of the age. His son John duly became a notable naturalist and wildlife artist.

Henri de Toulouse-Lautrec (1864–1901)

The early childhood work of Toulouse-Lautrec was preserved by his mother. It is illuminating and included here because the progress and development of his art can be followed. Thompson (1981) suggests that his draughtsmanship was limited in range until he attended art school at the age of 18. He writes, 'In common with most young children he produced schematic images of what he knew or had experienced rather than attempt to analyse rationally what he actually saw' (p. 38). Paine (2000) describes his work as a 6-year-old as showing an extraordinary expressive quality. From this age he was fond of drawing horses, circuses, and steeplechases. He had a predilection for caricature. He seems to have drawn from remembered reality rather than from his imagination. There is also some evidence to suggest that cartoon pictures of animals provided some inspiration (Pariser, 1995). He tended, therefore, to produce isolated images without reference to the context in which they existed.

Figure 7.9 seems to depict some practice occurring in getting the horses completed to his satisfaction. (But note, too, how the dog on the right-hand side is 'off the page'.) Some of his drawings echo the ways in which Nadia was not constrained by the edge of the paper on which she drew. Pariser (1995) states that Toulouse-Lautrec spent much of his childhood in practising his drawing skills making copious sketches such as Figure 7.9. The frequent copying and tracing and imitation of styles encouraged accelerated development of his graphic skills. This opportunity to practise was the result of his early ill health and an accident, which

Figure 7.9 Carriage and Horses (Chateau de Bosc) drawn by Henri de Toulouse-Lautrec
at about the age of 6–7. From Paine (1981), *Six Children Draw*. London:
Academic Press.© Elsevier and reproduced with kind permission.

severely injured his legs. His inability to participate in the physical activities typically enjoyed by those of his age led to him immersing himself obsessively in his
art. During his adolescence he enjoyed academic painting under the guidance of
specialist tutors. Unlike Millais, however, he does not appear to have spent much
time copying old masters or learning the rules of composition. There are other
factors in seeking an explanation for Toulouse-Lautrec's early talent. He came
from a wealthy family whose members were interested in the arts (his father
was an amateur sculptor and draughtsman) and who supported him at all times. As
he developed, he became increasingly concerned to depict visual appearances
accurately such as the legs of a trotting horse. Thompson (1981) notes that he
worked with rapidity to complete a drawing, having made a speedy sketch.
Toulouse-Lautrec said, 'When my pencil gets going I have to give it its head' (cited
in Thompson, 1981, p. 42).

Pablo Picasso (1881–1973)

Picasso is included here because he was one of the great artists of the last century
and there is some evidence for early precocity. His teenage drawings survive

in the Picasso Museum in Barcelona and in Paris and these show outstanding skill from the age of 12 suggesting precocious early development but few of his childhood drawings still exist.

It is recorded that Picasso showed an obsession and talent for drawing from an early age and that his first utterance was the Spanish word for pencil (Richardson, 1991). His father was a talented artist, who became a professor in the School of Fine Arts in Coruna. From about the age of 7, Picasso received formal teaching and training in techniques of art from his father. Picasso, like Millais before him, therefore, spent long periods copying work of the eminent masters. In addition he attended life-drawing classes. By the age of 13 his father believed that his son had surpassed his own talents.

Picasso had his own views on children's artwork. He said 'I have never done children's drawings. Never' (cited in Richardson, 1991, p. 29). Richardson, however, believes that this may have been part of the family view that Picasso had been 'a genius from earliest days' (pp. 62–63). Picasso said of himself 'I remember one of my first drawings. I was perhaps six . . . it wasn't a child's drawing. It was a real drawing, representing Hercules with his club' (cited in Richardson, 1991 p. 29). However, Richardson remains dubious about his child-hood precocity.

Figure 7.10 was drawn when Picasso was 9 years of age. For Richardson (1991, p. 62) his early work is 'what one would expect from a reasonably gifted child'. Picasso illustrates the audience in the arena with suggestive scribbled lines. The

Figure 7.10 Pablo Picasso (aged 9): Bull Fight and Pigeons, 1890. Pencil on paper Museu Picasso Barcelona. © Estate of Pablo Picasso/DACS (London), reproduced with kind permission.

childlike qualities are seen in the proportions between and within the figures, which are not quite correct and the figures have their own space. Fineberg (1997) argues that although it is possible to teach someone to draw pigeons and figures, the scribble of the crowd is what is 'gifted' in the drawing. He says, 'The seemingly "childlike" looseness and the playful sense of liveliness of the scribbled crowd in the background of Bullfight and Pigeons display a stunning sense of self-assurance in drawing for a nine-year-old. That free, gestural line is by no means haphazard . . . it brilliantly conveys the enthusiastic spectators' (1997, p. 5). He concludes that although Picasso may not have been a child prodigy, what was remarkable about him was 'the unique character of his way of seeing' which always characterised his art (p. 5). The drawing illustrates his prodigious talent, especially the study of pigeons.

Brian Hatton (1887–1916)

Celia Davies (1978), in her biography of Hatton, provides evidence of his early prodigious talent. Examples of a drawing made at the age of 2 and many of his sketches made while at primary school survive. It is apparent that he benefitted from his parents' great appreciation of art and encouragement of his talent. It was recorded that as a young child he preferred pencil and paper to any toys and would sit in his pram happily making drawings. He received early home tuition with his sisters. The local fairs, race meetings in Hereford, visits to the river and farms were all sources of early inspiration. Even the visits of a cart delivering manure to his garden or gypsies selling lace and pegs were sketched. Incidents involving horses were among his favourite early subjects. Figures 7.11–7.14 show some of his early work.

At the age of 8 he sent a drawing to the exhibition of the Royal Drawing Society (for young artists) and won the bronze medal. By the age of 11 he had won the gold. The competition was open to anyone under the age of 20 in the whole of Britain. This success led to a meeting with the eminent artist G. F. Watts who said of him, 'Of course for his age Brian Hatton's work is quite unsurpassed . . . the drawing of the team in The Reaper is quite astonishing' (cited in Davies, 1978, p. 13). In a letter to his mother (1898, cited in Davies, 1978, p. 17) Watts wrote, 'his work displays more than ordinary ability and power of observation'. The following year he won more prizes in competitions; the Director of the Society informing Mrs Hatton that Brian's work was far in advance of all other competitors. Among the drawings entered was a self-portrait done at the age of 11 in 1898 (see Figure 3.12). He continued to dominate the prize list in future years, regularly winning the G. F. Watts award who predicted that he felt certain that the young Brian Hatton would one day become more eminent than himself. He was sent away for his health and his letters to his parents from the ages of 9 to 15 when he was away from home contain delightful illustrations that indicate something of his talent (Figure 7.15).

The fact that he did have prodigious talent is revealed in an angry exchange of letters between a judge in a prestigious competition that Hatton had entered

Figure 7.11
Drawing of a horse and rider by
Hatton, aged between 7 and 8 years
old. Reprinted with the kind permission
of Hereford Museum, Herefordshire
Heritage Services, UK.

Figure 7.12
A collage indicating something of Hatton's
sense of humour from a young age, drawn
between the ages of 7 and 8. Reprinted with
the kind permission of Hereford Museum,
Herefordshire Heritage Services, UK.

Figure 7.13
Drawing by Hatton of horses being led that
was drawn between the ages of 7 and 8 and
again shows his early talent for movement
and the complexity of the subject matter.
Reprinted with the kind permission of
Hereford Museum, Herefordshire Heritage
Services, UK.

Figure 7.14
Drawing of sheep and a shepherd, drawn
by Hatton between the ages of 10 and 11,
showing his increasing maturity as an
artist. Reprinted with the kind permission
of Hereford Museum, Herefordshire
Heritage Services, UK.

and Dr Livingstone, in whose house he was staying when the picture was
completed. The question arose as to whether Hatton had met the requirements of
the competition, to draw from memory (rather than using any photographs or
other illustrations). It is apparent that the judges did not think that a picture of such
high quality could have been completed from memory. In his angry response,
Dr Livingstone stated that he had observed the picture being drawn and painted,
and said he could vouch for the fact that it was completed from memory.

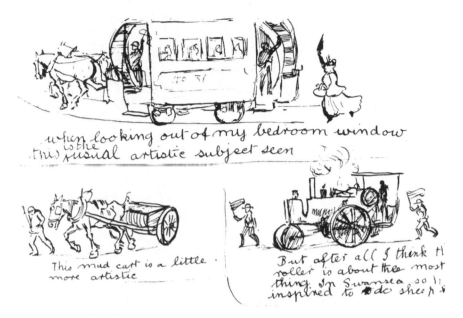

When looking out of my bedroom window this is the usual artistic subject seen

This mud cart is a little more artistic

But after all I think the roller is about the most thing in Swansea so I inspired to do sheep

Figure 7.15 Sketches by Hatton of views from his window in Swansea, probably of the Mumbles railway and related events. These were included in a letter he wrote to his parents at the age of 10. Note his use of perspective, movement and humour. Reprinted by kind permission of the Herefordshire Archive Service, UK.

In 1901 at the age of 13 and a half he sent in a portfolio of work to the Royal Drawing Society and swept the board of their prizes. In the following years, his work duly developed and he obtained valuable commissions from eminent people and had paintings accepted by the Royal Academy. In September 1914 on the outbreak of war, he volunteered to join the Worcester Yeomanry as a trooper. In November, he married Lydia Bidmead. In December 1915 he arrived in Egypt. On Easter Sunday, 23 April 1916 his regiment came under heavy attack by the Turks. He volunteered to ride off to get help from another regiment but was killed in the course of this mission. He was 28. The critic, W. S. Sparrow said of him that he possessed 'the rarest of all things – true genius' and 'he was a boy endowed with gifts of the spirit so extraordinary that the first period of his work from the age of ten, 1897, to that of nineteen, 1906, was a period not of rare promise only but also of wonderful achievement' (cited in Davies, 1978, p. 167). Another painter of the period Adrian Bury said he had 'a genius unique in the history of British art' (cited in Davies, p. 167). Figure 7.16 is a drawing by Hatton that compares remarkably with those of Nadia (Figure 1.4) and Leonardo da Vinci (Figure 1.5).

Figure 7.16 A galloping horse drawn by Hatton at the age of 7 or 8. This sketch was later developed into a major painting. Reprinted with the kind permission of Hereford Museum, Herefordshire Heritage Services, UK.

David Downes (b. 1971)

I originally met David in 1977 when he was 6 years old. His mother contacted me because he displayed outstanding drawing ability from an early age. He continued to develop his skills and was studied by Paine, in *Six Children Draw* (1981) and in *Artists Emerging* (2000). When he was very young he had severe speech and language difficulties. His coordination was very poor and at 3 years old he was unable to talk. David's ability to read preceded his ability to talk and his parents taught him language by labelling all the objects in the house. He developed speech from the age of 4 following visits to a speech therapist. Thereafter he made progress with all aspects of cognitive development.

In his second year of life David began to take an interest in geometric shapes on packets and in books and observing such features on television without showing any interest in the programmes. Once he was provided with pencils he began to draw, starting with the parapets of churches, endlessly repeating them. Tall buildings fascinated him, including churches (Figure 7.17), windmills, high-rise blocks and pylons. By the age of 4 and a half he was completing drawings of buildings, roads, hedges, and fences. His drawings (using ball-point pens, fibre-tipped pens, and pencils) incorporated visual depth, three-dimensionality, occlusion, and an awareness of proportion (Figure 7.18).

Once he had learned to talk, David's development proceeded well and he entered a local primary school although he needed some additional support. At the age of 5 he invented an imaginary world of places based on his experiences that he drew regularly. He said of 'Trottingham': 'This is my made up place;

Figure 7.17 Church drawn by David Downes at the age of 5. It is remarkable for the use of perspective and the solidity of the structure. Reprinted with the kind permission of David Downes.

Figure 7.18 Scene drawn by David Downes at the age of 5 years 9 months. Note the illusion of depth, created by variation in the size of the birds in the sky and the church in the distance. Reprinted with the kind permission of David Downes.

there's a place called Nottingham, so I thought there might be a place called Trottingham' (cited in Morgan, 1981, p. 28). As a child and subsequently as an adult David works entirely from memory and yet he shows considerable accuracy in the representations of the buildings he has observed. David has always

Figure 7.19 A sketch of a local church by David Downes at the age of 5. Like Figure 7.18, it shows an unusual ability to deal with perspective and the illusion of height and solidity in a child so young. Reprinted with the kind permission of David Downes.

been interested in architectural drawings of buildings (Figure 7.19) and urban landscapes.

It is pleasing to find that David has become a successful artist (Figure 7.20). He went to art school and on to the prestigious Royal College of Art where he completed an MA in communication design. His talent lies particularly in his architectural drawings for which he has received many important commissions and requests for projects, from the BBC, major city banks, Westminster Cathedral, and for the 2012 Olympic Games.

I was able to interview David in 2010, as a gifted artist his insights into the development of his artistic skills are a valuable resource. This is not only because he is an articulate adult, who was gifted in his early years, but also because his very early development was seen as unusually delayed. David has been considered as having mild atypical Asperger's syndrome but he does not meet the criteria for savant syndrome, since his general intelligence is above average. He describes his work as focusing on 'the juxtaposition of history and modernity in London . . . my work is a meeting of realism and imagination . . .' (Downes, n. d., para. 2).

Moreover, his subsequent success as a commissioned artist, with many exhibitions of his work, and the progress of his talent all provide support for the views of Treffert (1989, p. 314) who said, 'Training the talent can diminish the defect'. In David's case, he is totally self-reliant; he runs a successful business; he is highly articulate with a lovely sense of humour, and he is a very sociable person. As Paine noted (2000, p. 139) 'Whatever his ultimate achievement, it cannot now be insignificant and in the light of his history, it is already remarkable.'

Figure 7.20 The Albert Bridge by David Downes as a mature artist. Reprinted with the kind permission of David Downes.

Kieron Williamson (b. 2002)

In 2009 many press reports discussed the artwork of Kieron Williamson, then aged 7 who has been producing paintings, drawings, and pastel work since he was 5. He was producing pictures of phenomenal quality and he appears therefore from the accounts to be a prodigy (rather than savant) (Figures 7.21 and 7.22).

Kieron is able to draw in perspective and produce work with the skill of a much more mature and well-trained artist. Interviews with him indicate that he is able to discuss his ideas and his work fluently. In addition he is familiar with the work of eminent artists such as Picasso and Monet (unlike most autistic savant artists who have no apparent interest in or knowledge of other artists or what may be happening in the wider world of art). A local picture dealer said 'He has a very mature hand and has mastered certain techniques at an early stage which some artists take years to perfect' (cited in McVeigh, 2009, p. 13).

Kieron's mother has indicated (in private correspondence) that when he was a toddler (under 3 years of age) he went through the normal stages of drawing development (including scribbles and tadpole figures). He enjoyed all the usual toddler activities, sand play, water play, climbing, and other physical pursuits. Fine motor control may have been a little delayed but almost certainly within

Figure 7.21 Watercolour of houses by Kieron Williamson completed at the age of 6. The painting shows remarkable use of perspective, shadow effects, and mature use of colour. Reprinted with the kind permission of Michelle Williamson.

normal limits. Kieron was early in meeting most of his milestones. According to his baby book entry, Kieron was putting one to two words together at 20 months; he could say single words and make animal noises at 1-year-old, talking constantly at 2 years. There were no noticeable language delays, nor did he appear to present any behaviour problems that caused parental concern. He developed in normal ways along with his sister, Billie Jo.

His enjoyment of picture books appears to have begun at about 12 months. He began to take an interest in drawing realistically at about 5 years of age and his ability to employ perspective developed thereafter. Kieron's early drawings began following a family holiday at this time. Before the holiday he was reluctant to draw for himself; he would draw pictures at school but it wasn't a favourite pastime. He would instruct family members to draw dinosaurs or birds and he would confidently colour them in. After the holiday, he began to take the process of drawing much more seriously, insisting on the proper art materials and then he gave it his full attention. When he began a drawing, he would ask questions about getting started and enjoyed supportive input. He is described as being systematic and wanting to get things right; once having got underway with his paintings he did not then require further guidance. He had a few lessons at the age of 5 and then

Figure 7.22 Watercolour of a church by Kieron Williamson completed at the age of 6. This painting, like Figure 7.21, is remarkable for the mature use of colour and perspective. Reprinted with the kind permission of Michelle Williamson.

matured rapidly. One of his teachers says of him, 'His use of tone, colour and light is wonderful' (cited in McVeigh, 2009, p. 13).

He became rapidly proficient in drawing and painting in acrylics and watercolours after the age of 5. A local artist and gallery owner, Carol Ann Pennington, provided his first lessons of an hour a week in the summer holidays. She had observed his continuing efforts over the months and examined his other work from time to time. She noted how Kieron had a tendency to be quite tight and specific in his work, not liking error. Her style of work was, by comparison, loose, bright, and contemporary. She was able to influence him in this regard. He tried different techniques and media but prefers realism to abstraction. She also observed Kieron's ability to mix colours at a young age.

Initially, while in playschool he delighted in the use of black paint, but was finally encouraged to mix colours by using painting dinosaurs that required a mix of sandy, desert colours. He subsequently became confident to experiment with colours, being quite happy, for example, to include red in the sky, rather than the more obvious blue. The interest in colour came first, then the painting and then the process of drawing. Although his initial drawings were good, he did not value them. He started to enjoy sketching in year 2 at school by the age of 6. From about the age of 7 he has come to enjoy simple pen and wash watercolours or sketches. He is now also attempting to produce portraits and horses. From time to time he will try some new approach, making use of light, dark, and shadows. At the outset his favourite subjects were boats. He preferred complete scenes rather than single objects. Kieron would always include the horizon in his landscapes. However, painting or drawing something without a structured composition is beginning to develop. He has experimented with the use of a photograph and rulers to learn more about perspective and the concept of a vanishing point. But having understood the principle he has progressed with his technique, also learning from the comments and advice of other artists from time to time.

In that many talented artists come from a family in which there are others with similar skills, it is interesting to note that Keiron does not appear to have anyone in his immediate family who shares his high level of artistic skill. There are family members who can sketch and draw with some proficiency and enjoy craft activities. Kieron's interest in and delight with his artwork has been encouraged and praised (and much of his early work retained). This might also account for why he has been so prolific.

He is described by his parents as 'exuberant and hardworking'. He gives any enterprise his full attention and effort; this includes his schoolwork (where he receives high praise), his sporting interests and of course his art. The advice Kieron offers to others is complex and thoughtful: 'Start with acrylics, then water colours, then pastels and then oils'; and about landscape painting he says, 'Start with the sky first, top to bottom' and 'When you do distance, its lighter and when you do foreground it comes darker' (cited in Barkham, 2009, p. 10). He is delighted that his work is appreciated and valued; but is well able to balance this with his wide range of hobbies and leisure pursuits. He is clearly a sociable and talented person. It will, therefore, be of great interest to see how he develops as he grows older and more experienced.

Summary

The artistically gifted draw with a fluidity and speed; they do not need to erase or labour over their work. They appear to have the ability to memorise visual observations and then later set them down on paper with precision or in an aesthetically pleasing way (Gordon, 1987; Paine, 1981; Pariser, 1995; Milbrath, 1998). They have mastered the conventions of their culture, in depicting perspective and the norms of visual representation. What is evident from a brief examination of the lives of the renowned artists, who showed prodigious ability as children (Lievens, Millais, Landseer, Picasso, Toulouse-Lautrec, Scarlett Davis, and Hatton), is that they all came from homes (in some cases relatively affluent) in which they had a dominant culture of art. They had fathers who were gifted amateur artists, sculptors or draughtsmen, mothers who were supportive and encouraging of their talents (knowing where to send their child for further training) and they had early success that promoted and reinforced their interest in art. The two examples of contemporary artists who showed prodigious talent at a young age, Downes and Williamson, have also been fortunate to have encouraging and supportive parents (although not necessarily coming from artistic backgrounds). They too seem to have spent a great deal of time as young children enthusiastically practising their skills. Such factors relate to the views of Howe (1989) who noted the importance of gaining enjoyment from practice as a factor in becoming even more outstanding. In Howe's words: 'People are likely to gain an unusual degree of competence at an area of expertise if they become sufficiently interested in it to devote a substantial proportion of their time towards it, giving it their undivided attention' (p. 165). He goes on to ask whether talent can be reduced to motivation, attention, time and effort.

It is the case that all these non-autistic artists appear to have had a special ability for realistic depiction from their early years, which was then carefully nurtured, usually by their parents. In some cases this skill is recorded to have been observed at a remarkably young age (in the case of Hatton, at 2 years). While the term 'genius' is a term open to misuse, it is one which is frequently attached to those who display extraordinary talents at a very young age outside the realm of normal development. Whereas Snyder speculates that it may be that some intellectual giants had autistic traits (as discussed by Fitzgerald, 2004), Howe in *Genius Explained* (1999) examines the view that 'genius' is a special, somewhat mysterious, possibly innate gift. He examines the lives of some exceptionally creative people about whom the term has been applied. They include Darwin, the Brontë sisters, George Eliot, Michael Faraday, and Einstein. His thesis is that genius is the product of environment, personality, and dedicated effort rather than being a mysterious quality that is beyond comprehension. He argues that such people had an extraordinary degree of commitment, concentration on goals, dedication to practice, aligned with a driving ambition to succeed. He says: 'I am not convinced that there is anything about the lives and achievements of geniuses that is in principle any less amenable to explanation than the lives and achievements of other people ... That geniuses are special is undeniable, but the view that they are special for reasons that are mysterious needs to be challenged' (p. 8).

David Schenk (2010) also explores the question as to whether there is such a thing as innate talent and aptitude, which is passed through the genes, or whether it is something which can be developed. He, too, suggests that it is the latter, in which practice and dedication are the crucial factors together with good teaching, which produces outstanding ability. Schenk says that the genetic argument has been overstated and that our DNA is open to continual influence by external factors. There is a constant interaction between nature and nurture, the genes and the environment. Schenk disputes the view that people are born with innate talent (for music, art, calculation). Rather, everyone is born with a potential that can be developed given the right environmental influences. For example, in societies in which musical pitch plays an important part in everyday life, such as in China, everyone simply gets better at it. The success of runners from particular societies (such as Kenya) is attributed to the fact that running is a predominant feature of day-to-day life from an early age. The qualities that produce particular success in people (such as tenacity and diligence) are not, therefore, seen as the product of genetic inheritance but rather as cultural features.

This view has been criticised on the grounds that while people may have potential for improved ability that is not the same as developing the extraordinary abilities associated with those with whom the term genius is widely accepted, such as Einstein, Edison, and Newton. They were people who stepped beyond exceptional talent by inventing new ways of seeing and understanding aspects of the world in which they lived. In this view there is a difference between talent and genius which involves a dimension beyond proficiency. Most of the prodigious child artists discussed became very proficient artists but few became geniuses who broke traditions and were truly innovative, Picasso being the outstanding exception.

Drake and Winner (2009) provide suggestions as to the similarities and differences between autistic savants and non-autistic artists. While it is difficult to assess these with regard to artists of the past, it is possible to make some deductions based on comments made about their childhood experiences and the drawing process that emerged, from friends and family. It is, fortunately, possible to make a better assessment with regard to living artists, who have shown early precocious talent such as David Downes and Kieron Williamson.

What can the drawings of gifted children inform us about the skills of savants?

From what is known about the childhood drawings of Lievens, Scarlett Davis, Landseer, Millais, Toulouse-Lautrec, Picasso, Hatton, Williamson, and Downes, it can be stated that they had the following in common:

- They had a great deal of support and encouragement to develop their talent.
- They exhibited above average IQ and good language skills.
- They all practised their skill intensively and all had some training to progress further.
- Many spent time copying the old masters or in life classes from a young age.
- All appear to have been perfectionists.
- Since none of the children classified as gifted in drawing in Drake and Winner's (2009) study used a local proximity strategy (which is used by savants), it can be supposed that this is true of the non-autistic prodigies discussed above.
- Together with good general intelligence, it is likely that all displayed intact central coherence, executive functioning, and global advantage over local processing advantage.
- They all demonstrate superior visual memory and heightened visual analysis either innate or acquired. The question of whether any display eidetic ability is uncertain, although the ability of some to retain images and reproduce them at a later time is recorded (for example, Brian Hatton and David Downes).

- The subjects of the drawings of child prodigies vary considerably but human figures and birds and animals, especially horses, are notable themes; horses would have been commonplace at the time these artists lived. Some have shown an interest in architectural drawing.
- The childhood drawings of these artists illustrate the problems that arise in assessing what is meant by art and the rules and systems that we bring to bear in analysing the ways in which drawings are made and judged.

Conclusions

The special skills of young prodigious artists seem to be an exceptional visual memory and aptitude for visual analysis. Such skills were no doubt developed initially from long periods copying eminent masters, practising obsessively and subsequently working from memory. This is seen, for example, in the work of Hatton, whose ability to remember scenes he was able to depict was challenged, but was shown to be based on remarkable memory. It is apparent also in Landseer's work, whose early drawing of animals had to be from observation and recall, since they were not static subjects. David Downes has confirmed in discussion that he was able to study a scene for a period of time (in a work place, for example, where no sketching or photography was permitted) and then return home and draw it in fine detail. No doubt Picasso, Lievens, and Millais had similar skills. In the same way, Kieron Williamson must have an extraordinary ability to comprehend a landscape, absorb its detail and reproduce it on canvas. Communication with his mother confirmed that he does not copy from photographs but transforms images he has remembered in the way that his prodigious artist predecessors have done.

It does not seem to be the case that all precocious artists who develop their skills at an abnormally young age necessarily go on to become highly successful talented artists as mature adults. On the other hand, some very successful artists appear to have been comparatively late developers, showing no such youthful ability. It was suggested by the art critic Roger Fry that Cezanne, regarded as the founding father of modernism in art, was not a good draughtsman. He said of him that he lacked the skills of a good illustrator. He represented 'the most direct and simplest aspect of things – the aspect that is of primitive art' (Fry, 1989, p. xxiii). Yet the work he produced in his later years has come to be seen as groundbreaking and revolutionary.

It is apparent that Nadia is a special case of savantism because her drawing was so outstanding at such a young age (from the age of 3) and because the skills withered so dramatically. In her creative period (from 3 to 12 years) Nadia shares some of the qualities of other savant artists such as Stephen Wiltshire, in particular. Both appear to have had a superior visual memory, speed, and fluency of line. She also had some of the discrepancies that Drake and Winner (2009) found in other autistic savant artists. These include below average IQ (she certainly did not have a strong verbal IQ); she made use of local processing strategy (she was able to complete block design tasks, jigsaws, and inset puzzles but she could not speak). She used a local proximity strategy: that is, the drawing often started with a detail, moving to other separate details so that the final outline emerged last. She also accords with the features described in weak central coherence theory (where there is focus on the small features of a drawing rather than the global whole; little context for the picture; and there being no constraints by the placing of the drawing in relation to the size of the paper, so that parts of the drawing 'fall off the edge').

The mystery of exactly how the prodigies have achieved their talent remains unresolved; the work on autistic savants has not yet provided the key to unlock it. There are similarities in the way each displays their talents; but there are also significant differences. It may be that in due course research on neurological explanations will be fruitful. But as yet there is no single explanatory theory to account for the prodigious talents that appear from time to time both in savants and non-autistic prodigies. We can but view their work and marvel.

8   The challenge of Nadia

Overview

In the last 30 years, since Nadia was a child and drawing prolifically, research in psychology has proceeded at an accelerated pace. In writing this book I have had to range over a wide field. I have climbed foothills and discovered mountain ranges beyond in areas such as perception, cognition, neuropsychology and, of course, autistic spectrum disorder (ASD). There has also been a paradigm shift away from behaviourism in favour of explorations of the contents of the 'black box' of mind. In this concluding chapter I am offering interested readers and students signposts into those mountains in the knowledge that a bright new generation of psychology students will be venturing forth.

Paine (1981) commented that Nadia is 'the person who most challenges all our comfortable assumptions about drawing and we cannot reasonably ignore the questions her work raises about the nature of learning, the facility of drawing and the possibilities of teaching' (p. 5). In this final chapter the question 'where does Nadia fit?' is addressed; which theories best explain her talent and which fail to take account of her abilities and subsequent development? How can acquired skills apparently evaporate and what can the case of Nadia contribute to an understanding of developmental psychology and ASD?

A word of caution is needed before beginning a review of Nadia and current theories. Nadia is diagnosed as autistic. Recent research on ASD is acknowledging that the condition is not a unitary one but multidimensional and the search for a single explanatory theory may well be abandoned (Happé et al., 2006). Several researchers (Phillips & Silverstein, 2004; Rajendran & Mitchell, 2007) have pointed out that impairments in the three key areas in the triad can occur independently so that any conclusions drawn from a group of children with ASD need not apply to any single individual with a diagnosis of ASD. Klin (2009) and Mottron et al. (2006) characterised ASD as a continuum of subtypes. My experience as a practitioner has noted the differences between children with a diagnosis of ASD as much as the similarities (Selfe, 2002). Nadia is a unique individual and given the diverse nature of ASD, conclusions drawn in this chapter may only apply to Nadia since this is an ideographic study. However, it is hoped that the case of Nadia gives us insights into autism as well as into cognitive development in children.

Nadia is an unusual case of savant syndrome. First, her ability to draw visually realistic images emerged at the age of 3 without any period of practice. Her very young age and lack of any evident practice mark her out from other savants with drawing skills. Second, her original skills at graphic depiction have largely been lost or she no longer chooses to use them. This is not entirely unique, Palo and Kivalo (1977, as cited by Howe, 1989) noted there are other recorded cases of savant syndrome where special skills have emerged and then disappeared. In view of Nadia's amazing facility for drawing over a period of at least 7 years, this is an added dimension to be explained.

Summing up features of significance about Nadia, we know that she has or had the following:

- Severe learning difficulties and an extremely low intelligence quotient (IQ).
- Extremely poor receptive and expressive verbal abilities.
- A diagnosis of ASD made when she was 7 years of age and confirmed by subsequent assessments.
- Abnormal neurological electrical activity in her right hemisphere. She is left handed.
- Some apparent body and facial asymmetry as an adult with right-sided weaknesses and supposed left hemisphere dysfunction.
- An early emerging ability to draw visually realistic images mainly from pictures but occasionally from life that waned and largely disappeared in her teenage years.
- A good visual memory for designs and heightened visual analysis compared with other cognitive skills but these relative strengths were still below average on standardised norms.
- A local drawing strategy (in which a drawing started with the depiction of details, moving to other parts before the completion of the whole (see Figure 2.5). This is in contrast to the global strategy adopted by most children and adults (Drake & Winner, 2009).
- Supposed weak central coherence and enhanced perception (attention to the detail rather than the whole) in line with research into cognitive deficits in ASD (Frith, 1989; Happé & Frith, 2006).

Nadia can be considered in relation to the key perspectives expounded in Chapter 6 and the related theories about savant syndrome (cognitive, neurological, and ASD). Her case can also be addressed in relation to theories of ASD discussed in Chapters 4 and 6, and especially to theories about autistic savants. Furthermore, her achievements can be examined with regard to the theories of graphic representation and particularly the work of Phillips et al. (1978) and Sheppard et al. (2008), as discussed in Chapter 3. This has some relevance to theories of perception and particularly to the work of Gibson and to Marr. It would be useful, therefore, to begin this chapter by considering existing theories that account for the work of artistic savants and the significance of such theories for Nadia.

Theories: how they relate to Nadia

There are a number of explanatory theories for savant talents (Treffert, 1989, 2009), but not all are able to take account of the phenomenal work of Nadia. Her very young age and severity of cognitive disability when she was producing her earliest drawings appears to be unmatched by any other recorded savant. Her subsequent loss of skill is also relatively unusual. There are some well-researched and worthy theories that are not so relevant to discussions about Nadia such as Tantam's theory (2009) about non-verbal deficits and executive functioning theories. The fact that they are not given much consideration in this chapter does not indicate that they are not considered relevant or important theories (see Chapter 4 for a description of these theories).

Compensation and reinforcement

Treffert (1989) suggested that savants may make use of the special abilities they have developed as psychological mechanisms to compensate for global defects or to gain approval from others and a sense of self-worth. Howe (1989), too, suggests that frequent praise provides the motivation for constant practice. The characteristics of the compensation and reinforcement theory are as follows:

- A compensatory drive in savants to develop a skill in one area to off-set defects in another.
- This, together with positive reinforcement, increases the amount of practice and concentration that the savant adopts in relation to the skill.
- The developed talent becomes a form of coping mechanism and wins approval from those around them, especially parents who achieve satisfaction from the skill of their child.

A more negative view is that the focus on the skill, which is in some cases, of little social value, becomes a habit or compulsion that acts as a shield against other social interactions and then becomes increasingly difficult to break. This may result in the savant failing to develop other types of stimulation or interests that may have a more positive value.

The notion that Nadia's drawing may have resulted from compensation effects and from reinforcement has some merits. She commenced drawing after a period when her mother had been in hospital for several months and they were reunited. Nadia's parents took a great deal of trouble to encourage and promote her skill. This phenomenal islet of ability delighted her mother.

Along with the idea of compensatory mechanisms goes the notion of the channelling of concentration on a narrow band of behaviours but, as Treffert (1989) pointed out, savant skills are reinforced after they have emerged. Savant skills do not appear to develop slowly shaped by reinforcement. They pre-date reinforcement mechanisms. In Nadia's case her very first drawings were exceptional and her mother was certain that Nadia had not gone through a phase of drawing that was developmentally typical of ordinary children, even at an accelerated rate. We also have to explain why the skill waned despite encouragement and compensation. Reinforcement by parents' and teachers' attention and approval continued unabated and increased even as her skills were beginning to wane. It is true that Nadia's mother died when Nadia was 9 and her mother would have been the most important figure in her life in respect of reinforcement. But by this time the drawings had already begun to change. She drew less often and she regularly drew more childlike symbolic images. The absence of her major reinforcer, her mother, must have affected her motivation to draw but this does not fully account for her decline in ability and interest in drawing.

Memory and savant skills

An exceptional visual memory must form the basis for Nadia's drawing ability although the mechanisms for this and an explanation for the added ability to organise visual recall into the motor sequence required to set down the image, remain elusive. Nadia had the ability to recall images having looked at them closely for a period of time as if they were photographically recalled. But in addition, she could rotate them subsequently so that the same object was seen from a different viewpoint (see Figures 2.7 and 2.9). Visual imagery involves a dynamic reconstruction of those features of the optic array that the viewer considers to be significant and to which he or she has attended (Gibson, 1979). The images produced by autistic subjects are not photographic reproductions; they are constructions. But the additional skill Nadia showed in rotating images and retaining their volumetric properties, has not been adequately explained.

What is the evidence for eidetic imagery in Nadia's case? Did Nadia draw perfect representations of images previously seen? Some of her drawings, particularly the pelican drawings were remarkably like their originals (see Figures 2.20 and 2.21). The evidence for an unusually accurate visual memory can be judged from Nadia's remarkable drawing, inspired by the picture by Toulouse-Lautrec, where incidental detail such as the tag on the jockey's cap, is recalled and recorded. This drawing was done days after viewing the original (see Figure 1.7).

Theories involving eidetic imagery have been superseded by more dynamic theories of perception although some form of extraordinary memory is still evoked by current commentators (Pring, 2008). Research on eidetic imagery has become unfashionable in the face of new theories of perception. The work of Gibson (1979) and also of Marr (1982) on perception suggested a new paradigm that changed the direction of research. Gibson's analysis dissolves any distinction between visual and eidetic imagery since all perception is viewed as necessarily constructivist and dynamic (Selfe, 1983).

The proof of this was that the very strong images produced by my autistic subjects of pictures, scenes or objects were not photographic reproductions (Selfe, 1983). They were constructions. Stephen Wiltshire's famous view of St Pancras Station (see Figure 5.13), for example, reveals that the number of Gothic windows on the front elevation although symmetrically placed, is different from the actual number. Some elaborate reconstruction has taken place in Stephen's head.

The eidetic theory of memory, as defined by its original proponents (Haber, 1969), does not hold for Nadia although there is ample evidence that she had an extraordinary access to long-term visual memory. I witnessed her drawing on many occasions. These were not copied from pictures but were drawn from memory (on rare occasions, she drew from life). Generally, the inspiration for her drawings came from children's picture books in which the quality of the pictures was sometimes rather crude although photographically realistic. She studied such pictures with close attention and days or weeks later would execute a similar drawing. However, like Stephen Wiltshire, Nadia's drawings also showed many changes from the original; she was able to change the direction of the viewpoint in some cases and add embellishments. Explanations in terms of eidetic memory have to be regarded with caution in Nadia's case but the argument for some sort of special mechanism allowing ready access to long-term memory for pictorial images is compelling.

Although evidence to support the idea of retaining a photographic image for inspection by the mind's eye is not tenable, Gibson pointed out that a picture image is a very special instance of perception. It is already two dimensional. The problem of representing depth and volume is solved in representations of pictorial images (Jolley, 2008). Nadia's main source for her drawings and particularly her early drawings was pictures in books for young children. But what does defy comprehension is that Nadia was able to rotate images and present the object in a different orientation. Somehow Nadia had an awareness of the depth and volume of the horses and pelicans and this was gained from observation of pictures only. At the age she was drawing she had very limited experiences of actual animals. She lived in an urban situation. She may have encountered horses in life and on television but it was unlikely she had ever seen a real pelican. It remains baffling to understand how she knew the volumetric properties of the animals she depicted when she changed the orientation of the flat image seen in a picture book.

Long-term memory: storage and retrieval

There has been a long running debate about storage and retrieval mechanisms in memory beginning with Atkinson and Shiffrin (1968). Do normally functioning adults store much more information than they can retrieve? Atkinson and Shiffrin suggested that they do. This would account for the fact that we do know if we have seen something previously when it is presented although we had forgotten all about it. It would appear that artistic savants are able to retrieve images from long-term storage readily. All authors who discuss the issues relating to savant syndrome emphasise their phenomenal memory, although they are less explicit about the precise mechanisms involved (O'Connor & Hermelin, 1987b; Pring, 2008; Sacks, 1995b).

Pring (2008) reviews the explanations of savant artistic ability and the role played by memory. She asserted that: 'It is a challenge to find a way of measuring the acquisition of, or indeed memory for talent related material in savant syndrome' (p. 214). She concludes that:

- savants are able to produce visually accurate, more complex outputs sometimes months after seeing the original image;
- savants appear to encode data unusually effectively rather than having increased memory capacity;
- active processing produced more accessible memories compared with passive learning conditions;
- savants have been found to have an enhanced ability to segment a pattern into its constituent parts (Pring et al., 1995).

Many savants including Nadia focus on the small details in their drawing: 'The sense that the image has been reproduced on a piecemeal basis, without regard to the holistic impression seems to support the weak perceptual coherence theory described with the cognitive style seen in autism' (Pring, 2008, p. 223).

It was evident that Nadia possessed the ability to retain an image for several weeks seemingly without active rehearsal (at least in terms of drawing it). Moreover, she produced a horse and rider image periodically over the space of at least 5 years. Presumably the trace was laid down in long-term store (Baddeley, 2004) to be retrieved whenever she wished but it is also evident that the original image was subject to changes and decay. Not enough is known currently about storage and retrieval of visual information in long-term memory to enable a fuller understanding of the process in Nadia. Nor is there a good understanding of the mechanism that allows retrieval of an image to be translated into the planning and execution of a drawing. The problem, too, is that Nadia lost her skills, which is unusual if the long-term storage mechanisms were implicated, and suggests some sort of change or deterioration in neurological functioning coinciding with the onset of adolescence.

The role of practice

Although recognising the importance of practice in most areas of life, one has to discount this as an explanation for Nadia's drawings. Nadia's skill emerged from about the age of 3 and disappeared by the age of 15. She repeated the same subject matter frequently over that period (especially horses and cockerels) but it could never be said that she improved her drawings, in the way that practice would imply. They were similar but not necessarily better. Indeed, some of her earliest drawings (Figures 2.1–2.3) were among the most remarkable of all.

Children with ASD will spend inordinate amounts of time practising their obsession. Some commentators see autism and its deficits as being an essential prerequisite for the development of savant skills (Happé & Frith, 2009). But only 50% of the subjects with savant syndrome have a diagnosis of ASD. The emergence of Nadia's drawing ability pre-dated any history of practice or intense interest in drawings or in looking at pictures according to conversations with Nadia's parents.

Howe (1989) highlighted the role of practice in all savant skills. He suggests that savants and children with autism become focused on a narrow range of activities and spend many hours in their obsessional interests. He also points out the feats of non-savants who have practised a particular skill to perfection, such as musicians and acrobats. He says that intellectual limitations may be an advantage in sustaining attention to detail. The concept of 'practice' is complex (Pring, 2008). It is necessary to distinguish between unconscious exposure to the topic of interest and the gradual accrual of a knowledge system, leading to complex cognitions. Equally, skills such as musicianship, maths and art can exist in people who otherwise have no outstanding abilities (Howe, 1989).

Nadia paid a great deal of studious attention to the pictures that inspired her later productions. Yet, there was little evidence for intensive practice especially at the outset. She studied the pelican picture provided for her (Figure 2.20) for no more than 10 minutes and produced the first drawing 2 or 3 weeks later. The first image was the sharpest and most exact. The drawing did not improve thereafter, quite the contrary. Nadia's earliest drawings were recognisable as visually realistic depiction. Later, Nadia certainly did draw frequently and there was a stage of obsessive interest when she would draw on her bedroom walls but the ability to draw realistic images appeared unbidden and unpractised.

Genetic explanations of savant syndrome

There is no evidence that anyone in Nadia's family had any particular artistic skill although all her family members are able graduates. The inheritance of a particular ability or talent and certainly that of 'ancestral memory' (Treffert, 1989, p. 262) is therefore discounted. However, Howe (1989) says that the inheritance of innate talents has some merits. Rimland (1978) suggested that savant skills run in families but LaFontaine (1974) found no such link. Howe (1989, p. 166) points out that there is circularity in the notion of the inheritance of talent. It is not defined independently of the achievements that are given as evidence for the existence of such talents. Howe proposes that the only way circularity can be avoided, is by defining the talent explicitly and precisely and independently of achievement.

Research on the genetics underlying autism has proliferated. Geschwind (2008) states 'Autism is a heterogeneous neuro-developmental syndrome with a complex genetic aetiology' (p. 391). He goes on to point out that it is still not clear whether autism comprises 'a vast collection of different disorders akin to intellectual disability or a few disorders sharing common aberrant pathways' (p. 391). He believes that the direction of future research will be to try to identify unifying principles in the brain circuitry of autistic individuals.

Kelleher and Bear (2008), suggest that the neurological deficits in ASD are global rather than specific. They studied single gene disorders with a high incidence of ASD, such as Fragile X syndrome, and proposed that 'aberrant synaptic protein synthesis may represent one possible pathway leading to autistic phenotypes, including cognitive impairments and savant abilities' (p. 401). Other studies have implicated abnormalities with synaptic transmission involving the neurotransmitter serotonin (Boylan, Blue, & Hohmann, 2007).

Although this area is promising, we have no information available about Nadia's genetic inheritance, DNA or neurological functioning apart from the very early electroencephalogram (EEG). From the little information available, it would appear that no one in her immediate or extended family has any sort of genetic disorder, although Geschwind (2008) points out that most mutations known to cause autism are *de novo* mutations, occurring spontaneously.

Neurological explanations

It is highly likely that Nadia has structural and functional brain abnormalities. Research into cognitive models of ASD parallel those of neurological research and increasingly employ similar metaphors so that notions about local and global processing mirror those of abnormalities in connectivity, frontal lobe dysfunctions, abnormal migration of cells and compensatory brain plasticity. Overconnectivity in areas of the brain, allied to failures in apoptosis, offers a possible explanation for savant syndrome as it could account for intense activity in the neural networks of the brain at a local level and failures with integration at a global level (Cohen, 2007).

Since the original study of Nadia huge strides have been made in our understanding of underlying brain mechanisms involved in cognition. This has resulted from advances in brain imaging (magnetic resonance imaging [MRI], positron emission tomography [PET]). Neurological findings in relation to autism have been described in Chapter 4 and those related to savant syndrome in Chapter 6. These findings can be combined and summarised as follows.

- It is now generally accepted that the brain shows specific areas related to certain activities and there are functions that appear to be lateralised. Imaging techniques have confirmed that the left hemisphere is implicated in the use of language, mathematical computation and orderly, conceptual analysis. The right hemisphere is generally involved in tasks involving spatial relationships (Gazzaniga et al., 2002; Ozonoff & Miller, 1996).
- Research on neurological functioning in savants has been much more limited but has also tended to support Treffert's original assumptions (1989) on left hemisphere damage and right cerebral dominance in savant subjects.
- Differences in overall brain volume between some children with ASD and matched controls, and a particular abnormality with the amygdala have been identified (Sparks, Friedman, Shaw, Aylward, Echelard, Artru, et al., 2002).
- Further studies using MRI and autopsy data have confirmed that a proportion of people with ASD have larger brains with a thicker cortex than usual. This has led to the speculation that in such brains there has been limited brain

pruning, a process whereby the brain appears to reorganise circuitry (Boylan et al., 2007).

- It has been hypothesised that people with ASD have a developmental bias towards the proliferation of short-range circuitry over long-range connectivity (Belmonte et al., 2004). This may result in the overconnectivity of neural networks in specific areas that might account for local processing advantage and difficulties with global processing.

The savant may develop unusual and idiosyncratic neuronal circuitry (Wallace et al., 2009). This may be a compensatory alternative to typical brain function. In his latest work, Treffert (2009) retains the notion of lateralised functions in the brain but also draws upon the concept of brain plasticity. The idea of 'paradoxical functional facilitation', whereby one neurological area takes over the functions of a damaged area, is fundamental to his explanation of savant ability. It is likely that structural abnormalities coupled with idiosyncratic brain circuitry, produce the cluster of symptoms and skills found in the prodigious savant (Frith & Frith, 2003; Wallace et al., 2009).

In the original study of Nadia I reported on an EEG examination conducted when she was 5 years old that had shown abnormal electrical activity in her right hemisphere. Although she is left handed, many studies (e.g., Knect, Drager, Deppe, Bobe, Lohmann, Flöel, et al., 2000; Pujol, Deus, Losill, & Capdevila, 1999), have established that the majority of people who are left handed have language functions lateralised in the left hemisphere, along with almost all people who are right handed. I concluded that the discovery of abnormal activity and supposed damage to the right hemisphere was confusing and did not accord with predictions that damage would be mainly localised to the left hemisphere since Nadia had impaired language abilities.

Unfortunately, Nadia has not had any further neurological investigations. It would not be ethical to subject her to intrusive examinations and she would not be able to cooperate with normal brain scans. However, it is now evident that the right side of her body is less developed than the left side suggesting that the left hemisphere is not as efficiently developed as the right. This ties in with her left-handedness although her brother is also left handed so this might be genetic rather than resulting from damage centred in the left hemisphere. There is then, some tentative new evidence that supports the left hemisphere damage hypothesis; although, Belmonte et al. (2004) have described research into ASD as a fragmented tapestry, and nowhere is this more evident than in neurological studies.

Brain dysfunction and privileged access to lower level processing

The work of Snyder (2009) and Patterson and Erzinclioglu (2008) investigating the effects of brain dysfunction on drawing skills, have also produced helpful insights into Nadia's unique talent. The circuitry of the brain is not fully understood, but the fact that similar artistic skills have suddenly emerged and subsequently faded in patients suffering brain degeneration, is of relevance to her case.

Miller et al. (1998), studied a group of patients with frontotemporal dementia who, as their disease progressed, went through a short period when artistic abilities appeared to flower in the absence of previous interest or talent. Miller suggested that the loss of function in the left anterior temporal lobe had brought about a paradoxical effect, actually facilitating artistic skills. Snyder (2009) reviewed this research and speculated that savant skills may be latent in everybody but were usually unavailable because of top–down inhibition. By this he means that normally functioning individuals cannot do other than impose structure on presented material, and this is the work of the intact brain. Savants, he claims, do not automatically impose interpretation on new information and they have privileged access to lower level, less processed information.

These findings provided some weak evidence for the hypothesis that a lack of conceptualisation and neurological dysfunction may actually have facilitated visually realistic drawing in some patients. This hypothesis is attractive especially because Nadia's exceptional ability evaporated as she acquired some language skills and her conceptual abilities improved. Both Mottron et al. (2009) and Snyder (2009) assume that there are unconscious processes going on in the brain that normally cannot be readily accessed. Snyder conceptualises savant skills in terms of the savant having 'privileged access to lower level less processed information' (p. 1399) and Mottron refers to 'decoding systems' along with the notion of a superior ability to detect patterns and similarities. This is reminiscent, too, of Baron-Cohen's (Baron-Cohen, 2003a; Baron-Cohen et al., 2009) theory regarding hypersystemising and the hypothesised savant ability to find underlying structure in aspects of their experience. Nonetheless, the problem of elucidating the underlying mechanisms precisely and defining exactly what might constitute 'privileged access' or 'lower level, less processed information' remain.

Executive functioning

The concept of executive dysfunction is a difficult one in relation to people with severe and global learning difficulties and ASD. Executive functions are those involved in non-routine behaviours when reflection, adaptation, flexibility, planning and making a considered choice are required. In ASD there are supposed specific weaknesses in these top–down processes and with what could be regarded as 'intelligent behaviour'. In attempting any assessments with Nadia it is self-evident that she has profound difficulties in all the areas relating to executive functions and her sole strength was her spectacular drawing ability. Neurological models allied to executive functioning offer interesting insights but, again, neurological assessment of Nadia is not possible.

Weak central coherence theory

Weak central coherence theory is valuable in broadening an understanding of Nadia's drawing ability (Frith, 1989; Happé & Frith, 2006, 2009). The theory could help to explain why Nadia drew in the way she did, focusing on aspects of the original pictures she had seen, excluding most of the context and becoming absorbed by the details that fascinated her. Weak central coherence theory explains how people with autism have difficulty coordinating and integrating information in order to construct higher-level meaning in context. As originally investigated, it was proposed that people with ASD have difficulty in comprehending the global picture but appear to have an advantage over normal matched subjects in apprehending detail. This was demonstrable in various modalities. More recently weak central coherence theory has been used to explain savant skills and particularly savants with outstanding drawing skills (Mottron et al., 2006, 2009). Happé and Vital (2009) suggest that in drawing realistically the ability to notice and focus on detail probably aids production.

The local proximity approach to drawing individual objects described by Mottron and Belleville (1993), in the case of a subject known as E.C., is a close description of Nadia's drawing strategy. Certainly in her drawing she focused on detail, building the picture by adding contiguous elements or by using construction by local progression. Her approach to block design and other jigsaw type tasks when she was young was methodical and she matched individual elements to the global picture rather than assembling sections and bringing them together, indicating a preference for segmentation over a global approach (Selfe, 1983). In other respects a local processing bias was not evident nor could it be assessed because of her severe global delay and lack of cooperation. One of the problems with all research into ASD is that so much of it is conducted with children who are essentially atypical. They are frequently selected because they are cooperative, verbal, and more intelligent than the more typical child with ASD who is uncooperative and has poor language skills. Fombonne (2003) reports that 70% of children with ASD have a substantial learning difficulty (IQ below 70), but frequently studies exclude children with low ability.

Enhanced perceptual processing and pattern detection

Mottron et al. (2003, 2006) have hypothesised that autistic savants possess enhanced perceptual processing in specific circumstances. Savants are considered to have the ability to retain patterns and discover and apply rules and regularities in the world they observe (Mottron et al., 2009). Calendar calculators, for example, must process repeated patterns of dates and days of the week, in the same way musical savants have absorbed repeating patterns and regularities based on the scale and in chord sequences. In artistic talent, the savant is assumed to have applied the rules and regularities of linear perspective. Savant mathematical calculators discover the patterns ruling prime numbers or square roots (Mottron et al., 2009). Other examples are given from language and hyperlexia. All of this presents a compelling explanation of savant skills. Mottron et al.'s (2009) suggestions possess parallels with Baron-Cohen's (Baron-Cohen, 2003a, 2006; Baron-Cohen et al., 2009) hyper-systemising theory. Both theories propose that the savant is engaged in detecting and replicating the rules and regularities that occur in aspects of human experience that are not random. But the question inevitably arises, why these very specific and limited patterns and regularities? Also the rules and regularities of prime numbers and calendar calculation are highly complex and represent some very abstruse calculations. The calendar structure repeats every 28 and 400 years. This is not something that is easily evident especially to someone who cannot count change in money or tell the time.

Nadia was able to use linear perspective in her early drawings. Could she have an unconscious understanding of projection systems at the age of 3? She certainly was able to use foreshortening and hidden line elimination. She could rotate images while preserving aspects of their volumetric properties. But all of this seemed to be unconscious and effortless. She did not appear to be applying rules of perspective, measuring with her pencil and aligning and adjusting objects, as would an artist consciously aiming for linear perspective.

Hyper-systemising and hyper-attention to detail

Baron-Cohen (Baron-Cohen, 2003a, 2006; Baron-Cohen et al., 2009) have argued that people with ASD have a way of perceiving, analysing and remembering information that he refers to as hypersystemising. Systemising is the process of recognising underlying logical structures and repeating pattern or events such as occur in engineering, mathematics, and music. Baron-Cohen suggests that people with autism have a special sensitivity to systemising that results in their insistence on rules and routines at one level and can also help to explain the prevalence of savant skills. The local processing bias provides an example of the autistic person's systemising ability. Attention to detail suggests a concentration on constituent parts and their underlying regularities rather than on the whole picture.

Baron-Cohen's theory is a compelling one and it makes a great deal of sense in considering the various manifestations of autistic behaviour in a person like Nadia. It explains why structure, repetition, and routines are so important and usually form the basis of intervention programmes such as TEACCH (Treatment and Education of Autistic and Related Communication Handicapped Children) developed by Schopler and colleagues (Mesibov, Shea, & Schopler, 2004). It also helps to explain some of the odd, obsessive preoccupations found in autism, such as neatly arranged collections of stones or engine parts, fascination with bus timetables, schedules and technical manuals. It also fits in with the routine of Nadia's life and her insistence on those routines.

However, there is a difficulty in understanding what is actually being claimed. For example, why do we see the same peculiar and circumscribed skills in savants? The list is actually rather limited given all the possibilities for systemising. The artist savant has a limited repertoire of drawing subjects. The skills represent islets of ability but why are they the same islets arising in children who know nothing about one another? Linear perspective architectural drawing in autistic savants crops up all over the world. There are calendar calculators in Australia, USA and China. But if Baron-Cohen is right and these people have learned the relationship between time and days and the calendar as a system, why are there no savants discovering other instances of regularity and repetition in nature such as the pattern of the tides, phases of the moon, and all the natural and man-made phenomena showing regularity? Nadia may have a systemising brain but the idea that she has 'discovered' the logic and regularities of linear perspective at such a young age, at any level, conscious or unconscious, seems very difficult to sustain in the face of her severe cognitive deficits.

Other useful explanatory theories

Rimland (1978) suggested that autistic children have a pathological inability to broaden their attention and relates this to the intense narrow concentration presumed to be necessary to develop savant skills (Treffert, 1989, 2009). This theory also has parallels with that proposed by Ramachandran (2004), who linked brain damage to isolated residual functioning and suggested that Nadia's brain effectively allocated all her attentional resources to the one functioning module. He concluded that Nadia has an isolated 'hyperfunctioning art module' in her brain.

Howe suggests that 'The developing ego of a young child may be threatened by certain reactions of other people to the extent that the child is pressed towards repetitive or stereotypes patterns of behaviour' (Howe, 1989, p. 59). The suggestion is that this may induce the patterns of inward concentration that promotes further attitudes of isolation. It is concluded that there are circumstances in which being intellectually impaired can provide advantages for the person in allowing them to concentrate on very narrow and specific behaviour.

Some new theories are not particularly relevant to Nadia but hold out interesting insights and possibilities to our general understanding of ASD. Tantam (2009) draws attention to difficulties with body language and non-verbal communication as important but neglected aspects of autism. His theory of 'the interbrain' is relevant to an understanding of Nadia's difficulties with social communication but it is difficult to relate this to her drawing ability.

Nadia and modern theories of graphic representation

Nadia breaks the well-established norms for the evolution of symbolic or canonical representation during early development, especially in relation to her severe intellectual impairments. But we now have a better understanding of the processes underlying graphic representation. The theoretical models suggested by Gibson (1979) and Marr (1982) point us to the possibility of view-centred depictions as well as object-centred depiction. Nadia's early drawing was view-centred or, put very simply, Nadia drew what she saw. But what she drew in the main were her representations of flat two-dimensional pictures. Due to her extremely limited cognitive development she was possibly unable to store internal representations of objects and their invariant structures. In her infancy she may have lived in a world of transitory visual impressions. However, she was able to recall and then record flashes of this experience. My early experiments with Nadia remain relevant

Figure 8.1
Nadia's drawing of a horse when she was aged 22.

Figure 8.2
Nadia's drawing of a galloping
horse when she was aged about 5.

(Selfe, 1983). Nadia could match objects as shapes and outlines even when black silhouettes of objects were presented but she could not match objects as representatives of different categories. Could it be said that she could not extract information about their invariant structure? This notion could also account for the waning of her talent. The drawings done in adolescence were increasingly those typical of early childhood. Canonical forms of gardens, people and flowers and even horses started to appear. Perhaps this was not because she was copying what she had seen other children doing but because, at last, she was representing invariant structure and was able to form internal representations of objects of her experience (see Figures 8.1 and 8.2). If so, is the second horse really the more elaborate and mature creation?

Recent experimentation on graphic skills in children with ASD has been undertaken (Sheppard et al., 2007, 2008). Individuals with ASD are less influenced by the conceptual properties of objects and more influenced by visual appearance. This bears on the hypothesis that Nadia's lack of conceptual ability is related to her early drawing skill.

Towards a revised theory

Deficits in abstract thought and conceptualisation

My original explanation for Nadia's prodigious ability and her subsequent loss of it was in terms of her extremely restricted cognitive development as evidenced by her lack of expressive or receptive language (Selfe, 1977, 1983, 1995). Testing showed that Nadia had profound difficulties not only with verbal expression but also with comprehension. But as her language abilities started to improve, so her drawing skills waned. I linked these two events and pointed out that canonical drawing, like verbal processes, was essentially a symbolic activity. Theories of representational drawing in young children had demonstrated that normally functioning children were concerned to set down the invariant structure of an object or, in Freeman's terms the canonical representation, rather than one fixed viewpoint. These canons or invariant structures represented the key features of the object. They were symbols that stood for the welter of experiences of that object. As Nadia's ability to make internal symbolic representations appeared to improve, her ability to draw a single fixed viewpoint waned. I argued that maturing ways of thinking and conceptualising may have 'swallowed up' this earlier ability to see the world without any symbolic interpretation.

Several authors have propounded theories of deficits in conceptualisation in savant syndrome since then (Arnheim, 1980; Hermelin, 2001; Howe, 1989). Howe (1989) suggests that Nadia's drawing skill may have been a result of her failure to have any understanding of the meaning of the objects she drew. In many respects these theories also tie in with the executive dysfunction theory of autism (Frith, 1991; Hill, 2004) as discussed in Chapter 4. Executive dysfunction theory points to deficits in autistic children in planning, sequencing, flexibility, and intelligent comprehension and action. Very broadly, executive functioning relates to aspects of intelligence such as the ability to categorise and form concepts.

Theories of deficits in forming internal symbolic representations have suggested the following:

- Drawing in typically developing children is dominated by their need to set down their conceptual understanding of an object (Harris, 1963). It is also referred to as intellectual realism (Luquet, 1927/2001); canonical representation (Freeman et al., 1977); the search for equivalents (Arnheim, 1980; Golomb, 1992); invariant structures (Gibson, 1979) or object centred depiction (Willats, 1987, after Marr, 1982).
- In typically developing children the production of a characterising or meaningful symbolic representation appears to be more important than attention to idiosyncratic detail or to a single viewpoint representation of an object.
- Artistic savants are more concerned or better able to record a single fixed view of static spatial configurations.
- Artistic savants represent aspects of their perception such as lines, edges and contours, which are non-symbolic aspects of visual experience, and this can be linked to deficits in conceptual ability.
- Visually realistic drawing in young savant subjects is thereby seen as a symptom of underlying pathology taken in conjunction with other deficits in functioning.
- In drawing, autistic savants represent objects as patterns, lines and shapes rather than as representatives of classes or categories of objects.

This theory of deficits in the ability to form symbolic representations or concepts can be criticised on several levels. On the one hand some commentators have objected to what they see as a narrow, reductionist, psychological interpretation.

Dennis (1978) commented that there was a failure to see Nadia as an artist and any explanation in terms of cognitive deficits was parsimonious and limited. On the other, judged by some psychologists and psychiatrists, the explanation is seen as partial and inconclusive. Treffert (1989, 2009) suggests that the theory of severe limitations in conceptualisation can only be a partial explanation and does not apply to other savant skills. Most savants do have spoken language even if their ability to converse is limited. They are able to form internal representations and categorise, at least as evidenced by their language abilities. Savant children with outstanding musical skills range in intelligence and calendar calculators must be able to make internal representations of calendars involving complex notions of time and number. The notion that they have such limited conceptual abilities, which permits them access to lower level perceptual functions, appears more difficult to sustain.

Language has been described as being 'omnipresent in human conceptual behaviour' (Patterson & Erzinclioglu, 2008, p. 283). Another obvious difficulty with the theory is that other children with no communicative language, severe learning difficulties and restricted conceptual abilities do not draw and do not show any special graphic skill in fact quite the reverse; they usually draw at their mental age level. Moreover, psychometric tests have been developed based solely on the fact that graphic depiction is normally a very reliable indicator and measure of intelligence or cognitive maturity.

Similarly, if severe specific language impairment led to compensatory enhanced perceptual skills one might expect all children with such deficits to show some ability with visual perceptual tasks and with jigsaw puzzles or construction tasks. It is clear that they do not. Similarly children with profound hearing loss and severe language delay are not especially gifted at perceptual skills or at drawing.

Nadia's skill has waned and completely disappeared. If she can be persuaded to draw at all, she now draws in line with her learning difficulties and her mental age. The conceptualisation hypothesis continues to have some merits especially in the light of new research on perceptual processes in autistic children. Moreover, non-autistic, typically developing children can be promoted to draw more realistically when they believe they are copying patterns (Sheppard et al., 2008) i.e., when objects are de-objectified.

Children able to produce outstanding realism in their early drawing in association with severe learning difficulties share many features in common apart from their savant skill. They all have learning difficulties and almost all meet criteria for an ASD diagnosis. Nadia and other autistic savants with extraordinary drawing ability share a particular unusual cognitive abilities profile. In this respect they are unlike many other children with global retardation whose IQ profile is uniformly low. The autistic savants I studied had very uneven IQ profiles with profound deficits with verbal abilities coexisting with islets of ability relating to visual and perceptual organisation and analysis, as well as visual memory. It may be that the limited conceptualisation hypothesis applies only to the situation where language and verbal conceptual development is severely restricted, but visual/motor development is not. This would be in line with Treffert's (1989) conjecture that savants have left hemisphere dysfunction and intact right hemisphere functions and also with Mottron et al.'s (2003, 2006) notion of enhanced perception in specific areas (e.g. block design). In conclusion, it would be safe to speculate that although the limited conceptualisation explanation requires a great deal more refinement and examination, it still has some buoyancy. Moreover, it finds support from both neurological studies and from other major theories of perception. Perhaps its greatest strength is that the theory links the extraordinary achievements with the undeniable deficits.

Deficits in perceptual development

Willats (2005) outlines the theory of David Marr (1982) that postulates that there are two allied mechanisms in visual perception. There are viewer centred percepts of ever changing visual sensations where spatial relations are defined relative to the viewer (viewer specific descriptions). There is also perception supposedly comprising an internal working representation of an object that is slowly elaborated through experiences of that object (object centred descriptions). So that, for example, one perceives through many exposures that a square box has four sides; a top and a bottom that consist of rectangular shapes, right angles and dimensions of equal length as well as learning the functions of such an object. According to Willats, when children are asked to draw an object on a piece of paper (two-dimensional surface) they draw their perceptual knowledge not from view specific images but from object specific internal representations. The depiction of depth relationships becomes highly problematic for the child under 7 because such depictions often contradict what the child knows from his object centred percepts. For example, lamp posts in a street appear to diminish in size with distance from the viewer, although they are the same size and houses do not have sides that look like trapeziums or parallelograms. However, in depicting depth, these kinds of distortions are precisely what are required.

Phillips et al. (1978) and Sheppard et al. (2008) have shown that children are more accurate in their depictions when depth cues are removed and they believe they are copying flat patterns rather than three-dimensional objects (see Lange-Küttner & Vitner, 2008, for a number of related papers on this issue). Doherty, Campbell, Tsuji, and Phillips (2010) have shown that young children are less susceptible to visual illusions (they used a version of the Titchener circles, see Figure 4.1). They suggest that this is because older children have more exposure to pictures and observing architecture, which causes them and adults to impose depth cues on visually presented materials such as the Titchener circles.

Happé and Frith (1996) had demonstrated the same for children with ASD. They found that autistic children were less susceptible to visual illusions. There is ample evidence, too, of ASD children's preference for local specific processing over global processing (Frith, 1989; Happé & Frith, 2006). Mottron et al. (2009) have investigated the notion that those with ASD do not integrate visuoperceptual information efficiently into coherent percepts, characterised by a predominantly local approach to visual processing to the detriment of holistic information analysis. Mottron et al. (2006) suggest that some specific abilities in autistic children to see embedded figures and do block design tasks amounts to 'enhanced perception' (Mottron et al., 2006, p. 27). Mottron is correct in pointing out that perception may be radically different especially in an autistic child like Nadia, but perception is only enhanced in as much as it is less trammelled by the processes that include the integration of previous percepts. This is why individual pieces can be aligned and matched in block design tasks without interference from the whole context or the overall pattern. But, it is object centred perception that allows for intelligent action. Nadia had an enhanced ability to do block design and jigsaw puzzles but had a reduced ability to understand the whole context and act meaningfully upon the world. Nadia has severe learning difficulties and it is possible that these problems with extracting information from the visual world and integrating that information to form percepts that is at the root of her learning difficulties.

Marr's (1982) theories lead to the view that for Nadia, perceptions of the world and of pictures were not integrated so that the object centred functions involved in perception may have been severely limited. Drawings of horses or of cockerels may have been remembered in their detail but little was extracted from the original pictorial information presented to add to an internal representation and hypothesis about horses or cockerels. The images she looked at were two-dimensional and little may have been deduced about three-dimensionality. She may have lived in a world where pictures of horses were not integrated into one internal representation of a horse. The images she saw were flat and her own image as a memory may have been similarly two dimensional. Problems of representing depth simply did not exist. It was only very much later when an ability, in Marr's terms, to build an internal representation of an object as a percept developed that access to the raw unprocessed image started to wane while her internal representation became much more the canonical form seen in early depiction in children.

This explanation would also apply to the architectural drawings preferred by so many artistic savants, such as Stephen Wiltshire. Perception is much more photographic where the world is perceived as a series of disparate, flat snap shots rather than being dominated by the internal representation of an object and all its relationships, in terms of volume, size, dimensions, angularity, etc. Perception is camera-like rather than computer-like. The central difference relates to Marr's notion of view centred and object centred representation of visual perception.

These notions also give us insights into the world of the infant with ASD. It could be that young children with autism, and especially the autistic artist savants, live in a highly confusing world like that of Alice in Wonderland. For them, everyday objects are not instantly recognised when presented closer or further way or at new angles because the brain's function of integrating images into working hypotheses or percepts about objects is severely impaired. Day-to-day objects are not recognised; changes in light and orientation confuse and this confusion may account for the withdrawal from social interactions and the insistence on repetition and routine and the very high levels of anxiety seen in very young autistic children. Their world is unpredictable because the mechanisms of perception and conceptualisation are severely impaired. The world for such children is truly a 'blooming, buzzing confusion' (James, 1890/1983, p. 488).

More questions than answers?

More than 30 years have passed since Nadia's work was brought to the attention of the academic world. Yet as Pring (2008) notes, 'The visual knowledge and understanding that must underlie the ability to portray linear perspective, to take account of size constancy and to use perspective knowledge and achieve rotational transformations, as Nadia did, are not well understood' (p. 222).

The temptations to build theories is very strong. The speculations in the last sections may be interesting but there are undeniable flaws, the principal one being that if Nadia did not have internal object centred representations, how was she able to rotate images and demonstrate their volumetric properties? It is still the case that as yet there is no comprehensive explanation for the exceptional ability she showed as an infant and its subsequent loss.

All the theories discussed above are helpful and illuminating but one is left with a large number of unanswered questions of a more general nature. Why do savants, including Nadia, show such a small and highly specialised number of skills; in particular, calendar calculation, linear perspective drawing, an ability to play the piano by ear, and circumscribed computational abilities? Although amazing and curious, these skills are very narrow and specific. The calendar calculator often cannot tell the time or do simple computations. Musical savants almost invariably play the piano and very few cases of the syndrome involving other instruments are recorded. Why not a much wider range of skills relating to the more regular patterns that exist in nature such as the laws that govern the tides; or weather or the seasons? Why are there no savants able to show skills related to height, distance, speed, or decibels, or provide calculations on the mathematics governing algebra or geometry?

Moreover, the savant skills displayed are all rather special and puzzling examples of the patterns that govern phenomena. Calendars are not obviously regular due to variations in the number of days in each month and leap years. Similarly, conventional Western musical notation is not entirely regular with equal intervals between notes unless the notation used is the chromatic scale. Prime numbers do not occur in a regular sequence and there is no known formula that will yield all the prime numbers. The rules of linear perspective as a projection system were invented in the Renaissance and were based on Euclidean geometry. The laws were only demonstrable in a man-made world of buildings and roads. It could be argued that savant skill areas are not so much about discerning patterns and regularities in phenomena as about reconciling irregularities and glitches in patterns and applying the highly complex rules that can be extracted.

Is there something like conscious thought behind the production of the savant skill or does it arise unbidden and in an unconscious way? Do savants understand what they are doing but do not have the words to express it? Did Nadia consciously apply rules of linear perspective? Do calendar calculators perform calculations or visualise calendars in their heads? Musical savants very rarely read music. Do they play by ear and have they memorised whole pieces of music? Could they hum what they are going to play?

Theories about underlying logical structures and privileged access invoke notions of human consciousness as a submerged iceberg with only part available to the conscious mind. How is the submerged knowledge of the assumed underlying system coded, in words or images or symbols? Or, like the homing pigeon that has no understanding of its extraordinary feat, can savants 'just do it'? Is it an epiphenomenona, a curious residue from underlying pathology, or some sort of special access to the deep structures of the human brain that are pre-wired into the system?

Most savants do not have the language skills to describe how they achieve their amazing skill and those who do describe huge feats of memory usually do so in terms of imagery. Tammet (2006), a savant with multiple talents, states that he perceives numbers as images and colours. A talented artist, with mild Asperger's syndrome, described to me how he looks at scenes by standing still on one spot and when he comes to draw them the view is there in his mind's eye and he can just set it down on the blank canvas with no thought and certainly no conscious application of the principles of linear perspective.

Final words: why did Nadia's skills wane?

One of the fundamental questions in developmental psychology is whether the course of learning in infants is best understood as a continuous process or whether there are sharp discontinuities or stages in development. Stages in development are distinguished by qualitative as well as quantitative changes in learning skills (McDevitt & Ormrod, 2010). An example of this is the fundamental change in locomotion from crawling to walking; the abrupt and dramatic change from single word utterances to two-word sentences and generative grammar in language acquisition. Transition from one stage to another is marked by simultaneous changes in a number of other aspects of the child's behaviour. The ability to walk brings about a change in exploratory activity and generative grammar heralds the beginnings of symbolic play (McDevitt & Ormrod, 2010). It has also been noted that stage transitions are typically rapid. Such rapidity in the reorganisation of skills can be observed in skill acquisition in many human activities such as riding a bike. Van Geert (1998) produced a mathematical model that would explain how small-scale, quantitative changes could accumulate and lead to a qualitative change in learning. He used non-linear dynamics to explain how change could suddenly occur after passing a fluctuating marginal state between old learning and new forms of behaviour.

Computational models of cognition and information processing can be simulated on a computer, where input and output nodes are assumed to be highly interconnected and where there is parallel processing (Rumelhart & McClelland, 1986). Learning in a connectionist network is assumed to take place by altering the strength of connections between these nodes. Connectionist models can be used to simulate the progress of learning in infants such as in vocabulary acquisition, and such models have been found to be robust and to have predictive value (Elman, Karmiloff-Smith, Bates, Johnson, Parisi, & Plunkett, 1996; Elman, 2005). Connectionist models can also be used to illuminate the processes involving substantial and rapid changes. These are not just incremental changes in development but changes that involve transitions from one stage to another, and processes whereby learning appears to decay because of the incorporation of more efficient algorithms (Elman, 2005).

Neurologists (Cohen, 2007) have produced connectionist and computational models to understand the neurological abnormalities in ASD. They have shown that appropriate knowledge of the world exists in the brains of people with ASD but this is blocked by the presence of irrelevant connections related to overconnectivity and apoptosis, this being the natural process of neuronal pruning or die-back that appears to be disrupted in the brains of some autistic subjects (Sparks et al., 2002). Patterns of firing across synaptic connections between nerve cells in

Figure 8.3 Nadia, aged 42, with the author at their meeting in Nottingham in 2009. Photograph by Andy Beech.

the brain are known to strengthen or weaken their linkages and this leads to lasting changes in neuronal structures within the cortex. Changes in connectivity and brain structure occur throughout infancy and especially in adolescence. To quote Cohen (2007), 'Modelling exercises suggest that autism may be one of many social and language learning problems that can emerge from changes in the mechanisms responsible for development and pruning of connections in the brain' (p. 259).

Mathematical models are useful in explaining discontinuities and changes. These changes occur when the child moves from one task, which they master, to another. Schemas emerge and it would appear that once acquired, there is no going back, connections have been made and radical reorganisation has taken place. These models can possibly shed some light on Nadia's waning skill. The fact that there was a period when she was drawing both canonical and visually realistic drawings is suggestive of the fluctuating marginal state before her brain opted for the object centred depictions preferred by typically developing children. Her old skills were no longer available to her. Then during late adolescence her interest in drawing simply petered out. It seems that Nadia (Figure 8.3) remains an enigma and the words of Paine (1981, p. 5) remain relevant:

Many marvelled at the extraordinary facility shown in this child's drawings ... they defy analysis by any of the customary methods. At an age when Lautrec was still drawing horses in a fairly simplistic way, Nadia created images ... using many of the learned techniques of the sophisticated artist ... She is the person who most challenges all our comfortable assumptions about drawing.

References

Abell, F., Happé, F., & Frith, U. (2000). Do triangles play tricks? Attribution of mental states to animated shapes in normal and abnormal development. *Journal of Cognitive Development, 15*, 1–20.

Albright, D. (2004). *Modernism and music*. Chicago, IL: University of Chicago Press.

Allik, J., & Laak, T. (1985). The head is smaller than the body; but how does it join on? In N. Freeman & M. Cox (Eds.), *Visual order*. Cambridge: Cambridge University Press.

American Psychiatric Association. (1980). *Diagnostic and statistical manual of mental disorders* (3rd ed.). Washington, D.C.: American Psychiatric Association.

American Psychiatric Association. (1994). *Diagnostic and statistical manual of mental disorders* (4th ed.). Washington, D.C.: American Psychiatric Association.

Amir, N., Stafford J., Freshman, M., & Foa, A. B. (1998). Relationship between trauma narratives and trauma pathology. *Journal of Traumatic Stress, 11*, 385–392.

Anderson, J. R. (1990). *The adaptive character of thought*. Hillsdale, NJ: Lawrence Erlbaum Associates, Inc.

Anon. (1828, September 27). The cat Raphael: Gottfried Mind. *The Mirror of Literature, Amusement, and Instruction, xii (333)*, 200–202. Retrieved December 4, 2010, from http://www.gutenberg.org/files/15087/15087-h/15087-h.htm

Anon. (1874, March 15). Sir Edwin Landseer's early work. Retrieved November 9, 2010, from http://query.nytimes.com/gst/abstract.html?res=9D04EEDD1039EF34BC4D52D FB566838F669FDE

Anon. (2009, September). Scientists throw fresh light on autism. *Aberdeen University Magazine*, p. 63.

Aram, D., & Healy, J. (1988). Hyperlexia – a review of extraordinary word reading without meaning. *Journal of Child Psychology and Psychiatry, 13*, 267–278.

Arnheim, R. (1956). *Art and visual perception: A psychology of the creative eye*. London: Faber & Faber.

Arnheim, R. (1970). *Visual thinking*. London: Faber & Faber.

Arnheim, R. (1974). *Art and visual perception: A psychology of the creative eye. The new version*. Los Angeles, CA: University of California Press.

Arnheim, R. (1980). The puzzle of Nadia's drawings. *The Arts in Psychotherapy, 7*, 79–85.

Asperger, H. (1944). Die 'autistischen psychopathen' im kindesalter [Autistic psychopathology in childhood]. *Archiv für Psychiatrie und Nervenkrankheiten, 117*, 76–136.

Atkinson, R., & Shiffrin, R. (1968). Human memory: A proposed system and its control processes. In K. Spence & J. Spence (Eds.) *The psychology of learning and motivation* (Vol. 2, pp. 89–195). New York: Academic Press.

Baddeley, A. D. (1986). *Working memory*. Oxford: Clarendon Press.

Baddeley, A. (2004). *Working memory, thought and action*. Oxford: Oxford University Press.

Baddeley, A., & Hitch, G. (1974). Working memory. In G. Bower (Ed.), *The psychology of learning and motivation: Advances in research and theory* (Vol. 8, pp. 47–89). New York: Academic Press.

Baird, G., Simonoff, E., Pickles, A., Loucas, T., Meldrum, D., & Charman, D. (2006). Prevalence of disorders of the autistic spectrum in a population cohort of children in South Thames. *The Lancet, 368*, 210–215.

Barkham, P. (2009, December 29). The boy who paints like an Old Master. *The Guardian*. Retrieved November 29, 2010, from http://www.guardian.co.uk/lifeandstyle/2009/dec/29/boy-paints-like-old-master

Baron-Cohen, S. (2003a). *The essential difference: The truth about the male and female brain*. New York: Basic Books.

Baron-Cohen, S. (2003b, April 17). They just can't help it. *The Guardian*. Retrieved December 4, 2010, from http://www.guardian.co.uk/education/2003/apr/17/research.highereducation

Baron-Cohen, S. (2006). The hyper-systemising assortative mating theory of autism. *Progress in Neuro Psychopharmacology and Biological Psychiatry, 30*, 865–872.

Baron-Cohen, S., Ashwin, E., Ashwin, C., Tavassoli, T., & Chakrabarti, B. (2009). Talent in autism: Hyper-systemizing, hyper-attention to detail and sensory hypersensitivity. *Philosphical Transactions of the Royal Society of London, Series B, 364*, 1377–1383.

Baron-Cohen, S., Leslie, A., & Frith, U. (1985). Does the autistic child have a 'theory of mind'? *Cognition, 21*, 37–46.

Baudelaire, C. (1955). *The mirror of art*. London: Phaidon Press. (Original work published 1846.)

Belmonte, M., Allen, G., Beckel-Mitchener, A., Boulanger, L., Carper, R., & Webb, S. (2004). Autism and abnormal development of brain connectivity. *Journal of Neuroscience, 24*, 9228–9231.

Bennett, H. (1983). Remembering drinks orders: The memory skills of cocktail waitresses. *Human Learning: Journal of Practical Research and Application, 2*, 157–170.

Biro, S., & Leslie, A. (2007). Infant's perception of goal directed actions: Development through cue based boot-strapping. *Developmental Science, 10*, 379–398.

Boyatzis, C. J., Michaelson, P., & Lyle, E. (1995). Symbolic immunity and flexibility in preschoolers' human figure drawings. *Journal of Genetic Psychology, 156*(3), 293–302.

Boylan, C., Blue, M., & Hohmann, C. (2007). Modeling early cortical serotonergic deficits in autism. *Behavioural Brain Research, 176*(1), 94–108.

Brill, A. (1949). Some peculiar manifestations of memory with special reference to lightening calculators, *Journal of Nervous and Mental Diseases, 92*, 709–726.

Brink, T. (1980). Idiot savant with unusual mechanical ability: An organic explanation. *American Journal of Psychiatry, 137*, 250–251.

Buhler, K. (1949). *The mental development of the child*. London: Routledge & Kegan Paul. (Original work published 1930.)

Bruner, J., Olver, R., & Greenfield, P. (1966). *Studies in cognitive growth*. New York: John Wiley.

Burgemeister, L., Blum, H., & Lorge, I. (1959). *Columbia mental maturity scale*. New York: Harcourt Brace & Jovanovich.

Burt, C. (1921). *Mental and scholastic tests*. London: R. S. King.

Cain, A. (1969). Special isolated abilities in severely psychotic young children. *Psychiatry*, *32*, 137–147.

Camhi, L. (2006, June 18). When Picasso and Klee were very young. The art of childhood. *New York Times*. Retrieved November 29, 2010, from http://www.nytimes.com/2006/06/18/arts/design/18camhi.html

Casanova, M., & Trippe, J. (2009). Radial cytoarchitecture and patterns of cortical connectivity in autism. *Philosphical Transactions of the Royal Society of London, Series B*, *364*, 1433–1436.

Casanova, M., van Kooten, I., Switala, A., van Engeland, H., Heinsen, H., Steinbusch, H. W., et al. (2006). Minicolumnar abnormalities in autism. *Acta Neuropathologica*, *112*(3), 287–303.

Casson, H. (1987). Introduction. In S. Wiltshire, *Drawings*. London: Dent.

Castelli, F., Frith, C., Happé, F., & Frith, U. (2002). Autism, Asperger syndrome and brain mechanisms for the attribution of mental states to animated shapes. *Brain*, *125*, 1839–1849.

Charman, A., & Baron-Cohen, S. (1993). Drawing development in autism: The intellectual to visual realism shift. *British Journal of Developmental Psychology*, *77*, 171–186.

Charness, N., Clifton, J., & MacDonald, L. (1988). Case study of a musical monosavant: A cognitive-psychological focus. In L. Obler & D. Fein (Eds.), *The exceptional brain*. New York: Guilford Press.

Chase, W., & Ericsson, K. (1981). Skilled memory. In J. Anderson (Ed.), *Cognitive skills and their acquisition*. Hillsdale, NJ: Lawrence Erlbaum Associates, Inc.

Chomsky, N. (1972). *Language and mind*. New York: Harcourt Brace Jovanovich.

Clark, A. (1897). The child's attitude towards perspective problems. *Studies in Education*, *1*, 283–294.

Cohen, I. (2007). A neural network model of autism: Implications for theory and treatment. In D. Mareschal, S. Sirios, G. Westermann, & M. Johnson (Eds.), *Neuroconstructivism*. Oxford: Oxford University Press.

Collingwood, R. (1938). *The principles of art*. Oxford: Oxford University Press.

Coltheart, M. (2006). What has functional neuroimaging told us about the mind (so far)? *Cortex*, *42*, 323–331.

Courchesne, E., & Pierce, K. (2005). Brain growth in autism during a critical time in development: Implications for frontal pyramidal neuron and interneuron development and connectivity. *International Journal of Developmental Neuroscience*, *23*, 153–170.

Cox, M. (1986). Cubes are difficult to draw. *British Journal of Developmental Psychology*, *4*, 341–345.

Cox, M. (2005). *The pictorial world of the child*. Cambridge: Cambridge University Press.

Craik, F., & Tulving, E. (1975). Depth of processing and the retention of words in episodic memory. *Journal of Experimental Psychology*, *104*, 268–294.

Creak, E. (1961). Schizophrenic syndrome in childhood. *Cerebral Palsy Bulletin*, *3*, 501–504.

Davidson, J., & Sloboda, J. (1998). Innate talent: Reality or myth? *Behavioural and Brain Sciences*, *2*, 399–442.

Davies, A. M. (1983). Contextual sensitivity in young children's drawings. *Journal of Experimental Child Psychology*, *35*, 478–486.

Davies, C. (1978). *Brian Hatton – a biography of the artist (1887–1916)*. Suffolk: Terence Dalton.

Dawson, M., Mottron, L., & Gernsbacher, M. (2008). Learning in autism. In J. Byrne & M. Roediger (Eds.), *Learning and memory: A comprehensive reference* (Vol. 2). Oxford: Elsevier.

De Clercq, H. (2003). *Mum, is that a human being or an animal?* Bristol: Lucky Duck Publishing.

Dennis, N. (1978, May). Book review of Selfe, L. 'Nadia.' *New York Review of Books*.

Deutsch, D., Henthorn, T., & Dolson, H. (2004). Speech patterns heard early in life influence later perception of the triton paradox. *Music Perception, 21*, 357–372.

Doherty, M., Campbell, N., Tsuji, H., & Phillips, W. (2010). The Ebbinghaus Illusion deceives adults but not young children. *Developmental Science, 13*, 714–721.

Downes, D. (n.d.) *Biography*. Retrieved November 29, 2010, from http://www. daviddownes.co.uk/biography.html

Draaisma, D. (2009). Stereotypes of autism. *Philosphical Transactions of the Royal Society of London, Series B, 364*, 1475–1480.

Drake, J., & Winner, E. (2009). Precocious realists: Perceptual and cognitive characteristics associated with drawing talent in non-autistic children. *Philosphical Transactions of the Royal Society of London, Series B, 364*, 1449–1458.

Dubery, F., & Willats, J. (1972). *Drawing systems*. London: StudioVista.

Dubery, F., & Willats, J. (1983). *Perspective and other drawing systems*. London: Herbert Press.

Duckett, J. (1977). Adaptive and maladaptive behaviour of idiot savants. *American Journal of Mental Deficiency, 82*, 308–311.

Duncan, J. (2001). *Frontal lobe function and the control of visual attention*. Cambridge, MA: The MIT Press.

Eames, K., & Cox, M. (1994). Visual realism in the drawings of autistic, Downs syndrome and normal children. *British Journal of Developmental Psychology, 12*, 235–239.

Elman, J. (2005). Connectionist models of cognitive development: Where next? *Trends in Cognitive Science, 9(3)*, 111–117.

Elman, J., Karmiloff-Smith, A., Bates, E., Johnson, M., Parisi, D., & Plunkett, K. (1996). *Rethinking innateness*. Cambridge: MIT Press.

Fineberg, J. (1997). *The innocent eye: Children's art and the modern artist*. Princeton, NJ: Princeton University Press.

Fitzgerald, M. (2004). *Autism and creativity*. Hove, UK: Routledge.

Fitzgerald, M. (2005). The genesis of artistic creativity: Asperger's syndrome and the arts. London: Jessica Kingsley.

Fitzpatrick, M. (2009, October 12). Making autism 'normal' won't help my son. *The Times*, p. 24.

Fombonne, E. (2003). Epidemiological surveys of autism and other pervasive developmental disorders: An update. *Journal of Autism and Developmental Disorders, 33*(4), 365–382.

Ford, P. M., & Rees, E. L. (2008). Representational drawing and the transition from intellectual to visual realism in children with autism. *British Journal of Developmental Psychology, 26*, 197–219.

Freeman, N. (1972). Process and product in children's drawing. *Perception, 1*, 123–140.

Freeman, N. (1975). Do children draw men with arms coming out of the head? *Nature, 254*(5499), 416–417.

Freeman, N. (1980). *Strategies of representation in young children: Analysis of spatial skills and drawing processes*. London: Academic Press.

Freeman, N., & Cox, M. (Eds.). (1985). *Visual order, the nature and development of pictorial representation*. Cambridge: Cambridge University Press.

Freeman, N., Eiser, C., & Sayers, J. (1977). Children's strategies in producing three dimensional relationships on a two dimensional surface. *Journal of Experimental Child Psychology, 23*, 305–314.

Freeman, N., & Janikoun, R. (1972). Intellectual realism in children's drawings of a familiar object with distinctive features. *Child Development, 43*, 1116–1121.

Frith, U. (1989). *Autism: Explaining the enigma*. Oxford: Blackwell.

Frith, U. (Ed.). (1991). *Autism and Asperger syndrome*. Cambridge: Cambridge University Press.

Frith, U. (2001). Mind blindness and the brain in autism. *Neuron, 32*, 969–979.

Frith, C. (2003). What do imaging studies tell us about the neural basis of autism? *Autism: neural basis and treatment possibilities. Novartis Foundations Symposium, 251*, 149–176.

Frith, U., & Frith, C. (2003). Development and neurophysiology of mentalising. *Philosphical Transactions of the Royal Society of London, Series B, 358*, 459–473.

Frith, U., & Snowling, M. (1983). Reading for meaning and reading for sound in autistic and dyslexic children. *British Journal of Developmental Psychology, 1*, 329–342.

Frostig, M. (1964). *The Frostig programme for the development of visual perception*. Chicago, IL: Follett.

Fry, R. (1989). *Cezanne. A study of his development*. Chicago, IL: University of Chicago Press.

Gaunt, W. (1942). *The Pre-Raphaelite tragedy*. London: Jonathan Cape.

Gazzaniga, M., Ivry, R., & Mangun, G. (2002). *Cognitive neuroscience* (2nd ed.). New York: Norton and Co.

Geschwind, D. (2008). Autism: many genes, common pathways? *Cell, 135*, 391–395.

Gibson, J. J. (1979). *The ecological approach to visual perception*. Boston, MA: Houghton Mifflin.

Giedd, J. (2004). Structural magnetic resonance imaging of the adolescent brain. *Annals of the New York Academy of Sciences, 1021*, 77–85.

Gilbert, S., & Burgess, P. (2008). Executive function. *Current Biology, 18*, 110–114.

Giray, E., & Barclay, A. (1977). Eidetic imagery: Longitudinal results in brain damaged children. *American Journal of Mental Deficiency, 82*, 311–314.

Goldstein, S., Naglieri, J., & Ozonoff, S. (Eds.). (2009). *Assessment of autism spectrum disorders*. London: Guilford Press.

Golomb, C. (1992). *The child's creation of a pictorial world*. Berkeley, CA: University of California Press.

Golomb, C. (Ed.). (1995). *The development of artistically gifted children*. Hillsdale, NJ: Lawrence Erlbaum Associates, Inc.

Gombrich, E. (1960). *Art and illusion: A study in the psychology of pictorial presentations*. London: Phaidon Press.

Goodenough, F. (1926). *Measurement of intelligence by drawings*. New York: Harcourt, Brace & World.

Goodnow, J. (1977). *Children's drawing*. Cambridge, MA: Harvard University Press.

Gordon, A. (1987). Childhood works of artists. *Israel Museum Journal, 6*, 75–82.

Grandin, T. (2009). How does visual thinking work in the mind of a person with autism? A personal account. *Philosphical Transactions of the Royal Society of London, Series B, 364*, 1437–1442.

Gray, C., & Gummerman, K. (1975). The enigmatic eidetic image a critical examination of methods, data and theories. *Psychological Bulletin, 82*(3), 383–407.

Haber, R. (1969). Eidetic imagery. *Scientific American, 202*, 36–44.

Hacking, I. (2009). Autistic autobiography. *Philosphical Transactions of the Royal Society of London, Series B, 364*, 1467–1473.

Hadjikhani, N., Joseph, R., Manoach, D., Naik, P., Snyder, J., Dominick, K., et al. (2007). Body expressions of emotion do not trigger fear contagion in autism spectrum disorder. *Social, Cognitive and Affective Neuroscience, 4*(1), 70–78.

Happé, F. (1996). Studying weak central coherence at low levels: children with autism do not succumb to visual illusions. *Journal of Child Psychology & Psychiatry, 37*(7), 873–877.

Happé, F. (1997). Central coherence and theory of mind in autism: Reading homographs in context. *British Journal of Developmental Psychology, 15*, 1–12.

Happé, F. (1999). Autism: Cognitive deficit or cognitive style? *Trends in Cognitive Science, 3*, 216–222.

Happé, F., & Booth, R. (2008). The power of the positive: Revisiting weak coherence in autism spectrum disorders. *Quarterly Journal of Experimental Psychology, 61*(1), 50–63.

Happé, F., & Frith, U. (1996). The neuropsychology of autism. *Brain, 119*(4), 1377–1400.

Happé, F., & Frith, U. (2006). The weak coherence account: Detail-focused cognitive style in autism spectrum disorders. *Journal of Autism and Developmental Disorders, 35*(1), 5–25.

Happé, F., & Frith, U. (2009). The beautiful otherness of the autistic mind. *Philosphical Transactions of the Royal Society of London, Series B, 364*, 1345–1351.

Happé, F., & Frith, U. (Eds.). (2010). *Autism and talent*. Oxford: Oxford University Press.

Happé, F., Ronald, A., & Plomin, R. (2006). Time to give up on a single explanation for autism. *Nature and Neuroscience, 9*(10), 1218–1220.

Happé, F., & Vital, P. (2009). What aspects of autism predispose to talent? *Philosphical Transactions of the Royal Society of London, Series B, 364*, 1369–1375.

Harris, D. B. (1963). *Children's drawings as measures of intellectual maturity*. New York: Harcourt Brace & World.

Heaton, P. (2003). Pitch memory, labelling and disembedding in autism. *Journal of Child Psychology and Psychiatry, 44*(4), 543–551.

Heaton, P. (2009). Assessing musical skills in autistic children who are not savants. *Philosphical Transactions of the Royal Society of London, Series B, 364*, 1443–1447.

Heaton, P., & Wallace, G. (2004). Annotation – the savant syndrome. *Journal of Child Psychology and Psychiatry, 45*, 899–911.

Heavey, L. (1997). *Memory in the calendar calculating savant*. Unpublished PhD thesis, University of London, UK.

Heavey, L. (2003). Arithmetical savants. In A. Dowker & A. J. Baroody (Eds.), *The development of arithmetic concepts and skills: Constructing adaptive expertise* (pp. 409–433). Mahwah, NJ: Lawrence Erlbaum Associates, Inc.

Heavey, L., Pring, L., & Hermelin, B. (1999). A date to remember: The nature of memory in savant calendrical calculators. *Psychological Medicine, 29*, 145–160.

Hermelin, B. (2001). *Bright splinters of the mind*. London: Jessica Kingsley.

Hermelin, B., & O'Connor, N. (1964). Effects of sensory input and sensory dominance on severely disturbed, autistic children and on subnormal controls. *British Journal of Psychology, 55*, 201–206.

Hermelin, B., & O'Connor, N. (1970). *Psychological experiments with autistic children*. London: Pergamon.

Hermelin, B., & O'Connor, N. (1986). Idiot savant calendrical calculators: Rules and regularities. *Psychological Medicine, 16*, 885–893.

Hermelin, B., & O'Connor, N, (1990). Factors and primes: A specific numerical ability. *Psychological Medicine, 20*, 163–169.

Hermelin B., & O'Connor, N. (1991). Talents and preoccupations in idiots-savants. *Psychological Medicine, 21*, 959–964.

Hermelin, B., O'Connor, N., & Lee, S. (1987). Musical inventiveness of five idiots-savants. *Psychological Medicine, 17*, 685–694.

Hermelin, B., & Pring, L. (1998). The pictorial context dependency of savant artists: A research note. *Perceptual and Motor Skills, 87*, 995–1001.

Hermelin, B., Pring, L., Buhler, M., Wolff, S., & Heaton, P. (1999). A visually impaired savant artist: Interacting perceptual and memory representations. *Journal of Child Psychiatry and Psychology, 7*, 1129–1139.

Hill, A. (1975). An investigation of calendar calculating by an idiot savant. *American Journal of Psychiatry, 132*, 557–560.

Hill, E. (2004). Evaluating the theory of executive dysfunction in autism, *Developmental Review, 24*, 189–233.

Ho, E., Tsang, A., & Ho, D. (1991). An investigation of the calendar calculation ability of a Chinese calendar savant. *Journal of Autism and Developmental Disorders, 21*, 315–327.

Hobbs, T. (2004). *John Scarlett Davis: A biography*. Hereford: Logaston Press.

Horwitz, W., Kestenbaum, C., Person, E., & Jarvik, L. (1965). Identical twin – 'idiot savants' – calendar calculators. *American Journal of Psychiatry, 121*, 1075–1079.

Howe, M. (1989). *Fragments of genius: The strange feats of idiots savants*. London: Routledge.

Howe, M. (1999). *Genius explained – the origins of exceptional ability*. Cambridge: Cambridge University Press.

Howlin, P., Goode, S., Hutton, J., & Rutter, M. (2009). Savant skills in autism: Psychometric approaches and parental reports. *Philosphical Transactions of the Royal Society of London, Series B, 364*, 1359–1367.

Hughes, C., Russell, J., & Robbins, T. (1994). Evidence for executive dysfunction in autism. *Neuropsychologia, 32*, 477–492.

Humphrey, N. (1998). Cave art, autism and the evolution of the human mind. *Cambridge Archaeology Journal, 8*(2), 165–191.

Hunter, I. (1977). An exceptional memory. *British Journal of Psychology, 68*, 155–164.

James, W. (1983). *The principles of psychology* (with an introduction by G. Miller). Harvard MA: Harvard University Press. (Original work published 1890.)

Jolley, R. (2008). Children's understanding of the dual nature of pictures. In C. Lange-Küttner & A. Vinter (Eds.), *Drawing and the non-verbal mind*. Cambridge: Cambridge University Press.

Jolliffe, T., & Baron-Cohen, S. (1997). Are children with autism or Asperger's syndrome faster than normal on the embedded figures task? *Journal of Child Psychology and Psychiatry, 38*, 527–534.

Joynson, R. (1972). The return of mind. *Bulletin of British Psychological Society, 25*, 123–127.

Kanner, L. (1943). Autistic disturbances of affective contact. *Nervous Child, 2*, 217–250.

Karmiloff-Smith, A. (1990). Constraints on representational change: Evidence from children's drawing. *Cognition, 34*, 57–83.

Karmiloff-Smith, A. (2008). Nativism versus neuroconstructivism: Rethinking the study of developmental disorders. *Developmental Psychology*, *45*(1), 56–63.

Kelleher, R., & Bear, M. (2008). The autistic neuron: Troubled translation? *Cell*, *135*, 401–406.

Kellogg, R. (1969). *Analyzing children's art*. Palo Alto, CA: National Press Books.

Kerschensteiner, G. (1905). *Die Entwicklung der zeichnerischen Bedabung* [The development of talent for drawing]. Munich: Karl Gerber.

Kilner, J. M., & Frith, C. D. (2007). A possible role of primary motor cortex during action observation. *Proceedings of the National Academy of Sciences of USA*, *104*, 8683–8684.

Klin, A. (2009). Subtyping the autistic spectrum disorders: Theoretical, research and clinical considerations. In S. Goldstein, J. Naglieri, & S. Ozonoff (Eds.), *Assessment of autism spectrum disorders*. London: Guilford Press.

Klinger, L., Klinger, M., & Pohlig, R. (2006). Implicit learning impairments in autistic spectrum disorders. In J. Perez, P. Gonzales, M. Comi, & C. Niero (Eds.), *New research in autism: The future is today*. London: Jessica Kingsley Press.

Knect, S., Drager, B., Deppe, L., Bobe, H., Lohmann, H., Flöel, A., et al. (2000). Handedness and hemispheric language dominance in healthy humans. *Brain*, *123*(12), 2512–2518.

Kogan, M., Blumberg, S., Schieve H., Boyle, C., Perrin, J. Ghandour, R., et al. (2009). Prevalence of parent-reported diagnosis of autism spectrum disorder among children in the US. *Pediatrics*, *124*, 1395–1403.

LaFontaine, L. (1974). *Divergent abilities in the idiot savant*. Unpublished PhD thesis, Boston University, MA, USA.

Langdon Down, J. (1887). *On some of the mental affections of childhood and youth*. London: Churchill.

Lange-Küttner, C., & Vitner, A. (2008). *Drawing and the non verbal mind*. Cambridge: Cambridge University Press.

Laurance, J. (2010, March 2). MMR scare research withdrawn by 'Lancet'. *The Independent*.

Lean, G., & Lakhani, N. (2009, April 5). Vinyl flooring 'doubles chances of children being autistic', study shows. *The Independent*.

Lee, M. (1989). When is an object not an object? The effect of meaning upon the copying of line drawings. *British Journal of Psychology*, *80*, 15–37.

Leroy, A. (1951). Representations de la perspective dans les dessins d'enfants [Representations of persepctive in the drawings of children]. *Enfance*, *4*, 286–307.

Leslie, A. (1987). Pretence and representation; the origin of the 'Theory of Mind'. *Psychological Review*, *94*, 412–426.

Leslie, A., & Thaiss, L. (1992). Domain specificity in conceptual development evidence from autism. *Cognition*, *43*, 225–251.

Light, P. (1985). The development of view-specific representation considered from a socio-cognitive standpoint. In N. Freeman & M. Cox (Eds.), *Visual order: The nature and development of pictorial representation* (pp. 214–230). Cambridge: Cambridge University Press.

Light, P., & Humphreys, J. (1981). Internal spatial relationships in young children's drawings. *Journal of Experimental Child Psychology*, *31*, 521–530.

Light, P., & MacIntosh, E. (1980). Depth relationships in young children's drawings. *Journal of Experimental Child Psychology*, *30*, 79–87.

Lindsley, O. (1965). Can deficiency produce specific superiority: The challenge of the idiot savant. *Exceptional Children, 31,* 225–232.

Liss, M., Fein, D., Allen, D., Dunn, M., Feinstein, C., Morris, R., et al. (2001). Executive functioning in high functioning children with autism. *Journal of Child Psychology and Psychiatry, 42,* 261–270.

Lord, C., Rutter, M., Goode, S., Heemsbergen, J., Jordon, H., Mawhood, D., et al. (1989). Autism diagnostic observation schedule. *Journal of Autism Developmental Disorders, 19,* 185–212.

Lotter, V. (1966). Epidemiology of autistic conditions in young children: Prevalence. *Social Psychiatry, 1,* 124–137.

Lovaas, I. (1987). Behavioral treatment and normal educational and intellectual functioning in young autistic children. *Journal of Consulting and Clinical Psychology, 55,* 3–9.

Luquet, G. (2001). *Le dessin enfantin* [Children's drawings] (A. Costall, Trans.). Paris: Alcan. London: Free Association Books. (Original work published 1927.)

Luria, A. (1968). *The mind of a mnemonist.* New York: Basic Books.

McAlonan, G., Suckling, J., Wong, N., Cheung, V., Lienenkaemper, N., Cheung, C., et al. (2008). Distinctive patterns of grey matter abnormality in high functioning autism and Aspergers syndrome. *Journal of Child Psychology and Psychiatry, 49,* 1287–1295.

McDevitt, T., & Ormrod, J. (2010). *Child development and education* (4th ed.). Upper Saddle River, NJ: Prentice Hall.

McGregor, E., Nunez, M., Williams, K., & Comez, J. (Eds.). (2007). *An integrated view of autism: Perspectives from neurocognitive, clinical and intervention research.* Oxford: Blackwell.

McVeigh, T. (2009, November 29). Boy artist's landscapes sell for £17,000. *Observer.*

Marr, D. (1982). *Vision: A computational investigation into the human representation and processing of visual information.* San Francisco, CA: Freeman.

Mason, R., Williams, D., Kana, R., Minshew, N., & Just, M. (2007). Theory of Mind disruption and recruitment of the right hemisphere during narrative comprehension in autism. *Neuropsychologia, 46,* 269–280.

Matthews, J. (1984). Children drawing: Are young children really scribbling? *Early Child Development and Care, 18,* 1–39.

Matthews, J. (1999). *The art of childhood and adolescence.* London: Falmer Press.

Matthews, J. (2003). *Drawings and paintings: Children and visual representation.* London: Chapman.

Mesibov, G., Shea, V., & Schopler, E. (2004). *The TEACCH approach to autistic spectrum disorders.* New York: Plenum.

Milbrath, C. (1998). *Patterns of artistic development in children.* Cambridge: Cambridge University Press.

Miller, B., Boone, K., Cummings, L., & Mishkin F. (2000). Functional correlates of musical and visual ability in fronto-temporal dementia. *British Journal of Psychiatry, 176,* 458–463.

Miller, B., Cummings, L., Mishkin, F., Boone, K., Prince, F., Ponton, M., et al. (1998). Emergence of artistic talent in fronto-temporal dementia, *Neurology, 51,* 978–982.

Miller, G. (1963). The magical number 7+ or −2. *Psychological Review, 2,* 81–97.

Miller, L. (1989). *Musical savants: Exceptional skill in the mentally retarded.* Hillsdale, NJ: Lawrence Erlbaum Associates, Inc.

Miller, L. (1998). Defining the savant. *Journal of Developmental and Physical Disabilities*, *10*(1), 78–85.

Miller, L. (1999). The savant syndrome: Intellectual impairment and exceptional skill. *Psychological Bulletin*, *125*, 31–46.

Minsky, M., & Papert, S. A. (1972). *Artificial intelligence report* (Artificial Intelligence Memo No. 252). Cambridge, MA: MIT Press.

Moore, V. (1986). The use of a colouring task to elucidate children's drawings of a solid cube. *British Journal of Developmental Psychology*, *4*, 335–340.

Moore, V. (1987). The influence of experience on children's drawings of a familiar and unfamiliar object. *British Journal of Developmental Psychology*, *5*, 221–229.

Morgan, M. (1981). David Downes. In S. Paine (Ed.), *Six children draw*. London: Academic Press.

Morra, S. (2005). Cognitive aspects of change in drawings: A neo-Piagetian theoretical account. *British Journal of Developmental Psychology*, *23*, 317–341.

Morris, P., Gruneberg, M., Sykes, R., & Merrick, A. (1981). Football knowledge and the acquisition of new results. *British Journal of Psychology*, *72*, 479–483.

Mottron, L., & Belleville, S. (1993). A study of perceptual analysis in a high-level autistic subject with exceptional graphic abilities. *Brain and Cognition*, *23*, 279–309.

Mottron, L., & Belleville, S. (1995). Perspective production in a savant autistic draughtsman. *Psychological Medicine*, *25*, 639–648.

Mottron, L., Burack, J., Stauder, J., & Robaey, P. (1999). Perceptual processing among high-functioning persons with autism. *Journal of Child Psychology and Psychiatry*, *40*(2), 203–211.

Mottron, L., Burack, J., Iarocci, G., Belleville, S., & Enns J. (2003). Locally oriented perception with intact global processing among adolescents with high-functioning autism: Evidence from multiple paradigms. *Journal of Child Psychology and Psychiatry*, *44*(6), 904–913.

Mottron, L., Dawson. M., Soulieres, I., Hubert. B., & Burack. J. (2006). Enhanced perceptual functioning in autism: An update, and eight principles of autistic perception. *Journal of Autism and Developmental Disorders*, *36*, 27–34.

Mottron, L., Dawson, M., & Soulieres, I. (2009). Enhanced perception in savant syndrome: Patterns, structure and creativity. *Philosphical Transactions of the Royal Society of London, Series B*, *364*, 1385–1391.

Navon, D. (1977). Forest before trees: The precedence of global features in visual perception, *Cognitive Psychology*, *9*, 353–383.

Naglieri, J., & Chambers, K. (2009). Psychometric issues and current scales for assessing autistic spectrum disorders. In S. Goldstein, J. Nagliari, & S. Ozonoff (Eds.), *Assessment of autistic spectrum disorders*. New York: The Guilford Press.

Neves-Pereira, M., Muller, B., Massie, D., Williams, J., O'Brien, P., Hughes, A., et al. (2009). *Deregulation of EIF4E. Journal of Medical Genetics*, *46*(11), 759–765.

Norman, D., & Shallice, T. (1986). Attention to action: Willed and automatic control of behaviour. In R. Davidson, G. Schwartz, & D. Shapiro (Eds.), *Consciousness and self-regulation* (Vol. 4). New York: Plenum.

Nurcombe, M., & Parker, N. (1964). The idiot savant. *Journal of American Academic Child Psychiatry*, *3*, 469–487.

Nurmi, E., Dowd, M., Tadevosyan-Leyfer, O., Haines, J. L., Folstein, S. E., & Sutcliffe, J. S. (2003). Exploratory subsetting of autism families based on savant skills improves evidence of genetic linkage to 15q11-q13. *Journal of the American Academy of Child and Adolescent Psychiatry*, *42*, 856–863.

Ockelford, A. (1988). *Some observations concerning the musical education of blind children and those with additional handicaps.* Paper presented at the 32nd Conference of the Society for Research in Psychology of Music and Music Education at the University of Reading.

Ockelford, A., & Pring, L. (2005). Learning and creativity in a prodigious musical savant. *International Congress Series, 1282*, 903–907.

Ockelford, A., & Pring, L. (2006). *Learning and creativity in a musical savant.* Paper presented at the 4th Mary Kitzinger International Conference on Visual Impairment, Kingston University, July 2006.

O'Connor N., & Hermelin, B. (1978). *Seeing and hearing and space and time.* London: Academic Press.

O'Connor, N., & Hermelin, B. (1987a). Visual and graphic abilities of the idiot savant artist. *Psychological Medicine, 17*, 81–92.

O'Connor, N., & Hermelin, B. (1987b). Visual memory and motor programmes: Their use by idiot-savant artists and controls. *British Journal of Psychology, 78*, 307–323.

O'Connor, N., & Hermelin, B. (1989a). Low intelligence and special abilities. *Journal of Child Psychology and Psychiatry, 29*, 391–396.

O'Connor, N., & Hermelin, B. (1989b). The memory structure of autistic idiot-savant mnemonists. *British Journal of Psychology, 80*, 97–111.

Ormond, R. (1981). *Sir Edwin Landseer.* London: Thames and Hudson.

Orr, D. (2009, May 23). Simon Baron-Cohen: Ali G's smarter cousin and Britain's leading expert on autism. *The Independent.*

Orsini, G. (1961). *Benedetto Croce: Philosopher of art and literary critic.* Carbondale, IL: Southern Illinois University Press.

Osborne, L. (2003, June 22). Savant for a day. *New York Times Magazine*, p. 38.

Ozonoff, S., & Miller, J. (1996). An exploration of right-hemisphere contributions to the pragmatic impairments of autism. *Brain and Language, 52*(3), 411–434.

Ozonoff, S., Pennington, B., & Rogers, S. (1991). Executive function deficits in high functioning autistic individuals. Relationship to theory of mind. *Journal of Child Psychology & Psychiatry, 32*(7), 1081–1105.

Ozonoff, S., Strayer, D., McMahon, W., & Filloux, F. (1994). Executive function abilities in autism and Tourette syndrome: An information processing approach. *Journal of Child Psychology and Psychiatry, 35*(6), 1015–1032.

Paine, S. (Ed.). (1981). *Six children draw.* London: Academic Press.

Paine, S. (2000). *Artists emerging: Sustaining expression through drawing.* Aldershot: Ashgate Publishing.

Paivio, A. (1971). *Imagery and verbal processes.* New York: Holt, Reinhart & Winston.

Palo, J., & Kivalo, A. (1977). Calendar calculator with progressive mental deficiency. *Acta Paedopsychiatrica, 42*, 227–231.

Pariser, D. (1995). Lautrec: Gifted child artist and artistic monument. In C. Golomb (Ed.), *The development of artistically gifted children.* Hillsdale, NJ: Lawrence Erlbaum Associates, Inc.

Park, C. (1967). *The seige: The first eight years of an autistic child.* New York: Back Bay Books.

Patterson, C. C., & Siegal M. (1995). Deafness, conversation, and theory of mind. *Journal of Child Psychology and Psychiatry, 36*, 459–474.

Patterson, K., & Erzinclioglu, S. (2008). Drawing in neurogenerative disease. In C. Lange-Küttner & A. Vinter (Eds.), *Drawing and the non verbal mind.* Cambridge: Cambridge University Press.

Patterson, P. (2002). Maternal infection window on neuroimmune interactions in foetal; brain development and mental illness. *Current Opinion in Neurobiology, 12*, 115–118.

Peterson, C., Wellman, H., & Liu, D. (2005). Steps in theory-of-mind development for children with deafness or autism. *Child development, 76*(2), 502–517.

Philby, C. (2009, January 24). My secret life: Stephen Wiltshire. *The Independent.*

Phillips, W., Hobbs, S., & Pratt, F. (1978). Intellectual realism in children's drawings of cubes. *Cognition, 6*, 15–33.

Phillips, W., & Silverstein, S. (2004). Continuing commentary. *Behavioural and Brain Sciences, 27*, 594–600.

Piaget, J., & Inhelder, B. (1956). *The child's conception of space.* London: Routledge & Kegan Paul.

Picard, D., & Durand, K. (2005). Are young children's drawings canonically biased? *Journal of Experimental Child Psychology, 90*, 48–64.

Pilgrim, D. (2000). Psychiatric diagnosis-more questions than answers. *The Psychologist, 13*(6), 302–305.

Plaisted K., Grant, K., & Davis, G. (2009). Perception and apperception in autism: Rejecting the inverse assumption. *Philosphical Transactions of the Royal Society of London, Series B, 364*, 1393–1398.

Plaisted, K., Saksida. L., Alcantara, J., & Weisblatt, E. (2003). Towards an understanding of the mechanisms of weak central coherence effects: Experiments in visual configural learning and auditory perception. *Philosphical Transactions of the Royal Society of London, Series B, 358*(1430), 375–386.

Plaisted, K., Swettenham, J., & Rees, L. (1999). Children with autism show local precedence in a divided attention task and global precedence in a selective attention task. *Journal of Child Psychology and Psychiatry, 40*, 733–742.

Pring, L. (2005). Savant syndrome. *Developmental Medicine and Child Neurology, 47*(7), 500–503.

Pring, L. (2008). Memory characteristics in individuals with savant skills. In J. Boucher & D. Bowler (Eds.), *Memory in autism.* Cambridge: Cambridge University Press.

Pring, L., & Hermelin, B. (1997). Native savant talent and acquired skill. *Autism, 1*, 199–214.

Pring, L., & Hermelin, B. (2002). Numbers and letters: Exploring an autistic savant's unpractised ability. *Neurocase, 8*, 330–337.

Pring, L., Hermelin, B., & Heavey, L. (1995). Savants, segments, art and autism. *Journal of Child Psychology and Psychiatry, 36*, 1065–1076.

Pring, L., & Painter, J. (2002). Recollective experience in the visually impaired the role of sensory and conceptual processing. *British Journal of Visual Impairment & Blindness, 20*, 24–32.

Pujol, J., Deus, J., Losill, J., & Capdevila, A. (1999). Cerebral lateralisation of language in normal left handed people studied by functional MRI. *Neurology, 52*, 1038.

Pylyshyn, Z. (1973). What the mind's eye tells the mind's brain: A critique of mental imagery. *Psychological Bulletin, 80*, 1–24.

Rajendran, G., & Mitchell, P. (2007). Cognitive theories of autism. *Development Review, 27*, 224–260.

Ramachandran, V. (2004). *The emerging mind. 2003 BBC Reith Lectures.* London: BBC Publications.

Read, H. (1938). *Art and industry.* London: Faber and Faber.

Reynell, J. (1969). *Reynell developmental language scales.* Windsor: NFER.

Ricci, C. (1887). *L'arte dei bambini* [The art of children]. Bologna: Zanichelli.

Richardson, J. A. (1991). *Life of Picasso*. New York: Random House.

Rife, D., & Snyder, L. (1931). Studies in human inheritance. *Human Biology*, *3*, 547–559.

Rimland, B. (1978). Inside the mind of the autistic savant. *Psychology Today*, *12*(3), 69–80.

Rizzolatti, G. (1996). Promoter cortex and the recognition of motor actions. *Cognitive Brain Research*, *3*, 131–141.

Ronald, A., Happé, F., Bolton, P., Butcher, L. M., Price, T. S., Wheelwright, S., et al. (2006). Genetic heterogeneity between the three components of the autistic spectrum – a twin study. *Journal of the American Academy of Child and Adolescent Psychiatry*, *45*, 691–699.

Ropar, D., & Mitchell, P. (2002). Shape constancy in autism: The role of prior knowledge and perspective cues. *Journal of Child Psychology and Psychiatry*, *43*(5), 647–654.

Rubie-Davies, C. (2010). Teacher expectations and perceptions of student attributes: Is there a relationship? *British Journal of Educational Psychology*, *80*(1), 121–135.

Rumelhart, D. E., & McClelland, J. L. (1986). PDP models and general issues in cognitive science. In D. E. Rumelhart, J. L. McClelland, & the PDP Research Group (Eds.), *Parallel distributed processing: Explorations in the microstructure of cognition* (Vol. 1: Foundations). Cambridge, MA: Bradford Books/MIT Press.

Ruskin, J. (1843). *Modern painters*. London: Smith Elder and Co.

Russell, J. (1997). *Autism as an executive disorder*. Oxford: Oxford University Press.

Russell, J. (2002). Cognitive theories of autism. In J. Harrison & A. Owens (Eds.), *Cognitive deficits in brain disorders* (pp. 295–323). London: Martin Dunitz.

Rutter, M. (2000). Genetic Studies of Autism: From 1970s into the millennium. *Journal of Abnormal Child Psychology*, *28*, 3–14.

Rutter, M., Anderson-Wood, L., Beckett, C., Bredenkamp, C., Pastel, J., Groothes, C., et al. (1999). Quasi autistic patterns following early global privation. *Journal of Child Psychology and Psychiatry*, *40*, 537–549.

Rutter, M., Le Couteur, A., & Lord, C. (2004). *The autism diagnostic interview (revised)*. Los Angeles, CA: Western Psychological Services.

Sacks, O. (1985). *The man who mistook his wife for a hat, and other clinical tales*. London: Picador.

Sacks, O. (1995a). *An anthropologist on mars. Seven paradoxical tales*. London: Picador.

Sacks, O. (1995b). A neurologist's notebook: Prodigies. *The New Yorker*, pp. 44–65.

Schenk, D. (2010). *The genius in all of us*. New York: Doubleday.

Selfe, L. (1977). *Nadia: A case of extraordinary drawing ability in an autistic child*. London: Academic Press.

Selfe, L. (1983). *Normal and anomalous representational drawing ability in children*. London: Academic Press.

Selfe, L. (1995). Nadia revisited. In C. Golomb (Ed.), *The development of artistically gifted children*. Hillsdale, NJ: Lawrence Erlbaum Associates, Inc.

Selfe, L. (2002). Concerns about the identification and diagnosis of autistic spectrum disorders. *Educational Psychology in Practice*, *18*(4), 335–341.

Shah, A., & Frith, U. (1983). An islet of ability in autistic children. *Journal of Child Psychology and Psychiatry*, *24*, 613–620.

Shah, A., & Frith, U. (1993). Why do autistic individuals show superior performance on the block design task? *Journal of Child Psychology and Psychiatry*, *34*, 1351–1364.

Sheppard, E., Mitchell, P., & Ropar, D. (2008). Individuals with and without autism in copying tasks. In C. Lange-Kütter & A. Vinter (Eds.), *Drawing and the non verbal mind*. Cambridge: Cambridge University Press.

Sheppard, E., Ropar, D., & Mitchell, P. (2007). The impact of meaning and dimensionality on the accuracy of children's copying. *Journal of Autism and Developmental Disorders*, *37*, 1913–1924.

Sheppard, E., Ropar, D., & Mitchell, P. (2009). Perceiving the impossible. How individuals with autism copy paradoxical figures. *Autism*, *13*, 435–452.

Siegler, R. (1981). Developmental sequences within and between concepts. *Monographs for the Society for Research in Child Development*, *46*, 1–84.

Siipola, E., & Hayden, S. (1965). Exploring eidetic imagery among the retarded. *Perceptual and Motor Skills*, *21*, 275–286.

Skuse, D., Warrington. R., Bishop, D., Chowdhury, U., Mandy, W., & Place, M. (2004). The developmental, dimensional and diagnostic interview (3di). *Journal of American Academy of Childhood and Adolescent Psychiatry*, *43*(5), 548–558.

Sloboda, J., Hermelin, B., & O'Connor, N. (1985). An exceptional musical memory. *Music Perception*, *3*, 155.

Snyder, A. (2004). Autistic genius. *Nature*, *428*, 470–471.

Snyder, A. (2009). Explaining and inducing savant skills: Privileged access to lower level, less-processed information. *Philosphical Transactions of the Royal Society of London, Series B*, *364*, 1399–1405.

Snyder, A., & Thomas, D. (1999). Autistic artists give clues to cognition. *Perception*, *26*, 93–96.

Song, H., Onishi, K., Baillargeon, R., & Fisher, C. (2008). Can an agent's false belief be corrected by an appropriate communication. Psychological reasoning in 18 month old infants. *Cognition*, *109*, 295–315.

Sparks, B., Friedman, S., Shaw, D., Aylward, E. H., Echelard, D., Artru, A., et al. (2002). Brain structural abnormalities in young children with autism spectrum disorder. *Neurology*, *59*, 184–192.

Stutsman, R. (1931). *Merrill Palmer mental measurement of preschool children*. New York: World Books Yonkers.

Sully, J. (1895). *Studies of childhood*. London: Longmans Green.

Takeuchi A., & Hulse, S. (1993). Absolute pitch. *Psychological Bulletin*, *113*(2), 345–361.

Tammet, D. (2006). *Born on a blue day: A memoir of Aspergers and an extraordinary mind*. London: Hodder & Stoughton.

Tantam, D. (2009). *Can the world afford autistic spectrum disorder?* London: Jessica Kingsley Publishers.

Thomas, G., & Silk, A. (1990). *An introduction to the psychology of children's drawings*. London: Harvester Wheatsheaf.

Thompson, R. (1981). Toulouse-Lautrec. In S. Paine (Ed.), *Six children draw*. London: Academic Press.

Tolstoy, L. (1960). *What is art?* (A. Maude, Trans.). London: Macmillan Publishing. (Original work published 1896.)

Tredgold, A. (1914). *Mental deficiency*. New York: William Wood.

Treffert, D. A. (n.d.) *Ping Lian Yeak: An 11 year old specially gifted artist in Malaysia*. Retrieved November 29, 2010, from http://www.pinglian.com/

Treffert, D. A. (1989). *Extraordinary people: Understanding savant syndrome*. New York: Ballantine Books.

Treffert, D. (2006). *Extraordinary people: Understanding savant syndrome* (updated version). New York: Ballantine Books.

Treffert, D. A. (2009). The savant syndrome: An extraordinary condition. A synopsis: past, present, future. *Philosphical Transactions of the Royal Society of London, Series B, 364,* 1351–1357.

Treffert, D., & Wallace, G. (2002). Islands of genius: The mystery of savant syndrome. *Scientific American, 286,* 76–85.

Van Geert, P. (1998). A dynamic systems model of basic developmental mechanisms: Piaget, Vygotsky and beyond. *Psychological Review, 105*(5), 634–677.

Vasari, G. (1568). *The lives of the artists.* London: Penguin.

Viscott, D. S. (1970). A musical idiot savant: A psychodynamic study, and some speculations on the creative process. *Psychiatry, 33*(4), 494–515.

Wallace, G., Happé, F., & Giedd, J. (2009). A case study of a multiply talented savant with an autism spectrum disorder: Neuropsychological functioning and brain morphometry. *Philosphical Transactions of the Royal Society of London, Series B, 364,* 1425–1432.

Warner, M. (1981). Millais. In S. Paine (Ed.), *Six children draw.* London: Academic Press.

Watson, R. (1951). *The Vineland social maturity scale.* New York: Harper & Bros.

Wechsler, D. (1974). *Wechsler intelligence scales for children* (Version 3). London: Psychological Corporation.

Wheelock, A. (Ed.). (2008). *Jan Lievens: A Dutch master rediscovered.* Washington: National Gallery of Art.

White, S., Hill, E., Happé, F., & Frith, U. (2009). The strange stories: revealing mentalizing impairments in autism. *Child Development, 80*(4), 1097–1117.

Wilde, O. (1992). Preface. *The Picture of Dorian Gray.* Ware, UK: Wordsworth Editions. (Original work published 1891.)

Willats, J. (1987). Marr and pictures: An information-processing account of children's drawings. *Archives de Psychologie, 5*(5), 105–125.

Willats, J. (1997). *Art and representation: New principles in the analysis of pictures.* Princeton, NJ: Princeton University Press.

Willats, J. (2005). *Making sense of children's drawings.* Mahwah, NJ: Lawrence Erlbaum Associates, Inc.

Wiltshire, S. (1987). *Drawings.* London: Dent.

Wiltshire, S. (1991). *Floating cities.* London: Dent.

Wimmer, H., & Perner, J. (1983). Beliefs about beliefs: Representation and constraining function of wrong beliefs in young children's understanding of deception. *Cognition, 13,* 103–128.

Wing, L. (1996). *The autistic spectrum: A guide for parents and professionals.* London: Constable.

Wing, L., & Gould, J. (1979). Severe impairments of social interaction and associated abnormalities in children: Epidemiology and classification. *Journal of Autism and Developmental Disorders, 9,* 11–29.

Wing, L., & Gould, J. (1991). *Diagnostic Interview for Social and Communication Disorders* (DISCO). Bromley, UK: Eliot House.

Winner, E. (1996). *Gifted children: Myths and realities.* New York: Basic Books.

Wollheim, R. (1980). *Art and its objects* (2nd ed.). Cambridge: Cambridge University Press.

Woollett, K., Spiersw, H., & Maguire, E. (2009). Talent in the taxi: A model system for exploring expertise. *Philosphical Transactions of the Royal Society of London, Series B, 364*, 1407–1416.

World Health Organization. (1992). *The ICD-10 classification of mental and behavioural disorders: Clinical discriptions and diagnostic guidelines*. Geneva: WHO.

York, M. (2004, August 28). A portrait of the artist as a young girl. *New York Times*. Retrieved November 29, 2004, from http://www.nytimes.com/2004/09/28/nyregion/28artist.html?_r=1

Young, R., & Nettlebeck, T. (1995). The abilities of a musical savant and his family. *Journal of Autism and Developmental Disorders, 25*, 231–248.

Author index

Abell, F., 98
Albright, D., 176
Alcantara, J., 104, 105
Allen, D., 106
Allen, G., 4, 162, 211
Allik, J., 73
American Psychiatric Association, 5, 21, 24, 27, 87, 88, 90
Amir, N., 90
Anderson, J. R., 155
Anderson-Wood, L., 92
Anon. (1828), 127
Anon. (1874), 180, 182
Anon. (2009), 96
Aram, D., 124
Arnheim, R., 6, 59, 66, 142, 217
Artru, A., 210, 223
Ashwin, C., 7, 100, 104, 169, 170, 171, 212, 213, 214
Ashwin, E., 7, 100, 104, 169, 170, 171, 212, 213, 214
Asperger, H., 88
Atkinson, R., 149, 207
Aylward, E. H., 210, 223

Baddeley, A., 70, 149, 150, 208
Baddeley, A. D., 149
Baillargeon, R., 97
Baird, G., 89, 95
Barclay, A., 148
Barkham, P., 198
Baron-Cohen, S., 7, 16, 21, 83, 97, 99, 100, 103, 104, 166, 169, 170, 171, 212, 213, 214
Bates, E., 223
Baudelaire, C., 177
Bear, M., 209
Beckel-Mitchener, A., 4, 162, 211
Beckett, C., 92

Belleville, S., 82, 84, 85, 103, 105, 120, 166, 169, 213, 219
Belmonte, M., 4, 162, 211
Bennett, H., 155
Biro, S., 97
Bishop, D., 4
Blue, M., 210, 211
Blum, H., 15
Blumberg, S., 89, 95
Bobe, H., 211
Bolton, P., 158
Boone, K., 159, 163, 212
Booth, R., 169
Boulanger, L., 4, 162, 211
Boyatzis, C. J., 69
Boylan, C., 210, 211
Boyle, C., 89, 95
Bredenkamp, C., 92
Brill, A., 159
Brink, T., 160
Bruner, J., 15, 142
Buhler, K., 64
Buhler, M., 5
Burack, J., 82, 84, 85, 103, 105, 120, 154, 155, 166, 167, 169, 173, 203, 213, 219, 220
Burgemeister, L., 15
Burgess, P., 105, 106, 107
Burt, C., 64
Butcher, L. M., 158

Cain, A., 156
Camhi, L., 176
Campbell, N., 219
Capdevila, A., 211
Carper, R., 4, 162, 211
Casanova, M., 93, 160, 161
Casson, H., 135
Castelli, F., 98

Chakrabarti, B., 7, 100, 104, 169,
    170, 171, 212, 213, 214
Chambers, K., 92
Charman, A., 83
Charman, D., 89, 95
Charness, N., 112
Chase, W., 156
Cheung, C., 91
Cheung, V., 91
Chomsky, N., 60
Chowdhury, U., 4
Clark, A., 68, 76, 77
Clifton, J., 112
Cohen, I., 210, 223, 224
Collingwood, R., 176
Coltheart, M., 99
Comez, J., 90
Courchesne, E., 92
Cox, M., 6, 64, 66, 67, 68, 70, 71, 73,
    75, 82, 83, 172
Craik, F., 155
Creak, E., 4
Cummings, L., 159, 163, 212

Davidson, J., 154
Davies, A. M., 68
Davies, C., 189, 191
Davis, G., 104, 105
Dawson, M., 84, 154, 155, 166, 167,
    168, 173, 203, 212, 213, 219, 220
De Clercq, H., 163
Dennis, N., 218
Deppe, L., 211
Deus, J., 211
Deutsch, D., 154
Doherty, M., 219
Dolson, H., 154
Dominick, K., 109
Dowd, M., 159
Downes, D., 194
Draaisma, D., 3, 94, 123
Drager, B., 211
Drake, J., 172, 173, 177, 179, 200,
    201, 204
Dubery, F., 59
Duckett, J., 147, 148
Duncan, J., 107
Dunn, M., 106
Durand, K., 69

Eames, K., 83
Echelard, D., 210, 223
Eiser, C., 77, 78, 217
Elman, J., 223

Enns, J., 84, 85, 103, 105, 120, 166,
    169, 213, 219
Ericsson, K., 156
Erzinclioglu, S., 164, 211, 218

Fein, D., 106
Feinstein, C., 106
Filloux, F., 21, 103
Fineberg, J., 176, 178, 189
Fisher, C., 97
Fitzgerald, M., 122, 165, 174, 199
Fitzpatrick, M., 93
Flöel, A., 211
Foa, A. B., 90
Folstein, S. E., 159
Fombonne, E., 213
Ford, P. M., 69, 83
Freeman, N., 59, 66, 68, 71, 73, 75, 76,
    77, 78, 142, 217
Freshman, M., 90
Friedman, S., 210, 223
Frith, C., 82, 98, 160, 173, 211
Frith, C. D., 93
Frith, U., 3, 4, 5, 16, 21, 82, 84, 88, 93, 97,
    98, 99, 101, 102, 103, 112, 140, 146,
    147, 152, 156, 157, 168, 169, 204, 208,
    211, 212, 217, 219
Frostig, M., 15
Fry, R., 201

Gaunt, W., 186
Gazzaniga, M., 93, 210
Gernsbacher, M., 168
Geschwind, D., 209, 210
Ghandour, R., 89, 95
Gibson, J. J., 63, 144, 148, 206, 215, 217
Giedd, J., 161, 162, 211
Gilbert, S., 105, 106, 107
Giray, E., 148
Goldstein, S., 90
Golomb, C., 20, 66, 142, 172, 217
Gombrich, E., 60, 62, 70, 151
Goode, S., 3, 15, 91, 94, 113, 114
Goodenough, F., 15, 64, 142, 172, 173
Goodnow, J., 70, 75
Gordon, A., 198
Gould, J., 4, 89, 109
Grandin, T., 146
Grant, K., 104, 105
Gray, C., 148
Greenfield, P., 15, 142
Groothes, C., 92
Gruneberg, M., 155
Gummerman, K., 148

Haber, R., 147, 207
Hacking, I., 3, 94, 123, 146
Hadjikhani, N., 109
Haines, J. L., 159
Happé, F., 3, 5, 84, 87, 90, 93, 97, 98,
    99, 101, 102, 103, 105, 110, 112,
    114, 140, 146, 147, 156, 157, 158,
    161, 169, 203, 204, 208, 211, 212,
    213, 219
Harris, D. B., 15, 64, 66, 71, 142, 172,
    173, 217
Hayden, S., 148
Healy, J., 124
Heaton, P., 5, 115, 118, 146, 153
Heavey, L., 103, 117, 152, 153,
    169, 208
Heemsbergen, J., 94
Heinsen, H., 93
Henthorn, T., 154
Hermelin, B., 5, 16, 103, 111, 112, 113,
    115, 117, 118, 122, 123, 124, 132,
    134, 136, 140, 142, 143, 144, 145,
    146, 148, 150, 151, 152, 153, 154,
    158, 165, 166, 169, 176, 207,
    208, 217
Hill, A., 154
Hill, E., 97, 99, 217
Hitch, G., 149
Ho, D., 153
Ho, E., 153
Hobbs, S., 20, 79, 81, 82, 204, 219
Hobbs, T., 182, 183
Hohmann, C., 210, 211
Horwitz, W., 118
Howe, M., 5, 6, 111, 112, 113, 114,
    115, 117, 121, 125, 127, 136, 138,
    139, 141, 142, 145, 148, 152, 154,
    155, 156, 159, 199, 204, 205, 209,
    215, 217
Howlin, P., 3, 15, 91, 113, 114
Hubert, B., 84, 154, 155, 166, 167, 173,
    203, 213, 219, 220
Hughes, A., 96
Hughes, C., 106
Hulse, S., 153
Humphrey, N., 157
Humphreys, J., 60
Hunter, I., 139
Hutton, J., 3, 15, 91, 113, 114

Iarocci, G., 84, 85, 103, 105, 120, 166,
    169, 213, 219
Inhelder, B., 15, 61, 70, 175
Ivry, R., 93, 210

James, W., 221
Janikoun, R., 76
Jarvik, L., 118
Johnson, M., 223
Jolley, R., 207
Jolliffe, T., 103, 169
Jordon, H., 94
Joseph, R., 109
Joynson, R., 2
Just, M., 99

Kana, R., 99
Kanner, L., 88, 94, 118, 136
Karmiloff-Smith, A., 69, 70, 223
Kelleher, R., 209
Kellogg, R., 64
Kerschensteiner, G., 67
Kestenbaum, C., 118
Kilner, J. M., 93
Kivalo, A., 204
Klin, A., 90, 91, 110, 203
Klinger, L., 98
Klinger, M., 98
Knect, S., 211
Kogan, M., 89, 95

Laak,T., 73
LaFontaine, L., 154, 209
Lakhani, N., 96
Langdon Down, J., 125, 128, 138
Lange-Küttner, C., 219
Laurance, J., 96
Le Couter, A., 4, 109
Lean, G., 96
Lee, M., 82
Lee, S., 5
Leroy, A., 71
Leslie, A., 16, 21, 85, 97, 98, 99,
Lienenkaemper, N., 91
Light, P., 20, 60, 143
Lindsley, O., 141
Liss, M., 106
Liu, D., 99
Lohmann, H., 211
Lord, C., 4, 94, 109
Lorge, I., 15
Losill, J., 211
Lotter, V., 89
Loucas, T., 89, 95
Lovaas, I., 94
Luquet, G., 64, 65, 66, 67, 69,
    142, 217
Luria, A., 2
Lyle, E., 69

McAlonan, G., 91
McClelland, J. L., 223
McDevitt, T., 222
MacDonald, L., 112
McGregor, E., 90
MacIntosh, E., 20, 60
McMahon, W., 21, 103
McVeigh, T., 195, 197
Maguire, E., 157
Mandy, W., 4
Mangun, G., 93, 210
Manoach, D., 109
Marr, D., 60, 80, 206, 215, 217, 219, 220
Mason, R., 99
Massie, D., 96
Matthews, J., 64, 65, 66
Mawhood, D., 94
Meldrum, D., 89, 95
Merrick, A., 155
Mesibov, G., 214
Michaelson, P., 69
Milbrath, C., 172, 198
Miller, B., 159, 163, 212
Miller, G., 70
Miller, J., 21, 105, 210
Miller, L., 112, 113, 117, 153, 163, 168
Minshew, N., 99
Minsky, M., 61
Mishkin, F., 159, 163, 212
Mitchell, P., 5, 82, 83, 84, 85, 162, 203, 204, 216, 218, 219
Moore, V., 82, 85
Morgan, M., 193
Morra, S., 70
Morris, P., 155
Morris, R., 106
Mottron, L., 82, 84, 85, 103, 105, 120, 154, 155, 166, 167, 168, 169, 173, 203, 212, 213, 219, 220
Muller, B., 96

Naglieri, J., 90, 92
Naik, P., 109
Navon, D., 103
Nettlebeck, T., 153
Neves-Pereira, M., 96
Norman, D., 107
Nunez, M., 90
Nurcombe, M., 156
Nurmi, E., 159

O'Brien, P., 96
Ockelford, A., 118, 119, 122, 153, 154, 168

O'Connor, N., 5, 16, 113, 117, 132, 140, 143, 144, 145, 146, 150, 153, 154, 207
Olver, R., 15, 142
Onishi, K., 97
Ormond, R., 181, 182
Ormrod, J., 222
Orr, D., 94
Orsini, G., 176
Osborne, L., 164
Ozonoff, S., 21, 90, 103, 105, 106, 210

Paine, S., 125, 186, 187, 192, 194, 198, 203, 224
Painter, J., 154
Paivio, A., 16, 19
Palo, J., 204
Papert, S. A., 61
Pariser, D., 172, 174, 186, 198
Parisi, D., 223
Park, C., 118
Parker, N., 156
Pastel, J., 92
Patterson, C. C., 99
Patterson, K., 164, 211, 218
Patterson, P., 89
Pennington, B., 106
Perner, J., 97
Perrin, J., 89, 95
Person, E., 118
Peterson, C., 99
Philby, C., 136
Phillips, W., 20, 79, 81, 82, 203, 204, 219
Piaget, J., 15, 61, 70, 175
Picard, D., 69
Pickles, A., 89, 95
Pierce, K., 92
Pilgrim, D., 95
Place, M., 4
Plaisted, K., 101, 104, 105
Plomin, R., 5, 87, 90, 110, 203
Plunkett, K., 223
Pohlig, R., 98
Ponton, M., 163, 212
Pratt, F., 20, 79, 81, 82, 204, 219
Price, T. S., 158
Prince, F., 163, 212
Pring, L., 5, 103, 112, 117, 118, 119, 120, 122, 136, 139, 142, 148, 150, 151, 152, 153, 154, 155, 162, 166, 168, 169, 206, 207, 208, 209, 221
Pujol, J., 211
Pylyshyn, Z., 19

Rajendran, G., 203
Ramachandran, V., 215
Read, H., 177
Rees, E. L., 69, 83
Rees, L., 101
Reynell, J., 15
Ricci, C., 67
Richardson, J. A., 178, 188
Rife, D., 158
Rimland, B., 115, 160, 165, 169, 209, 215
Rizzolatti, G., 93
Robaey, P., 82, 84, 103, 166
Robbins, T., 106
Rogers, S., 106
Ronald, A., 5, 87, 90, 110, 158, 203
Ropar, D., 5, 82, 83, 84, 85, 162, 204, 216, 218, 219
Rubie-Davies, C., 95
Rumelhart, D. E., 223
Ruskin, J., 176
Russell, J., 99, 106
Rutter, M., 3, 4, 15, 89, 91, 92, 94, 109, 113, 114

Sacks, O., 118, 133, 149, 154, 163, 207
Saksida, L., 104, 105
Sayers, J., 77, 78, 217
Schenk, D., 199
Schieve, H., 89, 95
Schopler, E., 214
Selfe, L., 5, 20, 58, 59, 70, 73, 76, 78, 81, 82, 83, 91, 128, 142, 143, 144, 148, 150, 151, 154, 203, 206, 213, 216
Shah, A., 82, 101, 169
Shallice, T., 107
Shaw, D., 210, 223
Shea,V., 214
Sheppard, E., 5, 82, 83, 84, 85, 204, 216, 218, 219
Shiffrin, R., 149, 207
Siegal, M., 99
Siegler, R., 76
Siipola, E., 148
Silk, A., 65, 70, 73, 75, 78
Silverstein, S., 203
Simonoff, E., 89, 95
Skuse, D., 4
Sloboda, J., 153, 154
Snowling, M., 102
Snyder, A., 115, 162, 163, 164, 165, 211, 212
Snyder, J., 109
Snyder, L., 158
Song, H., 97

Soulieres, I., 84, 154, 155, 166, 167, 168, 173, 203, 212, 213, 219, 220
Sparks, B., 210, 223
Spiersw, H., 157
Stafford J., 90
Stauder, J., 82, 84, 103, 166
Steinbusch, H. W., 93
Strayer, D., 21, 103
Stutsman, R., 15
Suckling, J., 91
Sully, J., 67
Sutcliffe, J. S., 159
Swettenham, J., 101
Switala, A., 93
Sykes, R., 155

Tadevosyan-Leyfer, O., 159
Takeuchi, A., 153
Tammet, D., 137, 222
Tantam, D., 93, 108, 109, 160, 162, 205, 215
Tavassoli, T., 7, 100, 104, 169, 170, 171, 212, 213, 214
Thaiss, L., 98
Thomas, D., 163
Thomas, G., 65, 70, 73, 75, 78
Thompson, R., 175, 186, 187
Tolstoy, L., 176
Tredgold, A., 126, 127, 128, 129
Treffert, D., 120, 153, 160
Treffert, D. A., 3, 5, 6, 16, 101, 111, 112, 113, 114, 115, 117, 120, 121, 123, 124, 125, 128, 142, 147, 148, 149, 158, 159, 160, 162, 163, 166, 174, 194, 205, 209, 210, 211, 215, 218
Trippe, J., 93, 160, 161
Tsang, A., 153
Tsuji, H., 219
Tulving, E., 155

van Engeland, H., 93
Van Geert, P., 222
van Kooten, I., 93
Vasari, G., 175
Vitner, A., 219
Viscott, D. S., 121, 122
Vital, P., 101, 114, 169, 213

Wallace, G., 115, 120, 153, 160, 161, 211
Warner, M., 184
Warrington, R., 4
Watson, R., 121
Webb, S., 4, 162, 211
Wechsler, D., 15

Weisblatt, E., 104, 105
Wellman, H., 99
Wheelock, A., 179, 180
Wheelwright, S., 158
White, S., 97, 99
Wilde, O., 177
Willats, J., 6, 59, 60, 61, 70, 71, 142, 143,
    217, 219
Williams, D., 99
Williams, J., 96
Williams, K., 90
Wiltshire, S., 133, 134, 135, 136

Wimmer, H., 97
Wing, L., 4, 88, 89, 109
Winner, E., 146, 172, 173, 177, 179, 200,
    201, 204
Wolff, S., 5
Wollheim, R., 176, 177
Wong, N., 91
Woollett, K., 157
World Health Organization, 87, 90

York, M., 177
Young, R., 153

Subject index

Absolute pitch, 101, 118–119, 153–154
Abstract art, 177, 178
Abstract thought, 141–145, 216–219
Action representation, 65
Action schemas, 107
Affordances, 63, 144
Aggressive behaviour, 25
Aitken, Alexander, 139
Alignment, 66–67
Alzheimer's syndrome, 149
Amygdala, 210
Animal drawings, 9, 10, 13, 14, 17, 18, 19, 21, 22, 29–43, 56, 68, 126–127, 132, 157, 180–182, 185, 186, 187, 188, 190, 191, 192, 216
Applied behavioural analysis (ABA), 92
Architectural drawings, 131, 132–136, 137, 183, 184, 193–194, 195, 196, 197, 220
Arithmetical savants, 116–118, 153, 159, 213, see also Calendar calculators
Arousal, 105
Art, definition of, 176–177
Artistic savants, 116, 125–136, 141–142, 144, 145, 150–151, 154, 162, 167, 173–174
Asperger's syndrome, 5, 7, 87, 88, 93–94, 170
Assessment and assessment tools, 4, 92, 94–95
Attachment, 66–67
Attentional resources, 215
Atypical, mild Asperger's syndrome, 93–94
Auditory sensitivity, 104
Autism Diagnostic Interview Revised (ADI–(R)), 4, 109
Autism Diagnostic Observation Schedule (ADOS), 94
Autism spectrum disorder: assessment, 92, 94–95; attentional resources, 215; brain

abnormalities, 92–93, 98, 99; classical autism, 87; comorbidity, 92; definition, 4–5, 6; diagnostic issues, 21, 90–91, 93–95, 109–110; drawing, 82–85; early diagnosis, 94; empathising/ systemising theory, 100–101; enhanced perceptual functioning, 82–83, 84–85, 103; executive function, 21, 105–108; explosion in research on, 4, 21; first use of term, 88–89; interbrain, 108–109; labelling issues, 95; non-verbal communication, 108–109; overdiagnosis, 90; prevalence, 89–90; recovery, 94; savant syndrome, 6, 113, 114; sensory abnormalities, 170–171; spectrum nature of, 87; subtypes and subgroups, 91; theories, 95–109; theory of mind, 21, 97–99; treatment, 91–92; triad of impairments, 87–88; weak central coherence theory, 21, 84, 101–105, 152
Automatic processing, 105–106

Beethoven, Ludwig van, 123
Behavioural checklists, 92, 94–95, 109–110
Binet, Alfred, 112
Bird drawings, 14, 37–41, 132, 181
Block design test, 15, 19, 91, 166, 169
Body language, 215
Boudreaux, Ellen, 121
Brain abnormalities, 16, 92–93, 98, 99, 159–162, 163, 210, 211–212, 219
Brain connectivity theories, 92, 98, 99, 160–161, 210, 211
Brain plasticity, 211
Brain size, 92, 105, 160, 210
British Abilities Scale, 150
Building drawings, see Architectural drawings

Burton, Richard, 157
Buxton, Jedediah, 117

Calculator savants, 116–118, 153,
    159, 213
Calendar calculators, 116, 117–118, 138,
    142, 148, 153, 213
Canonical representation, 18, 59, 66, 68,
    69, 142, 216–217
Carousel horse drawings, 9, 10, 29, 56
Cat drawings, 126
Categorisation, 16, 142
Cave art, 157, 158
Central coherence, 101
Central executive, 150
Cezanne, Paul, 201
Child Development Research Unit
    (University of Nottingham), 11–14
Christopher, 123–124
Classical autism, 87
Closed form, 66
Cockerel drawings, 14, 37–41, 132, 181
Coded information, 167
Cognitive abilities, 14–15, 23–24, 82, 91,
    172–173
Cognitive modality transposition, 140,
    143–144
Cognitive style, 104
Cognitive theories of savant syndrome,
    141–157
Columbia Mental Maturity Scale, 15
Comorbidity, 92
Compensation, 145–147, 205–206
Compulsion, 146
Computational models, 222–224
Conceptualisation, 16, 19, 141–145, 165,
    216–219
Connectionist networks, 223–224
Connectivity theories, 92, 98, 99, 160–161,
    210, 211
Constructivism, 63
Context-specific formulation, 95
Controlled processing, 105–106
Copying, 93, 108, 109
Corpus callosum, 160
Cortical arousal, 105
Cortical thickness, 92, 161–162, 210
Cox, David, 182
Creativity, 165, 168
Criticism of own drawings, 70
Croce, Benedetto, 176
Cronkite, Walter, 120
Cross-modality processing, 140, 143–144
Cube drawings, 73–75, 80, 81, 84

Davis, John Scarlett, 182–184
Deblois, Tony, 120
Declarative memory, 150
Dementia, 149, 162–164, 212
Depth representation, 72–75, 83–85
Destructive behaviour, 23, 25–26, 27
Detail-focused processing, 101–102, 103,
    104, 146, 169–171, 214–215
Developmental, dimensional and
    diagnostic interview (3di), 4
Diagnosis and diagnostic tools, 4–5, 21,
    90–91, 93–95, 109–110
Diagnostic and Statistical Manual
    (DSM-IV), 87, 88–89, 90
Diagnostic Interview for Social and
    Communication Disorders (DISCO),
    4, 109
Die-back, 211, 223–224
Digit ratios, 100
Directional sense, 125
Discursive thinking, 19
Dog drawings, 19, 42
Downes, David, 192–195
Draw a Man test, 172
Drawing savants, *see* Artistic savants
Drawing systems, 61–62

Eccentric children, 93–94, 95
Ecological approach, 63, 144
EEG, 16, 211
Eidetic imagery, 147–148, 206–207
EIF4E gene, 96
Ellen, 124–125
Embedded figure task, 101
Emotion processing, 100
Empathising/systemising theory,
    100–101
Enhanced perceptual functioning theory,
    82–83, 84–85, 103, 166–168, 213–214,
    219, 220
Episodic buffer, 150
Equivalents, 66
Evolutionary theories, 157–158
Executive function, 21, 99, 105–108,
    212, 217
Extreme male brain, 100
Eye contact, 88, 108

Face drawings, 50–51, 184
Fairground horse drawings, 9, 10, 29, 56
False belief tasks, 97–98
Feature processing, 104
Feet, Nadia's interest in, 14, 25, 52–55
Figurative graphic schemes, 70

Figure drawings: by Nadia, 19, 44–49; proportions, 71–72, 73; tadpole figures, 66–67, 69–70
Fine motor skills, 25
Food preoccupation, 23, 26
Fortuitous realism, 65
Fox drawing, 180
Fragile X syndrome, 209
Frontal lobe, 99, 107
Fronto–parietal connectivity, 99
Frontotemporal dementia, 162–164, 212
Frostig Developmental Test of Visual Perception, 15
Fuller, Thomas, 117
Functional MRI (fMRI), 98, 99

G. W. (case study), 161–162
Garden drawing, 57
Gender bias, 100, 113, 147, 160
Generalisation, 142
Genetic factors, 89, 96, 158–159, 199–200, 209–210
Genius, 199, 200
Gestalt theory, 59
Gibson's ecological approach, 63, 144
Gifted child artists: abstract art, 177; characteristics, 174; examples, 174–200; intelligence, 172, 173; visual analysis, 173
Gifted children, their rage to learn, 146
Giotto di Bondone, 175
Giraffe drawing, 43
Global processing, *see* Local versus global processing
Gould, Glenn, 122–123
Graphic equivalents, 59
Graphic motor schema, 81
Graphic representation; developmental progress, 63–82; modern theories, 58–63, 215–216
Gross motor skills, 25

Habit, 146
Harriet, 121–122, 138
Hatton, Brian, 72, 189–192
Hemispheric lateralisation, 160, 163, 210
Hidden line elimination, 76–79
High level processing, 104–105, 106, 107
Holman Hunt, William, 186
Homographs, 102
Horse drawings, 9, 10, 13, 14, 17, 18, 19, 21, 29–36, 56, 181, 185, 186, 187, 190, 191, 192, 216
House drawings, 73–75, *see also* Architectural drawings

Human drawings: gifted child artists, 184, 185; by Nadia, 19, 44–55; proportions, 71–72, 73; tadpole figures, 66–67, 69–70
Hyperlexia, 124
Hyper-systemising theory, 104, 169–171, 214–215

Idiot savant, 111, 112
Idiots, 112
Imagery, 15–16
Imaginal thinking, 19
Imbeciles, 111
Imitation, 93, 108, 109
Implicit learning, 139
Infantile autism, 165
Infection, 89
Inferior parietal lobule, 93
Inheritance, 158–159, 199–200, 209–210
Innate talent and aptitude, 199–200
Intellectual realism, 66, 67, 217
Intellectually impaired individuals, 112
Intelligence quotient (IQ), 90, 112, 172, 173
Interbrain, 108–109, 215
Internal model, 69
Internal representations, 16, 217–218
International Classification of Diseases–10 (ICD–10), 87
Intervention programmes, 94, 214
Invariant structures, 142, 217
Invariants, 64
Invariants of structure, 63

Joint attention, 108, 109
Jungreis, 159

Labelling: drawing, 20–21; with autism, 95
Landseer, Edwin, 180–182
Langdon Down, John, 111
Language: categorising and symbolising activity, 142–143; language development in diagnosis of autism, 90–91; literal understanding, 85; metaphor understanding, 85; Nadia's language abilities, 9, 12, 15, 17, 19, 20, 23, 24–25, 143, 216; savant skills, 116, 123–124, 137–138
Latent savant skills, 115, 163, 164–165, 212
Law of closure, 59
Learning difficulty, 111
Left anterior temporal lobe, 163, 164, 212
Left hemisphere dysfunction, 16, 160, 163, 210, 211, 219
Leg drawings, 14, 52–55

Lemke, Leslie, 120–121
Leonardo da Vinci, 13
Lievens, Jan, 179–180
Life-long learning, 146
Linear perspective, 58, 62, 71, 144, 151
Linguistic, discursive thinking, 19
Lion drawing, 42
Literacy savant skills, 116
Local proximity strategy, 103
Local versus global processing, 101, 102, 103, 104, 105, 169, 173, 219
London taxi driver 'knowledge', 157
Long-term memory, 149, 207–208
Long-term memory schemas, 154
Lovaas method, 94
Low level processing, 104–105, 106
Low level weak central coherence, 104–105

Mandala, 64
Marr's theory of vision, 60–61
Matching tasks, 16, 143
Mathematical models, 222–224
Mathematical savants, 116–118, 153, 159, 213, *see also* Calendar calculators
Maxi task, 97
Meaning, 20–21
Measles, mumps and rubella (MMR) vaccine, 96
Medial prefrontal cortex, 98
Medicalisation, 95
Memory: improvement techniques, 149, 156; long-term memory, 149, 207–208; Nadia's drawing ability, 206–208; savant syndrome, 112, 137, 138, 139, 142, 148–154, 155; short-term memory, 70, 149; working memory, 70, 98, 149–150
Mendelssohn, Felix, 123
Mental deficiency, 111
Mentalising, 97–99
Merrill Palmer Mental Measurement of Preschool Children, 15
Metaphor use, 85
Metaphysics, 7
Millais, John Everett, 184–186
Mimicry, 93, 108, 109
Mind, Gottfried, 126–128
Mind blindness, 98, 99, 169
Minicolumns, 93, 161
Mirror image drawings, 14
Mirror neurons, 93, 162
Mirroring, 93, 108, 109
MMR vaccine, 96

Modality-specific processing, 140, 143–144
Monosavant, 112
Morons, 111
Motor control, 25, 91
Motoric systemising, 170
Mozart, Wolfgang Amadeus, 122, 178
Multiple savant skills, 116, 136–138
Musical savants, 116, 118–123, 153–154, 162, 167–168, 221

Nadia: abstract thought, 216–219; aggressive behaviour, 25; attending the Child Development Research Unit, Nottingham, 11–14; attentional resources, 215; brain dysfunction, 211–212; cognitive functioning, 14–15, 23–24; compensation, 205–206; conceptualisation, 16, 142, 216–219; decline in drawing skills, 18, 20, 21, 56–57, 204, 224; destructive behaviour, 23, 25–26, 27; detailed focus, 214–215; diagnosed with autism, 11, 17; drawing in adulthood, 27; drawing materials and surfaces, 12, 14, 28; drawings by, 9, 10, 13, 14, 17, 18, 19, 21, 22, 28–57, 157, 216; early development, 8–9; early diagnosis, 9, 11; early theories and explanations, 15–16; EEG, 16, 211; eidetic imagery, 206–207; enhanced perceptual functioning, 213–214; evolutionary explanation of her abilities, 157–158; executive function, 212; family background, 8–9; fashion interest, 25; father's death, 26; general health, 23; hyper-systemising, 214–215; inherited talent, 209–210; language abilities, 9, 12, 15, 17, 19, 20, 23, 24–25, 143, 216; late childhood development, 16–19; leisure and hobbies, 26–27; love of photographs, 27; matching skills, 16, 143; media interest, 18; memory, 206–208; middle age, 22–27; modern graphic representation theories, 215–216; mother's death, 17–18; motor control, 25; musical interests, 25; neurological explanations, 210–211; obsession with shoes and feet, 14, 25; original study on, 14–16; pattern detection, 213–214; perceptual development, 16, 220; photographs of, 8, 22, 27, 223; picture book use, 9, 24–25, 42; practice, 208–209; preoccupation with food, 23, 26; privileged access to lower level processing, 212; reinforcement, 205–206; schooling, 9, 11, 17; self-harm, 26; self-help skills, 26; sleeping, 26; social and behavioural factors, 25–26; special case of savantism, 201–202, 203–204; starting drawing, 9; theories of savant talents, 205–215; verbal skills, 16, 19, 24–25, 143; weak central coherence theory, 212–213; writing ability, 25; young adulthood, 19–21

Naive perspective, 62

Navon figures, 103

Neural connectivity theories, 92, 98, 99, 160–161, 210, 211

Neurological dysfunction, 89, 92–93, 159–165, 210–211

Neuronal circuitry, 162, 211

Neuronal pruning, 211, 223–224

Non-declarative memory, 150

Non-linear dynamics, 222

Non-routine processing, 105–106

Non-verbal communication, 108–109, 215

Object centred description, 60–61, 217, 219

Object data structures, 80

Object representation, 65–66

Object specific, 60

Oblique projection, 62

O'Brien, Dominic, 149

Obsessions, 14, 25, 93–94, 95, 100, 214

Occipital gyrus, 98

Occipito-temporo-parietal connectivity, 98

Okapi drawing, 43

Olmstead, Marla, 177

Optic array, 63, 144

Orthographic projection, 62

Overlapping, 71

Paravicini, Derek, 119–120

Parietal lobe, 99, 161

Pathological concreteness, 145

Pattern detection, 166–168, 169, 213–214

Pattern drawing, 79–82

Peek, Kim, 123

Pelican drawings, 14, 41

Perceptual development, 15–16, 219–221

Perceptual matching, 16, 143

Perceptual thinking, 19

Perspective, 19, 20–21, 58, *see also* Linear perspective

Pervasive developmental disorders, 88

Phonological loop, 150

Photographic realism, 144–145

Pi recitation, 137, 139

Picasso, Pablo, 176, 178, 187–189

Picture books, 9, 24–25, 42

Picture exchange communication system (PECS), 92

Picture matching, 16, 143

Ping Lian Yeak, 131–132

Plasticity, 211

Potential talent, 199–200

Practice, 146, 154–157, 199, 208–209

Pre-Raphaelite Brotherhood, 186

Precocious artists: abstract art, 177; characteristics, 174; examples, 174–200; intelligence, 172, 173; visual analysis, 173

Prefrontal cortex, 98, 106–108

Pretend play, 85, 141

Primary motor cortex, 93

Privileged access to lower level information, 162–165, 212

Procedural knowledge, 139

Procedural memory, 150

Prodigious savants, 6, 113

Proportion within objects, 71–72

Proportions between objects, 75–76, 77, 151

Prototypes, 66

Pruning theory, 211, 223–224

Pullen, James Henry, 128–130

Pure autism, 165

Quasi-autism, 92

Radial cell minicolumns, 93, 161

Rage to learn, 146

Reading, 102, 103–104, 123, 124

Recovery from autism, 94

Reindeer drawing, 43

Reinforcement, 145–147, 205–206

Relative size, 75–76, 77

Repetitive behaviour, 215

Repetitive transcranial magnetic stimulation, 163, 164

Representational drawing; developmental progress, 63–82; modern theories, 58–63, 215–216

Resemblances, 167

Rett's syndrome, 88, 89, 90

Rewards, 146–147, 156

Reynell Developmental Language Scale, 15

Richard, 138

Romanian orphans, 108

Rote memory, 142, 152

Routine processing, 105–106
Rule shifting, 99
Rush, Benjamin, 117

Sally Anne task, 97, 98
Satie, Eric, 123
Savage, Matt, 121
Savant, meaning of term, 111
Savant skills: areas of expertise, 115–116;
    artificial induction of, 163, 164–165;
    definition, 114; latent, 115, 163, 164–165,
    212; narrow and specific range, 221;
    normal suppression, 165; overemphasis
    on, 3; *see also* specific skills
Savant syndrome: abstract thought,
    141–145; areas of expertise, 115–116;
    autism, 6, 113, 114; brain function,
    159–162, 163; characteristics, 112–113;
    cognitive theories, 141–157;
    compensation, 145–147; conceptualising,
    141–145; creativity, 168; definition,
    6–7, 114–115; eidetic imagery, 147–148;
    enhanced perceptual functioning,
    166–168; evolutionary theories,
    157–158; examples of extraordinary
    savants, 116–138; gender, 113, 147,
    160; genetic theories, 158–159;
    growing interest in, 5; historical context,
    111–112; hyper-systemising, 169–171;
    incidence, 113–114; memory, 112,
    137, 138, 139, 142, 148–154, 155;
    neurological explanations, 159–165;
    pattern detection, 166–168; practice,
    154–157; privileged access to lower
    information, 162–165; reinforcement,
    145–147; reporting problems, 115;
    sensory deprivation, 165–166; social
    isolation, 165–166; structured codes,
    166–168; systemising, 101; types of
    savant, 113; use of term, 112; weak
    central coherence, 168–169
Schemas, 107
Schopenhauer, Arthur, 176
Scribbling stage, 64–65
Search for equivalents, 142, 217
Secondary representations, 85
Self-awareness, 99
Self-criticism, 70
Self-fulfilling prophesy, 95
Self-harm, 26
Self-monitoring, 99
Sensory abnormalities, 170–171
Sensory deprivation, 165–166
Sensory hypersensitivity, 170–171

Sensory systemising, 170
Sentence reading, 102, 103–104
Serotonin, 210
Sheep drawings, 22, 190
Shoes, Nadia's interest in, 14, 25, 52–55
Short-range connectivity theory,
    161, 211
Short-term memory, 70, 149
Sleeping, 26
Social isolation, 108, 165–166
Soper, Eileen, 182
Soundscape Centre, 122
Spatial savant skills, 116, 124–125
Specialised schools, 122
Spectrum of autistic disorders, 87
Splinter skills, 113
Stages of development, 67, 222
Stereotyped behaviour, 215
Stockings of Cambridge task, 106
Structures, 100, 166–168
Superior parietal lobe, 161
Superior temporal gyrus, 98
Superior temporal sulcus, 93
Supervisory system, 107
Symbolic activity, 66, 141, 142–143,
    216–217
Synapses, 161
Systemising, 100–101, 169–170, 214

Tadpole figures, 66–67, 69–70
Talented savants, 6, 113
TEACCH, 92, 214
Temporal lobe, left anterior, 163,
    164, 212
Temporal poles, 98
Testosterone, 100, 160
Theory of mind, 21, 97–99
Three mountains task, 70
Time keeping, 124–125
Titchener circles, 102
Touch, 108
Toulouse-Lautrec, Henri de, 17, 186–187
Transcranial magnetic stimulation,
    163, 164
Treatment and education of autistic and
    related communication handicapped
    children (TEACCH), 92, 214
Treatment of autism, 91–92
Triad of impairments, 87–88
Twin studies, 158

Ventral premotor area, 93
Verbal abilities, 15–16, 19, 24–25, 91,
    143; savant skills, 116, 123–124

Viewer specific description, 60, 219
Vinyl flooring, 96
Viral infection, 89
Visual acuity, 170–171
Visual agnosia, 149
Visual illusions, 102, 219
Visual perception, 104, 219
Visual realism, 67–68, 70, 83
Visuospatial sketch pad, 150

Weak central coherence theory, 21, 84,
    101–105, 152, 168–169, 212–213
Wechsler Intelligence Scales, 15
Weight estimation, 167
Willats' theory of drawing systems, 61–62
Williamson, Kieron, 178, 195–198
Wiltshire, Stephen, 132–136, 137, 206–207
Wisconsin Card Sorting task, 106
Working memory, 70, 98, 149–150